RT SEA

Arctic Circle

YUKON RIVER

65°

Tanana River

Captain Cook
in
Alaska
and the
North Pacific

60°

Bligh I

Snug Corner Cove

nchorage

ion

May 16

May 12

C. Suckling

Mt. St. Elias

Yakutat Bay

Mt. Fairweather

Kayak I

Prince William Sound

Montague I

abeth

Dry Bay

May 4

Chichagof I

Baranof I

Mt. Edgecumbe

Kruzof I

May 1, 1778

GULF OF ALASKA

Prince of Wales I

DIXON ENTRANCE

Queen Charlotte Is

Voyage from May, 1778 to October, 1778

——— *Underlined names given by Cook*

145°

140°

135°

130°

Library of Congress Control Number: 2008924537

ISBN: 978-1-57833-408-7

First Printing May, 2008

Printed in U.S.A.
through **Alaska Print Brokers**

Book design: Vered R. Mares, 𝔗𝔬𝔡𝔡 𝔆𝔬𝔪𝔪𝔲𝔫𝔦𝔠𝔞𝔱𝔦𝔬𝔫𝔰

This book was typeset in 12 point Warnock Pro.

Additional copies of this book may be purchased from the publisher for $30.95 (including $4.00 postage and handling.)

Published by

𝔗𝔬𝔡𝔡 𝔆𝔬𝔪𝔪𝔲𝔫𝔦𝔠𝔞𝔱𝔦𝔬𝔫𝔰
611 E. 12th Ave.
Anchorage, Alaska 99501-4603
(907) 274-8633 (TODD)
Fax: (907) 929-5550
with other offices in Ketchikan, Juneau, Fairbanks and Nome Alaska
sales@toddcom.com • **WWW.ALASKABOOKSANDCALENDARS.COM**

Cover Art: Snug Corner Cove, Prince William Sound, Alaska showing *HMS Discovery* and *Resolution* at anchor May 16, 1778 by John Webber, shipboard artist.

-Table of Contents-

~*About the Author*~

James K. Barnett has been an Alaska attorney in private practice in Anchorage since 1974. He is the long time President of the Cook Inlet Historical Society (1998-present) and, among other things, helped organize a 1994 exhibition and international symposium at the Anchorage Museum celebrating the bicentennial of Captain George Vancouver's voyage to Alaska. He was co-editor and contributor to the symposium papers, Enlightenment and Exploration in the North Pacific 1741-185, University of Washington Press, 1997. A fourth generation Californian, his principal leisure pursuit is the early history of the west coast of North America, from California to Alaska. He served as deputy commissioner of the Alaska Department of Natural Resources (1983-87) and elected member of the Anchorage Municipal Assembly (1986-93).

~ Preface ~

No man emerges larger in the history of the Pacific than Captain James Cook, the celebrated eighteenth century British mariner and circumnavigator, whose three voyages of exploration were perhaps the most extensive sailing expeditions in the history of the world. The heroic quality of this master mariner and his achievement in discovery and exploration are well known, but most of what is written focuses on Cook's considerable achievements in the South Pacific. After all, his voyages penetrated into new, uncharted realms in these exotic lands. Some residents of Australia and New Zealand, even Tahiti and Hawaii, consider Cook to be their "founding father," as well as an icon of discovery and exploration in their earliest recorded history.

Outside of Hawaii, Cook's achievements in the North Pacific are largely unknown, probably because the North Pacific, with its gales, clouds, fog and rain, does not enjoy the same glamorous image as the exotic South Pacific. Yet during a single "summer of storms" in 1778, Cook and his crew sailed during his third voyage from Oregon to Alaska looking for an imagined passage to Europe. After reaching and testing the Arctic ice pack in late summer they turned back via the Aleutian Islands to winter in Hawaii.

The third voyage account is fascinating, providing the fullest descriptions and illustrations of any Pacific voyage of that era, a captivating record of the first substantial contact by Europeans with the native people of the Northwest coast of America. This publication offers an in-depth look at that summer, including the encounters with local people, told from the perspective of the English observers. It also follows the sailors as they returned from Hawaii in 1779 after the unfortunate death of Cook to test the Arctic a second time.

Cook spent nearly a full decade at sea and his voyage accounts offer the first significant record of the indigenous people of the far reaches of the Pacific Ocean, including the people of the Northwest coast. The native people had no written language and except for anecdotal recollections passed on through later generations there are no records of their impressions to match Cook's "discovery" of the region, brought home to an appreciative public through extensive journals and magnificent drawings. These contacts between European sailors and local people were a momentous occasion, a clash of cultures that gave an irrevocable turn in Pacific history as Europeans came to conquer, colonize and exploit the people and resources of the Pacific.

Where possible, the descriptions offered by the sailors and artists themselves are retained. If there are uncertainties in any journal passage, the modern spelling has been adopted. Otherwise the spelling, capitalization and abbreviations offered by the crewmen, no matter how idiosyncratic, have been preserved. In addition, many of the original drawings of this part of the voyage, principally the work of the brilliant John Webber, are presented to acquaint the reader with the "first impressions" of the English crew with this vast coast and the many people and cultures they encountered.

I am indebted to many scholars and friends who have written about the third voyage of Captain Cook and western exploration in the decades that followed, particularly as they have considered the first contact between the native inhabitants and Europeans on the Northwest Coast. I have not attempted to reiterate what has been written before except as it helps to understand Cook's expedition in relation to the first European contacts in Alaska and the North Pacific.

I am especially indebted to Flip Todd, publisher at Todd Communications, for conceiving this project and

Dr. William E. (Bill) Davis, Professor Emeritus of Alaska Methodist University, the predecessor to Alaska Pacific University. Bill is the secretary and former president of the Cook Inlet Historical Society, serving as a member of its board of directors for nearly 30 years. He has provided invaluable editorial assistance in the preparation of each chapter. In addition, Jo Antonson (Alaska State Historian), Dr. Nancy Yaw Davis (Dena'ina anthropologist), Marilyn Knapp (Curator of History for the Anchorage Museum), Aaron Leggett (Dena'ina historian at the Alaska Native Cultural Center) and Barbara Sweetland Smith (Russian historian and curator) have given important guidance to the project. Finally, my wife, Marilyn Barnett, has read every word of the manuscript several times and offered priceless support on its flow and content. This considerable support was essential to the completion of this project.

— *Jim Barnett*

~Chapter 1~

New Albion

In late June 1778 two British sailing ships under the command of Captain James Cook crept through the shrouded mists of the eastern Aleutian Islands in western Alaska, one of the loneliest and least-known spots on earth. Rain came in torrents as the vessels coasted along the rocky, broken shore. The crew rarely saw the land or water, or anything except the decks of their ships. Although the two craft were within hailing distance of one another, they could rarely see each other through the dense, gloomy fog. Instead, as they sailed blindly ahead a constant rain and mist created imagined outlines of the bays and inlets near shore. Distant breakers were a welcome sound, as they announced that the shoreline was at a safe distance. But a long period of silence spoke volumes, as it could signal approaching hidden rocks. The frightful monotony was occasionally broken by a cannon blast from one of the ships. And with each blast, the crew anxiously listened for an imagined answer from shore.[1]

It was in this way that the crew of the *Resolution* and *Discovery* faced their perilous journey on a desolate and remote Aleutian Island coastline more than two centuries ago. The captain, James Cook, was a veteran of Pacific exploration in the South Seas, Antarctica and now the North Pacific. He had an uncanny sense of it all, navigating in safety, barking orders to keep his ships away from danger ahead. Still, everyone was on edge. A heart-stopping cry of "Rock!" or "Breakers ahead!" could be heard periodically, but usually the ships edged forward silently in the treacherous shallows at a slow, methodical pace. They hoped for an opening to the north to take them safely past the rocky shore, but the shoreline was impenetrable.

Occasionally the fog would lift. On June 24th land, and then an opening to the northwest, came into view. Cook sensed it was a false opening, and one that would prolong their misery. It seemed a continuation of the continent, so he continued running with the islands to the west. Soon they entered another bank of fog. The mist quickly encircled them and their surroundings soon took the usual composition—gloom and mist turning steadily thicker. Only an easterly breeze moved the ships away, securing their safety for the night.

At daybreak on the 26th the ships resumed their westerly course. Again, fog and mist, and dreadful silence engulfed them. Nothing could be seen beyond the ship's bow. In his journal Cook wrote, "Daylight availed us little as the Weather was so thick that we could not see a hundred yards before us, but as the wind was now very moderate I ventured to run." He spread the sails to run with the wind. But no sooner had they unfurled the sails than they took them in, " ...we were (soon) alarmed at hearing the Sound of breakers on our larboard (left) bow." He brought the ships to a halt, anchoring in a coarse, sandy bottom and taking in all the sails. They hailed Captain Clerke, commander of the *Discovery* nearby. Clerke anchored as well, waiting for the weather to clear. It was a good thing they stopped.[2]

"The sound of breakers had been the sound of salvation," Cook later wrote. "The ships had been running straight for the shore, which was only three quarters of a mile off, the head of a bay guarded at each side by a high rock, with lesser ones attendant." Relieved that he was not in mortal danger, he was candid about their good luck, "Providence had conducted us through between these rocks where I should not have ventured in a clear day and to such an anchoring place that I could not have chosen a better."

Such was the skill and temperament of Captain James Cook. A soft-spoken insightful man of science and the sea, he explored more of the Pacific Ocean than any European before him. He completed the first accurate map of the Pacific. Yet, in his decade of sailing, each day brought new challenges and tested his abilities as mariner, diplomat, chart maker, scientist, and leader of men. Now, in June 1778 he was again at the helm, leading his third and most difficult voyage. He was sailing in and out of hostile wind, rain and fog to find his way north along the broken, rock-strewn Alaskan coast.

Many of the journal keepers among the crew described their terror and astonishment on this latest brush with death. George Gilbert, midshipman on the flagship, wrote, "We could not help being struck with horror at the sight of the dangers we escaped, having 3 or 4 patches of rocks above water (in front of us) about 1/3 mile from one another. ... a more providential escape from instant destruction being scarce to be met with.[3]" John Ledyard, an American who was corporal of marines on the *Resolution*, reported "... when the fog cleared up, and we found ourselves embayed with rocks, reefs, and an island, all within two cables (a cable is 1/10th nautical mile or 608 ft.) length. We were not only amazed to find ourselves in such a frightful situation, but were still more astonished to conceive how we got there, as the least accidental deviation from the course we had steered would have been fatal.[4]"

William Ellis, the surgeon's mate on *Discovery*, offered his view of the near catastrophe:

> ... as we were running on, the weather being very thick and foggy, the Resolution

hailed the Discovery, and desired her to come to immediately, as there was a noise and at no great a distance from us, which exactly resembled the surf breaking upon the shore. Both ships very soon let go their anchors. ... This was a most providential escape; if we had stood on five minutes longer, we must in all probability have been on shore, or if we had varied our course either to the right of left, we should have run the risk of being upon the rocks.[5]

Clerke's journal was understated, if not ironic: "very nice pilotage, considering our perfect Ignorance of our situation.[6]" He had been with Cook on each of his three voyages, and they always managed to get through the tough spots, no matter the circumstance. So his report showed more confidence in his captain, and more certainty of Cook's brilliant navigational skills.

Captain Cook was exhausted after two long and arduous voyages to the South Pacific. Beginning in 1768 he had spent six of seven years at sea, and he deserved a comfortable retirement. Yet he answered England's call to return to the Pacific to find the imagined ice-free passage through present-day Alaska that would link the North Pacific Ocean back to Europe. Now, with two more years at sea, he had cheated death again, and was still moving north, searching for the elusive passage.

In his first two voyages in the Pacific, Cook disproved the claims of the armchair geographers in Europe that there was a great inhabitable Southern continent. The world's continents were in balance, they speculated, and since most of the continental land mass was concentrated in the northern hemisphere, there must be an equally large landmass in the south. While Cook's earlier efforts in the

Pacific were magnificent by all accounts, his principal contribution was to prove this speculative Southern continent did not exist.

So it was logical to send Cook to solve the final riddle, whether the elusive Northwest Passage, the so-called Strait of Anian, existed. For three centuries, since the discovery of America, European navigators had searched in vain for the location of this rumored short route from Europe to the riches of the Orient. It was roughly in the latitude of present-day Oregon and Washington that Jonathan Swift placed the fantasyland of "Brobdingnag" in *Gulliver's Travels.* Even the British Parliament added to the interest in the imagined passage, offering a handsome reward to the explorers who found the route. In 1745 it offered a £20,000 prize for the discovery by merchant vessels of a passage from the east by way of Hudson's Bay. Now it was extended to the discovery of such a passage from the west, and made available to men in government service. While the search would prove futile, the theoretical geographers convinced the Admiralty that the passage existed, because of tales of imagined and mystical voyagers passed down through the ages.[7]

Cook's voyage instructions from the Admiralty, issued in July 1776, were meticulous to a fault, and unmistakable on this point:

> ... in the beginning of February, or sooner if you shall judge it necessary, (you shall) proceed in as direct a Course as you can to the Coast of New Albion, endeavouring to fall in with it in the Latitude of 45° 0' North; and taking care, in your way thither, not to lose any time in search of new Lands, or to stop at any you may fall in with, unless you find it necessary to recruit your wood and water.

... Upon your arrival on the Coast of New Albion, you are to put into the first convenient Port to recruit your Wood and Water and procure Refreshments, and then to proceed Northward along the Coast as far as the Latitude of 65°, or farther, if you are not obstructed by Lands or Ice; taking care not to lose any time in exploring Rivers or Inlets, or upon any other account, until you get to the before-mentioned Latitude of 65°, where we could wish you to arrive in the Month of June next.

When you get that Length, you are very carefully to search for, and to explore, such Rivers or Inlets as may appear to be of a considerable extent and pointing towards Hudsons or Baffins Bays; and, if from your own Observations, or from any information you may receive from the Natives (who, there is reason to believe, are the same Race of People, and speak the same Language, of which you are furnished with a Vocabulary, as the Esquimaux) there shall appear to be a certainty, or even a probability, of a Water Passage into the aforementioned Bays, or either of them, you are, in such case to use your utmost endeavours to pass through with one or both of the Sloops, unless you shall be of the opinion that the passage may be effected with more certainty, or with greater probability, by smaller Vessels, in which case you are to set up the Frames of one or both of the small Vessels with which you are provided, and when they are put together, and are properly fitted, stored, & victualled, you are to dispatch one or both of them under the care of proper Officers, with a sufficient number of Petty Officers, Men and Boats, in order to attempt the said Passage; with such Instructions for their rejoining you, if they should fail, or for their farther proceedings if they should succeed, in the attempt, as you shall judge most proper.

But nevertheless if you shall find it more eligible to pursue any other measures, than those above pointed out, in order to make a discovery of the before mentioned Passage (if any such there be) you are at liberty, and we leave it to your discretion, to pursue such measures accordingly.[8]

It is fortunate that such precise instructions left Cook to his own discretion, as his instincts proved the crew's salvation many times. As with the earlier voyages, Cook suspected the geographers were wrong. He agreed to abandon his comfortable retirement to find and map this last unknown temperate coast. He could not have known this would be his most dangerous voyage and his final, fatal venture in the Pacific.

Cook sailed in the *Resolution,* the legendary ship he commanded in his second voyage. She was tired and forlorn from the outset. Repairs were required at her first stop and the ship gave Cook trouble during most days at sea, requiring repairs at nearly every anchorage on the voyage. After twenty months from England, and following his discovery of Hawaii, they sighted land on the Northwest Coast in early March 1778. They made landfall on March 7 at Yaquina Bay on the coast of modern-day Oregon, in the Latitude of 45° as prescribed. Winter was scarcely over. David Samwell, the surgeon's mate, wrote it was a country "high and craggy & mostly covered with snow.[9]"

Their spring arrival witnessed a bleak, blustery, miserable storm with unbridled fury. Although coastal storms are well known in this region today, Cook had no expectations on his arrival. He was distressed. He had an enormous task in the summer ahead, with precise instructions. He was to hold the coast and explore to the north, all the way to present day Alaska. The most pressing obstacle was the persistent storm with constant squalls of rain, hail, sleet and snow as well as a monstrous wind driving him in the wrong direction.

At last, about 100 miles south of the entrance to the Columbia River, a five-mile long rocky promontory with a sheer 1,000-foot face appeared out of the mists. Cook called this headland *Cape Foulweather*, no doubt because of the poor weather and dubious beginning of his exploration on the coast. Despite all measures to hold his latitude storms drove the ships south 150 miles astride Cape Blanco. In his journal, Cook lamented "There was no choice but to stretch to the Southward to get clear of the coast, this was done under courses and two close reefed top sails being rather more sail than the ships could bear but it was necessary to carry it to clear the land.[10]"

"We have now very disagreeable Weather," Clerke wrote in typical understatement, "fresh Gales with hard squalls of Wind sleet & snow; and a very heavy Westerly Swell." The five-week passage from Hawaii to Oregon had been marked by gradually worsening weather, and now they were facing a strong gale of windblown fury and a swirling sea. Clerke looked for a safe anchorage, but no harbor could be seen through the driving rain. "It is really rather a lamentable business that these Northwesters and this very unsettled Weather should so far intrude upon us," he wrote, "that we can neither forward our Matters by tracing the Coast, nor have the Satisfaction of getting into a Harbour to take a look at the Country. ... we can't look at the shore, but continue to dance about in the Offing here and make the best Weather of it we can.[11]"

Westerly swells and winds prevented them from moving away from the coast. They worried that the ships would be driven against the rocks. The astronomer William Bayly, who sailed with Clerke on the *Discovery*, said they were all anxious, even desperate:

> Our situation was very disagreeable all the morning, we began within 5 or 6 leagues (a marine league is three nautical miles of 6,080 ft.) at most off shore, with a gale of Wind & a great sea right on it as could blow, & had it increased it would have brought us under our Courses, we must have inevitably gone on shore, & its highly probable all perrished.[12]

In his journal the surgeon's mate Ellis reflected the drama of squalls, sleet and snow in his initial coastal experiences:

> The next day we had a strong breeze from the westward. The air was much colder than yesterday, with open cloudy weather, but very unsettled and squally, with showers of hail. The wind not proving favorable for exploring the coast, we stood to the southward, to avoid getting too near land. ... The land near the shore was of a moderate height: the hills were covered with straight tall trees of the fir kind, and where they were but thinly scattered, the ground

was covered with snow. ... During the night,
we had frequent squalls with showers of hail
and snow ... the squalls were generally too
heavy, as to oblige us (to strike all our sails)
... (it was) dark and cloudy, with a nasty
moist atmosphere...[13]

The American John Ledyard, reported "we had the
ruggedest weather we had yet experienced. The weather
was cold, the gales of wind were successive and strong, and
sometimes very violent. Our ships complained. ..."[14]

Cook must have read the account of Frances Fletcher,
Francis Drake's chaplain, who told of the *Golden Hind's*
suffering along this coast in 1578:

The winds were such as if the bowels
of the earth had set all at liberty, or as if all
the clouds under heaven had been called
together to lay their force upon that one
place. The seas ... were rolled up from the
depths, even from the base of the rocks, as
if they had been a scroll of parchment... the
impossibility of anchoring or spreading any
sail, the most mad seas, the lee shores, the
dangerous rocks, the contrary and most
intolerable winds ... all offered us such
small likelihood of escaping destruction,
that if the special providence of God himself
had not supported us, we could never have
endured this woeful state ...[15]

Cook and Clerke were seasoned Pacific mariners, who
in three voyages had challenged the harrowing passage of
Cape Horn, shipwreck on the Great Barrier Reef, and the

travails of fog, sleet and snow in the Antarctic ice pack. Yet their first reports after just two weeks on the Oregon coast offer deep respect, if not terror, for its inhospitable weather and seas. Failing to find a safe harbor, they spent two miserable weeks tacking repeatedly against the wind in a frenetic pattern often taking the ships as far as 200 miles out to sea. This third voyage on "this most horrible coast in the world" challenged the seafaring skills of all.

The storm finally relented. Beaten and weary, after a few days the crew regained Cape Foulweather, and managed to observe the shore. The land was of "moderate height," but rugged and "diversified with hill and Valley and almost every where covered with wood." Seals, porpoises, and whales were in abundance near shore. These were spring whale migrations and probably the seal rookery at Oregon's Seal Rocks. After a few hours of calm, the breeze came again, this time from the southwest, and the expedition was finally underway, bearing north toward Alaska. Sighting land periodically, the ships sailed northward, gradually increasing their latitude.

Cook called this area of the coast *New Albion*, after his instructions from the Admiralty. Despite the intervening centuries, the Admiralty felt secure in its claim to the coast of California and Oregon by virtue of the visit two centuries earlier by the legendary British captain Francis Drake, who reached this coast in 1579 as privateer and pirate, sailing for Elizabeth I.

After the discovery of the New World by Columbus, the two major European seafaring nations were Spain and Portugal. These two powers signed the Treaty of Tordesillas in 1494, giving Portugal title to all territories east of a line through the mid-Atlantic and giving Spain everything west of it. It was later discovered that Brazil lay to the east of this line, and so it was ceded to Portugal, but in effect this agreement left to Spain the European "rights" to invade and conquer the vast central American empires, ultimately extending all the way to Alta California (today's state of California).

In the twenty years after Columbus, the Spanish established colonies in Haiti, Cuba, Jamaica, and Puerto Rico. In 1513 Vasco Nuñez de Balboa became the first of the great "conquistadores." He pressed the Spanish claim to the American mainland and was the first European to see the Pacific Ocean from America, looking over its vast expanse from the steaming jungles on the western side of the Isthmus of Panama. Following Balboa, Hernando Cortés invaded Mexico, conquering the temples of Montezuma and enslaving the Aztec Nation in 1519. Anticipating a short distance to the Orient, Cortés established a naval base on the west coast of Mexico, and commissioned a series of coastal voyages to determine America's potential landward connection to China.[16]

After repeated failures, the Portuguese João Rodrigues Cabrilho, better known by his Spanish name, Juan Cabrillo, was the first European to reach modern day California, arriving in two small ships in San Diego harbor on September 28, 1542. Though Cabrillo later died from a gangrene infection, his pilot took command of the expedition and ran to the north along the coast before rough seas and violent winds turned him back at Cape Mendocino in northern California. This expedition, which probably reached the northernmost point of sixteenth century expeditions, was unknown to later Mexican viceroys and explorers.[17]

In the same year, the Portuguese pilot Ferdinand Magellan left Spain for the Spice Islands. As he entered the straits that now bear his name at the southern reach of South America, his fleet of five tiny ships was hammered by rain, sleet, snow and 40-foot waves. It was a miracle that anyone survived, but three ships remained. The decimated crew left the strait and entered a broad ocean in an unusual calm, and ironically Magellan named it the "Pacific," the quiet ocean. It was a dismal, ruined voyage. Magellan was killed in a skirmish in the Philippines and most of his remaining crew were drowned, killed or died of scurvy. But one ship and a meager crew returned safely to Spain, completing the first circumnavigation of the world.[18]

The Spanish decided the risk of mounting expeditions around Cape Horn was too high to bring the treasures of the Orient back to Spain. So they instead took advantage of new world colonies, using the prevailing trade winds to fetch the treasures of Cathay to the capitals of Europe via Mexico. These voyages were undertaken once each year in lumbering Manila Galleons until 1815. Yet in the course of hundreds of sailings, encountering the West Coast on each return, little was learned about the North Pacific. Instead, when the ships reached the coast, they simply turned south and headed for the safety of Acapulco.[19]

England was not party to the Treaty of Tordesillas. But England only began overseas explorations after unifying the British Isles under Elizabeth I in the middle of the sixteenth century. Often the Queen simply subsidized English privateers to prey on Spanish shipping in the Atlantic; Drake was her finest corsair. He was nothing if not bold. He devised a plan to strike at the Spanish New World colonies from their unprotected western flank. After entering the Pacific in the renowned *Golden Hinde* at Cape Horn, Drake made repeated raids on Spanish towns and ships, capturing considerable loot.

To avoid the anticipated Spanish fleet to the south, he decided to escape through the undiscovered Strait of Anian, or Northwest Passage. In so doing, he made the greatest headway toward Alaska in the two centuries of exploration that followed Columbus. The northern reach of his trip is unknown, but it was probably the latitude of Oregon, in the same latitude that Cook approached two centuries later. But Drake ultimately was discouraged by the cold and repeated northwesterly gales, and abandoned his effort to find a passage to Europe. Given the cold weather he encountered in June, including snow-covered terrain, his voyage may have ended beyond Oregon, even as far north as southern Alaska. Determining the actual reach of his voyage has stymied scholars ever since.[20]

Drake returned to the area of San Francisco Bay, which he called "New Albion," the Latin version of "New England." He stayed there for six weeks in the summer of 1579. The name was intended to flaunt his discovery at Spain. Eighteenth century American colonists at war with England would have been surprised that the original New England, established nearly fifty years before the Pilgrims landed at Plymouth Rock, was Drake's anchorage in modern day California!

In that era voyagers rarely left journals, and their maps were kept secret for commercial and political advantage. So most of the information about the voyage comes from second-hand accounts, and these accounts are generally silent about the North Pacific, deliberately concealed from the public. So today no one is quite sure exactly where he stopped, or what transpired on the coast. Most scholars think the anchorage was in the area of modern day Drake's Bay north of San Francisco, though others place the anchorage nearer to San Francisco, and one places it in Oregon. Others have speculated Drake discharged some of his crew to lighten the ship before crossing the Pacific, becoming the first European settlers of modern-day California. If he was north of San Francisco

Bay, which is likely, Drake would have been in contact with the Coast Miwok Indians, the first European contact with native people on the coast north of Mexico.[21]

Drake finally returned by way of the Pacific and Cape Horn, reaching England in 1580. His voyage was the first circumnavigation of the globe by an Englishman, and the first ship of any nation to make the voyage under one commander. Drake also was the first European to set foot in California north of Santa Barbara, pushing the imagined Northwest Passage even further to the north.

The only Spanish voyage north from Mexico during these same two centuries was by Sebastian Vizcaino, who sought a harbor in California for the Mexican galleons on their return from the Orient. Other than naming every feature along the coast, names that continue in use today, his most notable achievement came in 1602 at Monterey. He thought Monterey was an excellent site for a settlement, likening it to Castile. But it was not a natural harbor and the superlatives afforded the port were so fantastic that in 1769 the Portola Expedition searched for it in vain until they found San Francisco Bay by mistake.

The crew on Vizcaino's ships was so overcome with scurvy that only a few could walk, but they reached the latitude of Oregon, observing "Aguilar's River." Claims of finding this river stimulated armchair geographers anticipating the Northwest Passage. While all of Vizcaino's boats returned to Mexico, the death by scurvy of two-thirds of the crew confirmed that the price was too high to search for ports or treasure in California. Even worse, on his return Vizcaino's scribe popularized the notion that California was an island. It took a century for this miscalculation to be corrected.[22]

The voyagers on Cook's vessels were aware of this history. James King, second lieutenant on the *Resolution*, in scholarly style, asserted in his journal:

This part of the continent of America has not
as far as we know ever before been seen; for there
is no certain account of any navigators being so
high as 44° latitude excepting Sir Francis Drake
and (Sebastian) Vizcaino. Both these navigators
landed on the continent at 38° of latitude.
Both were stopped from proceeding farther
to the north than 44° from the rigour of the
climate, the former even though it was June ...[23]

The Admiralty assumed Drake's claim to the area
encompassed Oregon, so in 1776 Cook was instructed
to rejoin the continent at Drake's point of departure, as
if their voyages were separated by a matter of a months,
rather than two centuries. By redoubling his voyage in the
teeth of the spring storm, Cook almost certainly retraced
the northern reaches of the Vizcaino and Drake voyages,
and now moved north into what Cook assumed were
uncharted waters.

As Cook left his southernmost point on the coast, a
hundred miles off the area astride Cape Blanco, the storm
that had been with him for two weeks abated. There were
even short periods of calm. Finally, a breeze arose from the
southwest and brought fair weather, allowing him to steer
closer to the Oregon shore for the first real inspection.

The vessels were probably too far out to sea when they
passed the outlet of the Columbia River, so it remained
undiscovered. If the outlet was noticed by anyone, the
journals took no special note. On Sunday, March 22, the
favorable winds held; they passed coastal Washington in
a few hours. The land was flat and forested, then as night
approached Cook noticed a large "hillock" that appeared
to be an island of rocks in the afternoon shadows. At first
it "flattered" them into thinking there would be an opening

large enough to find a harbor, but as they approached for a closer inspection the opening seemed to be closed off by low land. He called this point *Cape Flattery*, a name still used to mark the northwesternmost point of the state of Washington.[24]

In the days of sail, the coast of Oregon and Washington were notorious for the hazardous sailing conditions that Cook had stumbled upon, and Cape Flattery was soon known by mariners to be one of the most vicious headlands in the world. To the north Cook seemed to see an opening and a harbor, but a gale soon sprang up and he went further off, giving greater protection from another near miss with the coast. This onset of bad weather prevented him from discovering and exploring the Strait of Juan de Fuca, which he missed even though Cape Flattery heralded its southern entrance.

In his journal he wrote that he was probably now in the latitude of Vizcaino's "Aguilar's River" and the other speculative passageways to Europe. Other claims of inland passages by other explorers such as Juan de Fuca in 1592 and Bartholomew de Fonte in 1640 were known. Passages appeared on contemporary Spanish maps, often showing a chain of rivers and channels through Canada that emptied into Hudson's Bay. However, Cook was a man of science who did not trifle with rumors and speculation. He doubted the claims of such geographical fantasies and appeared to enjoy the fact that no such passage existed.

Even though he was quite wrong, Cook gave an ironical commentary on his own skepticism about the imaginations of the armchair geographers in Europe. "It is in this very latitude we were now in where geographers have place the pretended *Strait of Juan de Fuca*, but we saw nothing like it, nor is there the least probability that iver any such thing existed."[25]

In the dim of night the ships either went further out to sea or simply overlooked the passage before them. But they did not see the wide entry north of Cape Flattery. It is now the entrance to Puget Sound and Southern British Columbia. Had he seen it, Cook certainly would have explored it, and gained an appreciation of the complexity of the islands, inlets, channels and inland waterways extending from Puget Sound to southern Alaska. But the hostile weather dominated his thinking, so he abandoned the shore. He left the first discovery of the sites of the present day cities of Seattle and Vancouver to others.

The next morning the ships were well offshore and clear of the strait. They only came close to the land again several days later. Then they observed a land of high, snow-capped mountains and deep forests we know today as Vancouver Island. Given the height and distance of the mountains from shore, Cook could not have imagined this was an island. He called it Hope Bay, in hopes an anchorage could soon be found. By midday he saw two indentations in the land, and chose the southern most opening to seek out shelter and fresh water.

~Chapter 2~

Master Mariner

James Cook was one of the most able and enlightened sailors that England ever produced. A nation of seafaring prosperity and achievement, the British people were ready for Cook like few other men in their history. He started as an ordinary seaman with few connections in a society where connections were indispensable. But his skill, intelligence and determination yielded quick results. At the pinnacle of his career, he explored, charted and returned to his appreciative nation reports from the far reaches of the earth's surface. He found more unexplored lands than any other man in Western history.

Cook was a Yorkshire farmer's son who took to the sea at an early age. Born in 1728, he abandoned his father's calling for a life at sea. He started as an apprentice on a North Sea collier, sharpening his mind and seafaring skills in Whitby, a center of shipbuilding and trade on England's eastern coast. In 1755 he began his service in the British Navy, and his advancement from ordinary seaman to master's mate confirmed his skill, perseverance and commitment for a naval career.

During the French and Indian Wars, he served in Canadian waters, notably in the siege at Quebec in 1759. During that battle he helped pilot boats for General Wolfe so English soldiers could land at the foot of the cliffs below the Plains of Abraham, surprising the French and sealing the British victory. Later Cook became a master surveyor and learned the art of marine chart making. During his early career he learned the mysteries of cartography and gained insights into geography, astronomy and the imagined features of the known world. He surveyed the

Gulf of St. Lawrence and the coasts of Newfoundland with maps that are so accurate they are used to this day.[1]

In 1768 he led the first of three journeys into the Pacific upon which his fame is based. Unknown and newly commissioned as a lieutenant, Cook was sent to the South Seas on the bark *Endeavor.* This ship was brought out of the coal trade for just £2,800 to join a venture of nine European Nations to observe the transit of Venus as it passed across the face of the sun to determine the distance of the earth from the sun. Scientists were stationed in all parts of the world to observe the transit as the Europeans assumed measurements taken from different locations would provide more accurate and quantifiable results.

This viewing is an opportunity that presents itself to scientists in dual sightings eight years apart about every 120 years. The two opportunities in the eighteenth century came in 1761 and 1769. In 1761 Europe was at war, thus limiting scientific voyages. So scientists of the western world did not want to miss the opportunity to observe the Transit on their second chance in 1769. No less than 77 stations and 151 separate reports from around the world were documented, many requiring voyages to new, unexplored regions such as Tahiti. Among others, there was a joint Franco-Spanish expedition to Baja California. But Cook's was the most remote, as European scientists insisted that the Transit of Venus be observed from the Pacific. The English astronomer Thomas Hornsby in 1771 used the information gleaned to conclude the mean distance of the earth from the sun to be 93,726,900 English miles or 153 million kilometers.[2]

The powerful Royal Society led the scientific effort in London. As a result, a representative of the Society, the wealthy and esteemed Joseph Banks, accompanied Cook. At Banks' own expense he brought a complement of artists and naturalists on the voyage to record the flora, fauna, and sea life, as well as the peoples they met, their customs, and their daily lives. The *Endeavor* was just 106 feet long, and 29 feet in the beam. All told, 11 civilians, 71 naval personnel and 12 marines were crowded into an area no larger than a singles tennis court! Leaving Plymouth in mid-summer, Cook rounded Cape Horn in a matter of months, with a passage so comfortable that Banks and his botanists had time ashore to inspect and collect specimens at Tierra del Fuego.[3]

A few months into their adventure the expedition arrived in Tahiti. They established tents for the observation of Venus on a promontory they called "Point Venus," fronting on Matavai Bay, where they stayed three months. The crew was kept busy refitting the ship and her rigging and gathering supplies, while the officers carried out a survey of the island and its coastline. Banks and his party zealously collected thousands of exotic specimens, turning the already crowded vessel into a giant laboratory. Banks' artists Sydney Parkinson and Alexander Buchan made a resplendent record of the voyage that is still held in high regard.[4] On June 19 the voyagers observed the transit with imperfect results.[5]

Cook carried instructions from the Admiralty to execute when his scientific tasks were finished. Leaving Tahiti in mid-1769, he explored to the west. He first visited the other major islands of modern day French Polynesia, then journeyed to New Zealand. In eight weeks he performed a running coastal survey of the New Zealand coastline, showing it was composed of two large, narrowly separated islands. He then discovered and traversed the fertile eastern shore of Australia, finding Botany Bay. Cook named, but otherwise passed Port Jackson, to the north, which later settlers found to be the superior resting spot. Nonetheless, Cook's discovery of Botany Bay set in motion the British conquest of Australia and the founding of a host of British settlements near modern-day Sydney.[6]

Sailing north in the dark, *Endeavor's* keel was mangled at high tide on the Great Barrier Reef. A gaping hole in her hull nearly swamped the vessel. After 24 desperate hours, throwing some 20 tons of iron, stone ballast and six cannons overboard, the crew managed to slide her off the reef. These desperate measures once again proved the worth of Cook as he coaxed his ship to shore, where it was hauled out and hastily repaired at a place still called "Endeavor River," near modern-day Cooktown. The near sinking occurred offshore a place Australians now call Cape Tribulation. This harrowing incident convinced Cook of the folly of using single ship on a voyage of such consequence and especially so far from home. He decided, then and there, that in future voyages such projects would be undertaken with two vessels.[7]

With temporary repairs made, Cook and his crew exited the reef, calling it "the Labyrinth." They sailed on to Dutch Batavia, modern-day Jakarta, to further repair and overhaul the vessel. Batavia was a European seafarer's haven in the Orient. But it was built in swamps infested with mosquitoes, well known for malaria, typhoid and other causes of death. During the 10-week shore side repair, virulent and lethal diseases infected virtually every member of Cook's crew, and 31 perished. Leaving Batavia at last, they rounded the Cape of Good Hope, returning to England, completing a circumnavigation of the globe in three years.[8]

While his visit to Tahiti lasted just three months, the reports in England on their return were larger than life. Newspapers were full of colorful accounts of exotic islands, native peoples and their customs, and curiosities collected by Banks and his party. Cook's crew applauded their captain's achievements as diplomat, scientist and navigator, and he gained instant fame through Banks' incredible tales to a receptive London society. The Admiralty, usually understated, advised Cook they "extremely well approve of the whole of your proceedings." After all, he had charted 5,000 miles of previously unknown coastline. King George III granted an hour-long audience with the returning hero, personally bestowing a promotion to the rank of Commander. Cook later modestly told a friend the king "was pleased to express his Approbation of my Conduct in Terms that were extremely pleasing to me."[9]

Almost immediately there was talk of another voyage to the South Seas, this time to find the imagined Southern continent. The *Endeavor* had been sold into merchant service and was ultimately scuttled in the siege of Newport in the American Revolution, so two replacements were purchased, both Whitby colliers. These ships, the *Resolution* and *Adventure*, were commanded by Cook and Captain Tobias Furneaux respectively. Relatively large but flat-bottomed with a shallow draft, these vessels could put in close to shore for observations and more easily be careened, beached on shore, for repair. Banks wanted to accompany the voyage again, but his grand plans to renovate the *Resolution* to house an even larger entourage were dismissed by Cook and the Admiralty.[10] Instead they were accompanied by a new group of artists and naturalists. In less than a year, July 13, 1772, a complement of 200 men sailed for the South Pacific. Cook first returned to New Zealand and Tahiti, then charted an array of islands of the South Pacific: Tasmania, Norfolk Island, Tonga, Easter Island, New Hebrides, New Caledonia, and the Marquesas.

Cook's contacts with native peoples were also far more diverse than on the first voyage and he recorded in his journal the complexities of the local people he encountered, including their customs, religions, leadership and even the reception on shore. Many were not as friendly as the Tahitians. For example, while in Ship Cove, New Zealand, Captain Furneaux and his men from the *Adventure* had a disastrous experience with the Maoris. A party sent from the ship to gather a last load of water and foodstuffs was attacked, and all the men were killed, and some were reported eaten.[11]

Furneaux and Cook were often separated in their voyage and Furneaux and his crew suffered terribly when alone. After weeks of continuous strong gales in the second year, Furneaux's ship was leaking, his men were cold, wet and sick and his stores were spoiled. Reaching the longitude of Cape Horn, but well south of it, Furneaux abandoned the voyage and Cook. He returned to England after two years at sea, arriving a full year before Cook.

The public was spellbound by Furneaux's early reports of the voyage, including his gruesome reports of an attack on his crew by cannibals in New Zealand. The nation was also fascinated by a young islander called Omai, whom Furneaux brought willingly back to England to experience the world and share his exotic customs with an inquisitive British public. Sir Joseph Banks was especially fond of the Tahitian. In the two years Omai was in London, Banks regularly dressed him as a fashionable English gentleman and introduced him to English society. He attended the opera, met with nobility, and dined with celebrated statesmen and authors like Samuel Johnson. While he learned some English, Omai was usually in the company of crewmembers, who could roughly interpret for him in his native language.[12]

In the final year of the voyage, Cook adopted an enormous zigzag route in order to touch and chart as many islands as possible. At the same time, he plunged southward to seek land near the South Pole. With each foray, he drove the *Resolution* headlong toward Antarctica. Each time he encountered fog, ice, gales and other fearsome conditions until the ice pack prevented further progress. For one period Cook was at sea 122 days consecutively, for another 117 days. Once he sailed for ten thousand miles over uncharted seas without sighting land. His course took him twice within the Antarctic Circle, proving to speculative geographers that there was no great Southern continent as had been imagined since before Columbus. But the travail overcame Cook and his crew and they retreated to Tahiti and then finally returned to England, in late July, 1775. Like the first voyage, Cook circumnavigated the globe in three years. Cook lost just four men, and only one to sickness.[13]

Returning to England a year after Furneaux, Cook had a tumultuous reception wherever he went. His fame spread through Britain and the world thanks to his navigational and scientific achievements. King George eagerly heard the report of his voyage and then bestowed another promotion, this time to post captain. But the two voyages were long and arduous and Cook was exhausted. At the age of 46 he took a high-ranking position at a Naval Hospital with a secure retirement. He spent time with his family and he and his wife Elizabeth soon announced they were having another child. He was elected a Fellow of the Royal Society, a high honor in itself, to be counted among the leading British scientists and scholars. Later the Society awarded him the Copley Gold Medal, the highest scientific honor it could bestow. It was a brilliant end to a phenomenal career, or so it seemed.[14]

Retirement apparently did not suit Cook. He longed for the sea. Rumors of another Pacific expedition to search for the speculative strait through the American continent circulated, and Cook was captivated. After all, the lands and waters of the North Pacific were still mostly unknown to Europeans.[15] He did not expect to command the new expedition but he was frequently consulted by the Admiralty about voyage details. At a dinner party with the Earl of Sandwich, the First Lord of the Admiralty, Cook was asked to advise about the pending journey. There was little doubt Cook was the most qualified to lead it. Cook's hosts impressed him with the grand scale and importance of the voyage and its benefits to science and navigation. To everyone's relief, Cook convinced himself he was the only one to take charge. In just six months after returning home, Cook had committed himself to another expedition.[16] By the time the Copley Medal was struck and ready for delivery, he had already left England. The British Nation was only too willing to take advantage of his considerable skills as captain, navigator, chart maker and diplomat on one more, and this time fatal, voyage of world exploration.

The third voyage was the most ambitious. He sailed again with the *Resolution*, but this time the consort was the *Discovery*, commanded by Charles Clerke. Clerke was one of Cook's favorite officers and served him well on both prior voyages to the Pacific, serving as Master's mate on the first voyage and second lieutenant on the second voyage. Cook received his final instructions the same week the American colonists declared their independence from Great Britain. Given his own celebrated status and the prospects of another famous voyage, Cook had his choice of officers, and he chose well. In addition to Clerke, Lieutenant John Gore was the second in command on the flagship, and James King was second lieutenant. Although just 21 years old, William Bligh was appointed as master of the *Resolution*. George Vancouver, who served as midshipman on the second voyage, returned as a Lieutenant on the *Discovery*.

Cook and his crew left Plymouth in the *Resolution*, sandwiched between a fleet of warships bound for the anticipated war in the American colonies. The *Resolution* had to sail alone, as the unfortunate Clerke was detained in debtor's jail. Clerke had guaranteed the debts of his brother, also a captain in the Royal Navy, and his brother left on an earlier voyage without settling with his creditors. Clerke was finally released and joined Cook with the *Discovery* in Cape Town. But Clerke had contracted tuberculosis while in prison and died from the disease during the voyage.[17]

Together the *Resolution* and *Discovery* had a crew of 181 men, including 20 from the earlier voyages. After they came together at the Cape of Good Hope, the two vessels sailed by way of Kerguelen Island in the Indian Ocean, to Tasmania, New Zealand, Tonga and Tahiti, all in just over twelve months. The principal reason to return to Tahiti was to repatriate Omai. Cook was not particularly fond of the Tahitian and was baffled by the fame he achieved in English society. Although Cook was sometimes amused by Omai, he found him to be haughty and insincere, wholly unable to handle his newfound wealth or political position. Once back in the Pacific, Omai enjoyed special status with the other chiefs. They designated a piece of land for him on Huahine, a nearby island in the "Society Island" group of islands and, before the ships left to a tearful departure, the carpenters built him a small house.[18]

As Cook continued on the third voyage his days of benevolent rule and respect for other human beings was on the wane. Since the first visit to Tahiti the native preoccupation with stealing items of clothing, nails, navigational instruments, animals and even shore boats had become well known. In the past, Cook had always reacted with diplomacy and a measured response, tolerating theft as a part of the experience on shore. If the stolen item was critical to the voyage, he would insist on its return by making cautious demands through the local leadership. It was usually recovered with little effect on the populace.

But on the third voyage, at least in the South Pacific and Hawaii, Cook abandoned such moderation.

The change started in New Zealand and it came first in relations with his crew. Cook had returned to the place where Furneaux's shore party had been decimated on the second voyage. The Maori were unmindful to their earlier treachery and, when Cook arrived, pretended normal relations. The crewmembers, especially those from the second voyage, demanded retribution. Cook would have none of that, so the murderers walked openly in the presence of the crew. Cook even had the artists on board draw a portrait of their leader. Many of the crew rebelled to the point of mutiny. Sullen and bitter, they responded with petty thievery on board. Cook was relentless. Although floggings were common aboard British ships, they increased in frequency. Rations were cut, and then cut again, as the captain insisted that the stolen items be returned. Tensions grew on board to the point of explosion. Cook seemed more at peace with the Maori than his own crew, who were resentful.[19]

After New Zealand, the expedition next arrived at Tonga. Here the anger arising from the split between captain and crew was meted out against the unsuspecting people on shore. Like most new encounters in these exotic islands, the Tongan people rowed and swam to the ships with both overwhelming joy and curiosity. But the Tongans soon took to petty thievery, similar to the prior encounters. As if by design, the women seemed intent on distracting the sailors as their men stole anything they could find. Cook was powerless to restore order. It seemed both his crew and the Tongans preferred the chaos and violence ensued. Cook and the loyal marines on board responded rashly, arresting chiefs and other Tongan men, demanding ransom for lost goods. Lashings were meted to both natives and crewmen, and often innocent people were accused and punished.

For the first time in the history of Cook's voyages his own men were ashamed of his behavior. Surgeon William Anderson was openly critical of the captain's orders in his journal. "I am far from thinking there was any injustice in punishing this man for the theft, as it cannot be determined what might be in the consequence of such practices had been permitted," he wrote. "But that he should be confined in a painful posture for some hours after or a ransom demanded after proper punishment for the crime had been inflicted, I believe scarcely will be found consonant with the principles of justice or humanity upon the strictest scrutiny."

The repressive measures had no effect. Cook refused to leave the place, which he dubbed the "Friendly Isles," and instead decided to start branding Tongan thieves by shaving half their heads as a "mark of infamy." In this way, Cook surmised, the crew could refuse boarding rights to returning thieves. The Tongans did not take this punishment lightly. Their chief soon planned to kill Cook in retribution during planned ceremonies on shore. Fortunately for Cook, the chief and his rivals could not agree on how to spring the trap and the feast proceeded uneventfully.[20]

At their next stop in Tahiti, Cook demurred to petty thievery as on prior voyages. But despite many prior visits to Tahiti without incident, he put one local to the lash and then cut off his ear. This punishment, unprecedented for Cook, was for stealing a goat, even though the animal was safely recovered. Fortunately for the Tahitians, and maybe Cook, the ships soon left the islands in December 1777 for the Northwest Coast. Clerke was already so ill from tuberculosis that Cook suggested he stay behind at

Tahiti. Although curable today, at the time of the voyage the disease was irreversible. After leaving Tahiti, Clerke was frequently so ill that he was unfit to command the *Discovery*. As it turned out, Burney, Clerke's first lieutenant, and Bligh were often in command of Cook's consort for the remainder of the expedition until Clerke died aboard the *Resolution* as they approached Kamchatka in August, 1779.

Expecting a long and tedious haul to North America, within weeks they came upon an unexpected paradise in mid-January, 1778. They chanced upon a chain of high volcanic islands that many consider Cook's greatest discovery. He named them the Sandwich Islands after the Earl of Sandwich, Lord of the Admiralty. Today they are the Hawaiian Islands. Cook was the first European to see them and, given their location in the central Pacific, the discovery was of unmatched strategic and commercial importance in the years to come.

As the ships approached the islands, canoes full of local people surrounded the expedition. Their features and customs suggested the people were directly related to the Polynesians seen in New Zealand and Tahiti. To the astonishment of the sailors, words they heard were in familiar Polynesian tongue—hogs, sweet potatoes, plantains, breadfruit, and fish—words the sailors had listened to every day in Tahiti. Once on shore, Cook's command over the people was powerful. He was revered as a god, which made him uncomfortable. When he passed crowds they would prostrate themselves on the ground, a gesture of respect and submission usually reserved for kings. They would not rise until he commanded them do so. He was certain by their reactions and mannerisms they had never seen Europeans before and he found them even more beautiful and accomplished in ways of the sea than the people of Tahiti.[21]

The visit was broken by the unnecessary killing of a Hawaiian by a landing party, as well as by Cook's continuing unhappiness with the pervasive pilfering. Now in Hawaii, with people who had never met Europeans before, Cook decided retribution and punishment was the means to stop theft. Clearly, his patience and tolerance were significantly reduced. But in their eagerness to make Cook feel welcome, the islanders carefully masked their own warlike nature.

Before he left Hawaii, Cook made many detailed observations about the customs and language of the islanders. He was particularly impressed with their canoes, seamanship and methods of navigation. He was also impressed by their ability to take to the water and swim, which most Europeans of the time could not do. He speculated on the patterns of migration to Hawaii, since these "South sea islanders" occupied a Polynesian nation that extended over 2,000 miles north from Tahiti and New Zealand. Using the empirical evidence before him, he surmised this widespread Pacific maritime culture had a kinship in language and customs with people throughout the "Polynesian Triangle," from Easter Island on the east, to New Zealand on the west, and Hawaii in the north.

Cook was right. Scholars agree today that the Polynesian migration to Hawaii was part of one of the most remarkable sailing achievements of mankind. This great migration probably began before the birth of Christ. Europeans were still sailing close to coastlines before developing navigational instruments that would allow them to venture onto the open ocean when voyagers from Fiji, Tonga, and Samoa began to settle islands in an ocean area of over 10 million square miles. The settlement took perhaps a thousand years to complete and involved finding and fixing the position of islands that were less than a mile in diameter on which the highest landmark was a coconut tree. So by the time Cook and other European explorers entered the Pacific Ocean almost all the habitable islands had been settled for hundreds of years.

The voyaging was all the more remarkable because it was done in modest canoes built with tools of stone, bone, and coral. The canoes were navigated without instruments by seafarers who simply depended on observations of the ocean and sky and other patterns of nature to discern the direction and location of islands. The dugout or outrigger canoes were fashioned from tree trunks with adzes or made from planks sewn together with a cordage of coconut fiber. Cracks and seams were sealed with the sap from breadfruit trees. An outrigger was attached to a single hull for greater stability on the ocean; two hulls were lashed together with crossbeams and a deck added between the hulls to create double canoes capable of voyaging long distances. The canoes were paddled when there was no wind and sailed when there was. The sails were usually woven from coconut leaves. These vessels were remarkably seaworthy as they made voyages of over 2,000 miles along the longest sea-lanes of Polynesia.[22]

Cook stayed in Hawaii just two weeks, as he could not spare any more time away from coastal exploration. A few days from the Oregon coast his crew was greeted by remarkable displays of the *aurora borealis.* Then, as they sighted land, a storm came, locking up the secrets of the coast for a tumultuous two weeks. In five weeks crossing from Hawaii the temperature had dropped forty degrees. Finally, at sunrise on March 7, 1778, "the long looked for Coast of new Albion" was revealed, and Cook came in contact with the west coast of North America for the first time.[23]

Across the continent, at the same time that Cook arrived on the coast, George Washington and his Continental Army were completing their first winter at

Valley Forge, Pennsylvania, in rebellion against the British King. During the weeks of Cook's voyage from Hawaii, American and French representatives signed two treaties in Paris in which France recognized the United States as an independent nation, beginning its open support of the colonists and the provision of military supplies to Washington's army. The British response was swift and the two nations soon declared war.

The respect for Captain Cook and the discoveries of his third voyage were of paramount significance to the western world, even while it was at war. Benjamin Franklin, then American ambassador to France, issued a letter of free passage, so that Cook would not be disturbed by the American allies when he returned to European waters in 1779. Cook was probably only vaguely aware of the American Revolution and certainly did not know of Franklin's letter of praise and protection. Yet the letter demonstrated the high regard Cook enjoyed throughout the western world and the anticipated success of his third voyage.

-Chapter 3-

Nootka Sound

The gale that greeted the expedition along the Oregon coast offered the crew a bleak and ominous welcome to the Northwest coast. When the storm finally subsided, the expedition turned north for Alaska. Since leaving Hawaii, the ships had been nearly two months at sea, so the sailors were in desperate need of water and a place to refit *Resolution*, which had sprung a serious leak. As they passed Cape Flattery, the landscape changed to snow-covered mountains and steep, thickly wooded valleys of cedar, spruce and hemlock. Rocks and breakers were everywhere along the shore, and all sides fell precipitously to crashing waves, making it doubtful any shelter could be found. James King, second lieutenant on the *Resolution*, said it was "as wild & savage a Country as one can well draw in so temperate a climate." They rarely saw a beach, let alone an inlet to follow to calm waters.

In the late afternoon of March 29 a narrow channel appeared, the first opening detected. The ships approached, hoping to at least find water. But they found more. An inner channel opened into a vast bay, studded with islands and a number of streams, all overwhelmed by high, snow-topped mountains. A fine anchorage was found in a deep, sheltered inlet with a central island. Cook called it *Bligh Island*, after the irascible master of the *Resolution*. The wind dropped to a calm, so the shore boats were hoisted to tow the ships further in. No sooner had the sailors started rowing than melodious whooping was heard from shore. In an instant over a hundred local residents came out in 30 or 40 massive cedar canoes, surrounding the ships.[1]

These people, clothed with animal skins and smeared with paint, were not nearly as attractive as the exotic islanders from the South Pacific. The English were accustomed to being greeted by natives in canoes, but this welcoming party was much different from those in Polynesia. As the local people approached, they stood in their dugout canoes and shouted an abrasive song in wild chorus. Some held rattles and waved their arms, pointing at the sky and shore. Others threw colorful ochre into the sky and some even danced in their excitement. It was an uncommon, savage welcoming ceremony. The people were in a near frenzy and kept it up for quite a while.

King described this first encounter:

> The first men that came would not approach the ship very near and seemed to eye us with Astonishment, till the second boat came that had two men in it; the figure and actions of one of these were truly frightful; he worked himself into the highest frenzy, uttering something between a howl & a song, holding a rattle in each hand, which at intervals he laid down, taking handfuls of red Ochre & birds feathers & strewing them in the Sea; this was followed by a Violent way of talking ... at the same time pointing to the Shore, yet we did not attribute this incantation to threatening or any ill intentions towards us; on the contrary they seem'd quite pleas'd with us; in all the other boats, someone or other act'd nearly the same as the first man did.[2]

Some local notables with superior airs and plumage soon arrived. They were well painted, almost gaudy in appearance, with their heads ornamented by many feathers tied to strings falling about their shoulders and back. These were clearly the leaders of the group. One orator seemed to stand out as the chief, so Cook offered him a piece of green cloth. The speaker was disappointed, so Cook gave him some iron tools. That achieved the desired result. Actually, the chief was ebullient. He now let it be known they were eager to trade. The local residents stayed all night along side the ships but were not willing to come aboard. They offered animal skins, fishhooks, bark cloth, weapons and carved masks. A favorite of the crew was the "sea-beaver," or sea otter. Cook speculated enterprising traders would find a profitable market for this "soft gold," and in the following decades it became the driving commercial force in the area. In return the local people first accepted anything the English offered, but soon displayed a preference for iron, especially knives, chisels and nails. A single nail would fetch a sea otter fur. There was the usual pilfering of things not offered for trade, but the thievery was not as bad as that experienced in the South Pacific.[3]

Cook called this first anchorage on the west coast "Ship Cove" in "King George's Sound;" the Admiralty later renamed it "Resolution Cove" in "Nootka Sound." "Nootka" was the name Cook thought the local people gave to it. It was later determined that "nootka" meant to "go round."[4] They were probably giving Cook advice as he looked for a more protected anchorage. But the name continues today to sometimes refer to the North Americans who lived along the seaward coast of Vancouver Island, Canada, and the Olympic Peninsula of Washington state.

Cook was more than relieved that he found the place, "We had got pretty near the inlet before we were sure there was one; but as we were in a bay I had resolved to anchor to endeavour to get some Water, of which we were in great want." Today the sound is a peaceful, mostly uninhabited spit of land just inside the reach of the tempestuous North Pacific, but at the time Cook and his crew assumed they were on the only hospitable shelter on the mainland for miles.[5]

The explorers could not have known this sound lay on a large island, an island of vast proportions, covered in deep forests of spruce, hemlock and cedar. But they certainly understood this was a rain-catching topography, with fog, clouds, drizzle, showers and downpours alternating for days, even weeks, on end. Today it is known to be a central part of the coastal rain forest that extends from the Olympic Peninsula to Southern Alaska. Winters are relatively mild, with periods of snow and rain trading off, but the region is the heart of the world's largest temperate rain forest.

They also could not foresee that in fifteen years, as a direct result of their discovery of plentiful sea otter, the area would become a hotly contested refuge for European mariners and fur hunters operating on the Northwest coast. The first to return were members of the present crew, leading their own expeditions. George Dixon, the armorer on *Discovery*, and Nathaniel Portlock, the master's mate on the consort vessel, returned here on separate voyages in 1785. It was Dixon who discovered a large island group north of Vancouver Island and gave it the name of his ship, *Queen Charlotte*. These are the Queen Charlotte Islands of today. The strait north of the island, which separates coastal British Columbia from Alaska, is Dixon Entrance.[6]

A nineteen-year old midshipman on the *Discovery*, George Vancouver, had an even greater part to play. After the rush for fur began, ownership and right to colonize this bit of real estate led to great conflict between England and Spain, testing on the European political stage their respective claims to the coast. Vancouver was commissioned to return here in 1792 as a part of a greater five-year voyage to chart the area and meet with the Spanish to resolve the international tensions and claims to the territory. He made a circuit of the island's vast coastline, proving its insularity, and mapped Puget Sound. As soon as the tensions eased, westerners quickly over hunted the sea otter population, and Nootka Sound fell into historical oblivion.[7]

This was the first time since his survey of Newfoundland that Cook had stepped on North American soil. What began as a simple stop for water turned into a stay of four weeks, longer than any other anchorage they made in the north that year. Within a day the Nootka were visiting and trading with the English without reserve, although the British rarely saw any women. Language did not impede them, "We soon became perfectly acquainted with each others inclinations," Clerke explained, "tho' our conversation was as perfectly unintelligible to both parties as tho' we had no such faculty as articulation amongst us." And, after the first day, the locals were no longer reluctant to board the ships. Clearly the Nootka people did not regard the English as superior or more powerful than themselves, or even godlike, as occurred in Polynesian encounters. Instead they approached with confidence and the four-week interchange was every much as a reciprocal relationship.

"A considerable number of Natives visited us daily," Cook wrote on April 1. "On their first coming they generally went through a singular ceremony; they would paddle with all their strength quite round both Ships, A Chief or other principal person standing up with a Spear, or some other Weapon in his hand and speaking, or rather hollaring all the time, sometimes this person would have his face covered with a mask, either that of the human face or some animal, and some times instead of a weapon would hold in his hand a rattle. After making the Circuit of the ships they would come along side and begin to trade without further ceremony. Very often indeed they would first give us a song which all joined with a very agreeable harmony."[8]

In spite of this daily intercourse with the locals, the crew took to their assignments. The ships required a considerable overhaul that consumed the attention of the captain and many of the crew. A blacksmith's tent was set up on shore. The foremast of the *Resolution* was rotten, and the mizzenmast collapsed within a few days, so both had to be replaced. The hull and rigging of both ships, severely battered off Cape Foulweather, also required attention. Trees had to be chosen, felled, trimmed, sawed and fitted. This task was time consuming and required careful work in view of the many anticipated years at sea ahead for the ship. Fortunately the local people assisted in carrying the massive timbers to shore. Once the vessels were re-rigged and re-masted with the stout local timbers, the vessels were careened at high tide and re-caulked for continued service.

John Rickman, a lieutenant on the *Discovery*, described the process:

> Being in great want of masts, most of those we brought out with us being sprung, our carpenters were sent into the woods to cut down such trees as they should find fit for their purpose. This they did without the least interruption from any of the inhabitants. They found trees from 100 to 150 feet high, without a knot, and measuring from 40 to 60 feet in circumference. In these trees the eagles build their nests. When they had cut down what best suited their purpose, the great difficulty was

to bring them to shore; and in this labour they were assisted by the natives.[9]

The development in the eighteenth century of small, square-rigged ships like the *Resolution* and *Discovery* had advanced exponentially over the centuries. In Viking times, one-masted ships were sufficient to carry a single sail and offered small vessels manageable way in anything of a breeze. The sail was stretched and hoisted on a pole, where it could stand fast against the mast. But as ships grew in size one sail was too large to handle, so the area of the sail was made changeable by separate ropes rigged from the deck. Later a small mast was added to the front of the ship, the bowsprit, which could be separately maneuvered to help steer, even if there was little wind. This was the kind of vessel still in use by Russian fur hunters encountered in the Aleutian Islands in the time of Cook.

During the last half of the eighteenth century, before iron came to be more widely used, the technology of English ships reached a peak. Since iron was only used for fastenings and fittings, most of the ship was constructed and supported by wood and hemp. Sails were deep, narrow, and square—affording the greatest amount of wind in the sail, with maximum turning capabilities. To get more sail area, ship builders extended the height of the masts, often through separate but interconnected spars and masts. Soon both fore and main masts carried three sails each, on top of the other: the lower sail, the topsail and the topgallant sail. As standing rigging became stronger and stouter in the larger square-rigged ships, additional sails were set in between the masts and before the foremast, called staysails and jibs. This meant, in the time of Cook, all manner of masts were regularly breaking or rotting with weather and wear. Replacement of ships' rigging, like that done in Nootka, was a constant pattern of shipboard life.[10]

Cook's flagship *Resolution* was the largest of the four ships he took on his three voyages. They were not warships, but colliers, or coal ships, all built in Whitby on the northeast shore of England. *Resolution* was built in 1770 and acquired by the Admiralty in 1771. After the return of the third voyage, she was sold into the merchant fleet again, even though she was thoroughly spent after two voyages of world exploration. *Resolution* was small by modern standards—461 tons and 110 feet in length, 30 feet wide, and a mere 13 feet to the depth of its hold. Nonetheless she carried a crew of 112 on the third voyage, making for very cramped quarters. The consort *Discovery* was even smaller, under 300 tons, and just 91 feet in length.

Colliers had simplified rigs so they could be handled by a few men. English ships had the luxury of large crews, especially on long voyages, When purchased by the Admiralty, the colliers were re-rigged with more cordage and tackles for use by such crews, which enabled the ships to spread more canvas in the wind. This improved ship handling, allowing the ships to cover the miles required of these extended passages faster, a hallmark of the British Navy at the time.[11]

The crew and civilian servants were berthed in hammocks slung above the stores on the lower deck. With about 80 men in hammocks, the available space was fully occupied around the clock; the crew slept in shifts while underway. The bulk of the stores were placed in the hold in the lower deck in casks or sacks, and access to this hold was limited to grating-covered hatches lifted by ropes and tackle.

The outer surface or hull of the ships was sheathed with carefully selected heavy wooden planking and waterproofed with caulk, a mixture of tar and hemp called "oakum". Unlike the spars and masts of a ship, however, this planking could not be replaced. It was not unusual for ships to be recaulked several times each year. This was done by careening the ships, or moving them to shore at high tide, where the crew would caulk the planking and remove marine crustaceans that adhered to the hulls. In Cook's case, because of the age and poor condition of the ships at the outset, such caulking and recaulking could only prolong the life of the ships for a short time.

Since the time of Drake, exploratory ventures had changed as the nations of Europe prospered. The Renaissance and Reformation had established the foundations of the modern state and new techniques of war and diplomacy had led to overseas expansion. At first, in the era of Cortez, Balboa and Drake, European expansion had a decided bent toward conquest and destruction. The explorers were obliged to find and return gold and other wealth to their homeland while, at the same time, attempting to Christianize the conquered populations.

By the time Cook arrived in Pacific waters, the goals of exploration had changed, from conquest to enlightenment. In the last half of the eighteenth century many Europeans, especially those in England and France, considered themselves the most civilized people in history. They had conquered most of unknown world and learned much from the older civilizations of the East. Now they believed they surpassed even the ancient Greeks and Romans in artistic and intellectual creativeness and so they concluded it was their obligation to explore and illuminate the uncivilized world. This view guided the era of the Enlightenment, assuming the "light" of science would help informed and unselfish minds improve mankind.

The practical usefulness of scientific activity became apparent to governments and monarchs. National governments often founded or chartered the first permanent scientific societies to foster these goals. The Royal Society of London for the Promotion of Natural Knowledge was chartered in 1662 and the French Académie Royale des Sciences was founded four years later. Both institutions provided honor and fame for scientists and a place to discuss their work. In return, the governments received practical inventions that helped them economically and advanced the reputation of those nations in the world. Beneath the academic and national rivalries, a new community of thought and activity became a part of European civilization.[12]

Enlightenment meant knowledge and knowledge meant science, particularly natural science. Scientists were supposed to spread knowledge and encourage its application in the social and economic advance of civilization, particularly in molding newly discovered lands and people in the image of European civilization. Advancements in navigation and cartography, and the understanding of the heavens, were therefore central to scientific inquiry in this era. Occasionally governments sponsored projects like the observation of the transit of Venus. They held a similar view of exploration, which was to stimulate the spirit of inquiry of newly discovered lands. So the British people were ready for Cook like few other men in their history. His voyages to the Pacific were the epitome of the spirit of the Enlightenment, since they featured the best of all scientific inquiry.

Cook was a champion of Enlightenment ideals of empirical observation and peaceful contact. The stop at Nootka was like none other on the voyage. Here each member of the crew applied his special expertise to scientific inquiry in the time on shore. The astronomers, King and Bayly, set up their observatory tents on an elevated rock near the ships and sighted the moon and stars to determine Nootka's location on the earth. The chart makers, Bligh and Edgar, went sounding and surveying, and constructing charts of the area. The surgeon, Anderson, a part time naturalist, cataloged and drew the profusion of birds that flocked around the sound. James Burney, James King and David Samwell, and later the two captains, did their best to record the language and songs of the local people. Those without special scientific expertise had other, more mundane tasks. The crew refilled the empty water casks and resupplied the ships with food and other provisions found on shore. But the record of the stay in Nootka was splendid, almost extravagant.

The Enlightenment did much for the arts associated with hydrography, navigation, geodesy, astronomy, bathymetry, chart making, and recordkeeping in voyage journals. The shape of the earth had been determined and lines of latitude and longitude placed on the globe. Latitudes at the Equator were set at 0° and the North and South Poles, still undiscovered, were set at 90°. The chart makers could easily determine latitudes, north and south, using a sextant in relation to the sun and stars. But the difficulty was with the meridians, the east and west directions. By the time of Cook's third voyage it had been generally accepted that the base meridian point for all calculations on land and sea, longitude 0°, would run through the Royal Naval Observatory at Greenwich, but the method of determining longitude when away from Europe was uncertain and the results unpredictable.

Two means existed to calculate longitude: lunar calculations and marine chronometers. Lunar observations of longitude, or the east-west position from Greenwich, required the use of the cycles and phases of the moon. After fixing the location of the moon, complex tables in the *Nautical Almanac* would tell mariners how to determine their longitude wherever they were. Such lunar fixes required precision and, in a place like Nootka, such precision was difficult. The astronomers had to be stationery, so at Nootka they set up tents, or observatories, which were equipped with a transit instrument, astronomical clocks and quadrants, barometers, thermometers, an azimuth compass and a reflecting telescope. They had to see the moon. While the constant rain confounded them, Cook, King and Bayly observed a series of hundreds of lunar distances in the cove and left a fine record of lunar observations in the four-week span on shore. The purpose of the multiple calculations was to ensure that random errors in the instruments were minimized. The calculated longitudes today prove they were successful. They apparently had it correct within three minutes, that is, $3/60^{th}$ of a single degree of longitude.

Another way to determine longitude was through chronometers. These portable timekeepers kept a close timekeeping rate under variable and adverse conditions. Some were the size of a modern stopwatch. They were the supreme accomplishments of mechanical technology of the day. More versatile than lunar observations or clocks, they could be taken in a moving vessel. Lunar observations required a shore post and observatory tent; clocks needed weights and a pendulum that could not function with any accuracy on ships.

At the time of Cook, chronometers were experimental. The objective was to carry Greenwich time, or some other known time from a base meridian, and compute the distance in longitude based on the time from Greenwich. Their accuracy was often little better than dead reckoning. Success required they be regularly and properly wound and that they keep a consistent rate of time over a long period, a demanding task on a three-year Pacific voyage. Their use also required periodic lunar observations from shore to verify accuracy between shore stops and to determine the predictability of the rates of change over an extended voyage.

The British government established a Board of Longitude to stimulate inventors and even offered cash prizes for the most accurate and dependable timekeepers. By the time of the second voyage the chronometers on board were considered to be fairly accurate. To ensure the greatest accuracy the expedition was outfitted with several chronometers built by different inventors for comparison purposes. Each was rated against the other with careful reports made to the Board of Longitude at the end of the voyage. It was an exacting business.[13]

Bligh was distressed about the accuracy of the charts later in the voyage, particularly in the Bering Sea. The errors were never his fault, he reasoned, just due to the sloppy work of his fellows. His irritation does not appear at Nootka where he supervised the preparation of charts by Edgar, Roberts, Burney and Riou, each of whose work is considered masterful by modern standards. Bligh's charts carefully depicted each island and shoal, and laid over lines of latitude and longitude that closely resemble modern charts. In the inner reaches of the bay he found sheltered anchorages that were so vast and secure that they could accommodate the entire British Navy. Altogether, his charts of the west coast of North America were brilliant, resulting in no small measure from his exceptional skills with navigational instruments and the chronometers on board.

James Cook was not simply an exceptional seaman but he was also a well-versed scientist, both in planning and implementing scientific expeditions. He understood, probably more clearly than any man during his time, that the health of his crew was critical to the success of his voyages. He made sure there were always fresh provisions and insisted his crew eat them, no matter how distasteful. On arrival at any new lands, like Nootka, he sought fresh water and provisions from shore. At Nootka, the sailors traded frequently for fresh fish and mussels. Even on board ships, antiscorbutics were administered frequently to prevent scurvy.

George Gilbert, midshipman on the flagship, described the food available on board, "We were allowed a small quantity of sowr Krout, twice a week to eat with our salt provisions; it is an excellent antiscorbutick and kept exceeding well all the voyage. We had likewise portable soup, three times a week boiled with our peas; which were very much the worst article of provisions we had onboard." Some of these provisions were probably meaningless in the effort to prevent scurvy, as this was the era before knowledge of vitamins and vitamin deficiencies. Cook's favorite ministrations were "sour krout" and "portable soup," but improved hygiene, sanitation and the frequent use of native foods when available were probably more beneficial. Nonetheless, fresh provisions and attention to diet was the hallmark of Cook's voyages and this attentiveness assured the health of his sailors.[14]

He was obsessed with hygiene and discouraged sexual relations with the local people. His directions at Nootka were not unlike his instructions in Tahiti and other exotic islands to the south, but his crew was more accepting to his dictates at Nootka. Few of the men were interested in trading for sex with the local women, although like most other lands the women seemed ready to provide it. At Nootka, the fathers often made the bargain, according to Samwell, exchanging their daughters' favors for simple items, like a pewter plate. But many of the crew found the local women were too caked in grease and dirt to meet the sensibilities of even these enthusiastic love-starved men. By the end of the four weeks Samwell reported some of the more persistent fellows overcame such pretensions. They devised a "Ceremony of Purification," where the women were first scrubbed clean with soap and hot water. After taking pains to cake on red ochre paint to make themselves appealing, the women were astonished to find the Englishmen scrubbing it off. Nonetheless, the experience was just about as pleasant as could be found in the Pacific, but done with less frequency.[15]

By the time the sailors arrived in Nootka, they had been away from Europe for nearly two years. They had been eating hardtack biscuits since they left home and in two years even the most carefully stored biscuits were infested with maggots and other insects. Consequently Cook and his men looked for fresh things to eat and drink. Spruce beer was a favorite. Made from the tips of spruce buds, it was brewed as a supplement to the crew's dwindling rations of alcohol. It went down smoothly, was rich in vitamins, and for people as afraid of drinking water as most 18th-century sailors were, it was the perfect beverage. And, if they drank enough, they would not notice how badly the hardtack was infested, or whether it crawled across the table!

While Cook was uncompromising about diet and cleanliness, he gave up his equally strict efforts to control thieving through the use of retribution and punishment that he had imposed in the South Seas, deciding instead to accept the inevitable losses. Clerke had resolved long ago not to bother with disciplining thieves, particularly if a visit was planned to be a short one. He felt it would only engender bad will that was a greater price to pay than the theft of trifles. The effects of Clerke's tuberculosis were also beginning to weigh on his health, so he had little energy to spend on recriminations with local people.

Although the English admired the sea otter pelts they acquired, they could only speculate as to their value. The discovery of the treasure trove came later in the voyage, when at Macao and Canton they were paid handsomely for the few pelts they had acquired. This realization, and the publication of the third voyage journals in 1784, led to a rush of European traders into the North Pacific, previously the exclusive domain of the Russians. The trade was to last some 50 years, throughout the Northwest Coast, including the islands off Kamchatka north of Japan.

John Ledyard, an American with well-honed commercial instincts, remarked about the variety of the skins available at Nootka. "The light in which this country will appear most to advantage respects the variety of its animals, and the richness of their fur. They have foxes, sables, hares, marmots, ermines, weazles, bears, wolves, deer, moose, dogs, otters, beavers … this animal was sold at Kamchatka, a Russian factory on the Asiatic coast for …near 12 guineas, and had it been sold in China it would have been worth 30 guineas." The beaver and sea otter were the prize and Ledyard speculated on the advantages of the land in the China trade. "We purchase while here about 1500 beaver, besides other skins, but took none but the best … it afterward happened (upon reaching China at the end of the voyage)," he explained, "that skins which did not cost the purchaser sixpence sterling sold in China for 100 dollars."[16] On reading reports like Ledyard's, a rush for fur ensued. By 1825 the sea otter had been hunted to virtual extinction.

The Admiralty's instructions on the third voyage required Cook "to survey, make charts, and take views of such bays, harbours, and different parts of the coast … as may be useful to navigation of commerce." He was also required "to note types of trees, soil, animals and fish and to make as accurate drawings of them as you can."[17] Cook accomplished this task with considerable success. Indeed, the third voyage yielded the best-known body of work from any of the early voyages on the west coast of North America.

Cook, King, Samwell, Ellis and Clerke all left extensive ethnographic records. Clerke was also an excellent naturalist, sighting and reporting local plants and bird life like none other. He saw eagles, swallows, a crested jay, thrush, wrens, hummingbirds and sandpipers. He also speculated that while there were few waterfowl, they were migratory—and March was too early to see them at this latitude. The snapdragons and columbine were starting to bloom, as well as water lilies, hedge mustards and violets. He lamented the early spring arrival on the coast, as "there were great numbers just making their appearance."[18]

One of the most remarkable achievements of Cook's voyages was to bring back a vivid and comprehensive pictorial record of the places visited. Earlier explorers had returned with notebooks and journals and the navigators had produced maps and charts. Some of the seamen could draw, but usually poorly. By contrast, the artists who went with Cook offered dramatic and imposing landscapes, as well as the facial expressions and dress of native peoples.

The legacy of the third voyage, surpassing the effort from Cook's earlier voyages, was the brilliant drawings by John Webber. Webber was born in London in 1751 to an emigrant Swiss sculptor. He studied in Switzerland, then Paris, and joined the voyage at just 27 as the official voyage artist. His prolific output of drawings in Nootka and along the Alaska coastline are the finest drawings of the west coast and its inhabitants made in the era of European coastal exploration. He observed landscapes, including plants, trees, birds, and he drew intricate detail of the faces of native people, including their weapons, ornaments and homes.

William Webb Ellis was the other active artist on the third voyage. He worked mostly in pencil and watercolor, making drawings of native peoples, landscapes and subjects related to the natural sciences. He was the surgeon's mate on the *Discovery* and was encouraged by Clerke to draw images because of his artistic talent. He had little formal training and, unlike Webber, had no commission from the Admiralty.

Webber and Ellis made an excellent team, and their efforts resulted in a remarkable record of the voyage. They worked frequently together, particularly at Nootka, as many of their views were drawn from the same location. At Nootka they produced exceptional drawings of the people, landscape and vessels at Ship Cove. At the conclusion of the voyage Webber's drawings were given to a team of engravers. He then supervised the engraving of sixty-one of these drawings that were published in a comprehensive folio atlas with the official account of the third voyage. These engravings were reprinted in the periodicals of the day and continue today as the best-known images of European exploration on the coast.

Webber lived into his eighties and, while he painted landscapes and portraits throughout Europe, his greatest accomplishments came from the voyage. In his later years he returned to his recollections of the voyage and offered new renderings to a seeming insatiable public. His legacy was to provide the highest level of artistic representation of native people and landscapes to the European populace and to record with accuracy the visual image of these people at the time of the first European contact. His widely disseminated drawings also became the new benchmark for pictures of exploration on the coast, a standard followed in turn by the Russian, French, Spanish and later English voyages to the area.[19]

On his return from the voyage, Ellis published one of the few unauthorized journals of the voyage. This was forbidden, and certainly rankled Banks and the Admiralty, but Ellis was in debt and threw caution to the wind. He soon joined an Austrian voyage of circumnavigation as principal artist but, before leaving Europe on the voyage, he was killed in a fall from the main mast of his ship. He was not quite thirty years old.[20]

−Chapter 4−

People of the Coast

Cook spent his longest period with the people of the Northwest coast during his month at Ship Cove in Nootka Sound. This time afforded Cook—as well as King, Samwell, Ellis and Clerke—the opportunity to prepare an extensive ethnographic record, a record that was matched only during the three voyages in Tahiti and Hawaii. It also was the first sustained period in which Europeans came in contact with the Indians of the Pacific Northwest. For some it was the beginning of the end, the first invasion of peaceable peoples by rapacious Europeans. For Cook, and the English observers of his voyages at the time, the contact unlocked the mystery of the coast and its people.

Cook's journal, along with those of his companions who wrote of the people of Nootka Sound, are the first record of western culture coming to the people of the Northwest coast. Luckily Cook, and other English explorers who came to the coast in the decades that followed, collected important artifacts now treasured by the British Museum and other European institutions. Cook's observations and conclusions, despite their Euro-centrism, still rate high with modern scholars. Even when confronted by cultures and practices he did not understand, Cook avoided over simplifying or denigrating the people, instead he reported factually and with keen insight, based on his earlier contacts in other Pacific regions and the scientific age of the Enlightenment in which he lived. His journal is the earliest written source material for the region and still captivates anthropologists who rediscovered the people a century later.

The people of Nootka Sound lived a rugged existence subsisting in a harsh environment. Their lives were far different than the easy pace of the exotic islands of the South Pacific. This difference and the manner of the people did not go unnoticed in the journals and the Nootkans suffered in the comparison. Rather than "noble savages," Cook and his crew found them to be "depraved savages." They were filthy, covered with lice, and never bathed. But their artistic skills were well honed, and they had a keener sense for trade than their contemporaries in Polynesia. They also showed no fear of Europeans, and seemed a friendly, inoffensive people who interacted well with Cook and his crew. Their easygoing nature and modest approach to the foreigners is evident since no one was shot during the four-week visit.

The local people were easy to speak with and they understood how to communicate with the English. Cook explained, "We had learnt little more of their language than to ask names of things and the two simple words yes and no." Much of their language was recorded in the logs. For Cook, most of his comments had to await his return to the sea before taking the time to summarize the place and its inhabitants. He frequently contrasted his Nootka experiences to those in the South Pacific, particularly when comparing the people. Among other things, he noted that the Nootka people did not regard the English as superior or more powerful than themselves, so the natives approached the sailors in trade with confidence. There was no submissive behavior or deification, as in Tahiti and Hawaii.[1]

Cook observed very few similarities in the appearance of the Nootkans. The broad flat faces and high cheekbones of these coastal people meant they were not related to the natives of the South Pacific. Unknown to Cook, this was probably the result of artificial enhancements at birth. Apparently the people placed a pad of bark firmly against the heads of children in their infancy, while in their cradles, to enhance the forehead as a thing of beauty. Cook found the Nootka were not very talkative, usually grave and silent, and "a docile, courteous, good natured people." They had straight, long black hair, usually flowing, and were short and stocky in build. They were also quick tempered, passionate and quick to react to the slightest provocation. They recognized the value of property and were less likely to steal than "many of our friends of the S. S. islands (presumed to mean South Sea Islands including Hawaii)." In all, Cook and the other observers of the local inhabitants guessed there were several thousand people of different tribes in the area.

The Nootka complexion was "swarthy," but Cook assumed it was more from face painting than their skin tone. Both sexes daubed themselves liberally with black, red and white ochre mixed with oil. They were covered with dirt and grease, and stank inordinately of fish, oil and smoke, since they probably never bathed. Although less attractive to Cook than the Polynesians, their music was pleasing, especially when paddling in cadence. The English found the songs rhythmic, complex and melodic. Canoeists often sang in unison, sometimes standing, keeping time by beating their paddles against the sides of the boats.[2]

King was especially fond of the singing, "A young man with a remarkable soft effeminate voice after ward sung by himself, but he ended so suddenly & unexpectedly, which being accompanied by a peculiar gesture, made us all laugh, & he finding that we were not ill pleased repeated his song several times." In response, the English offered their own music, "...we ordered the Fife & drum to lay a tune; these were the only people we had seen that ever paid the smallest attention to those or any of our musical Instruments, if we except the drum, & that only I suppose from its noise & resemblance to their own drums; they observed the profoundest silence, & we were sorry that the dark hindered our seeing the effect of this musick on their countenances.[3]

Clerke was not as complimentary as Cook or King. "The Natives here ... are exceedingly ill made, having large Knees, contracted Calves and protuberant Ancles: this deformity of the Limbs, I suppose to be owing to a pernicious custom they have of sitting upon their Legs. ... These are the dirtiest set of People I ever yet met with; they are continually rubbing their faces & Bodies over with one kind of filth or other by way of beautifying themselves, and by this frequent Repetition they have so ingrain'd the dirt into the Skin, that it is absolutely hard to tell, what colour our good Mother Nature originally gave them."[4] Indeed, beauty is in the eye of the beholder.

Ledyard, who was from Connecticut, reflected on the similarities of the Nootka people to other North Americans he had seen on the East Coast. "I had no sooner beheld these Americans than I set them down for the same kind of people that inhabit the opposite side of the continent. They are rather above the middle stature, copper-coloured, and of an athletic make. ... in their manners they resemble the other aborigines of North-America, they are bold and ferocious, sly and reserved, not easily provoked but revengeful; we saw no signs of religion or worship among them, and if the sacrifice it is to the God of liberty." He thought their language was "very guttural," and if written in English it "would very much abound with consonants." He was certain they were cannibals and sacrificed humans in ceremonies, but none of the other journals suggested that. Such speculation was presumably offered only to titillate his readers, based on the offering of human skulls and dried hands as items for trade.[5] Both Clerke and Ellis wrote such speculation was hasty and exaggerated.

Their clothes were mostly made from furs, including a cloak fashioned, in Cook's words, "like a round dish cover" that covered their shoulders and kept them warm and protected from the incessant rain. Their clothing was unique to each individual, shaped according to inclination or the size and configuration of the animal from which it was taken. There was little regard for covering private parts. They wore weaved hats that appeared to be "inverted flower pots." Ledyard said they had no coverings for their feet or legs; they walked barefoot on the uneven, rock-strewn soils.

They had no crops or livestock, though anthropologists later found evidence of some cultivation of plants in the region. But the English assumed they relied solely on a seasonally abundant environment that allowed them to hunt, fish and gather food in a manner that Cook and his crew could only begin to understand. They hunted seals, sea lions and occasionally whales throughout the year, but moved to the shores in the spring for seafood, and sought different kinds of fish, berries and roots in season— including the annual runs of herring and Pacific salmon. In the winter they gathered by clans in large planked houses and passed those quieter times with a ceremonial life steeped in traditions of potlatch, feasting, dancing and inter-tribal relations.

The Northwest Coast is a thin, lush coastline extending from California to Alaska. Native people have occupied the area for at least ten thousand years. All traditionally used special hunting and fishing techniques to subsist effectively on the superabundant food resources in the lush rain forests and rich marine environment. In the part of the coast Cook visited, villages were inhabited by kin groups of related families, or clans. The expedition landed in the midst of the southern peoples of modern-day British Columbia, the Nuu-chah-nulth. The archeological evidence is that these people in Nootka Sound, who were of the Mowachaht group, and the Nootka culture have survived in this area with an unbroken occupation of the local Yuquot village site for more than four thousand years. Today the term "Nootka" refers to all speakers of the Wakashan language, including the Nootkan, Nitinat, and Makah tribes. There are many differences, especially social organization and attitudes toward individual status, that separate these people of the Northwest coast from other North American tribes.[6]

Cook observed their large, cedar-planked houses, which were up to 150-200 feet in length. Each home was divided into family apartments with vents for fires inside. Cook said the houses were "as filthy as hog sties" and reeked of fish, fish oil and smoke. The crew had the greatest interest in the carved masks and large wooden images. These were assumed to have religious importance, but their significance was never understood. The seamen were also impressed with their well made, intricately carved dugout canoes. Some were over 40-feet long and reflected extraordinary craftsmanship. Their main weapons were bows and arrows, slings, spears and tomahawks. The tomahawks were made of stone, with decorated and carved wooden handles, suggesting more than just a practical use.[7]

Cook was surprised how hard the Nootka bargained when trading with the sailors. He wrote, "these people got a greater... variety of things from us than any other people we had visited." Their principal fascination was with iron. By the time they departed Nootka, Cook was fearful that no iron was left on board his ships. "Nothing would go down with them but metal and brass," he wrote, "...so that before we left the place, hardly a bit of brass was left in the Ship, except what was in the necessary instruments. Whole Suits of cloaths were striped of every button, Bureaus & ca of their furniture and Copper kettles, Tin canisters, Candle sticks & ca all went to wreck."

The Nootkans were skilled in commerce because trading was the way they established relations with neighboring tribes. The Polynesians had formalized, almost ceremonial exchanges filled with taboos and sanctions that restricted the free flow of trade. But the people of the Northwest Coast were different, much like capitalists of the modern day. It did not matter to them whether they were trading with people from neighboring tribes or Englishmen in ships. They always wanted to strike the best deal they could. They also had a sense of private property that the crew had not previously seen. For example, the English were asked to pay the chiefs for wood, water and grass by exchanging the ship's goats. John Webber gave the buttons off his coat so he could draw portraits of the people on shore. These experiences led Cook to comment that nowhere had he met people "who had such high notions of everything the Country produced being their exclusive property..."[8]

The Nootka people who first greeted the English seemed determined to monopolize trade for themselves. Five days after the expedition arrived in the sound, Cook observed some of the inhabitants arming themselves near one of his shore parties. Alarmed by this apparent threat, Cook ordered his party to rejoin the vessels. Observing all this, the Nootka men made signs indicating they had no hostile intentions against the English. They were protecting themselves against enemies from another tribe, later thought to be the Clayoquot. Cook observed canoes entering the bay and the two groups engaging in violent and angry speeches, after which they retreated.

"At length a party in about a dozen large Canoes, appeared of the South point of the Cove, where they laid drawn up in a body," Cook wrote, anticipating a fight. "At length the difference, whatever it was, was compromised, but the Strangers were not allowed to come along side the Ships nor to have any trade or intercourse with us: our first friends, or those who lived in the Sound seemed determined to ingross us intirely to themselves." Cook later learned these newcomers wanted to trade with the English but the Nootka prevented it.[9]

Ellis and Samwell both wrote of the incident at length. It was a fearful sight. Although there was no apparent provocation for the attack it was reminiscent of the episode in Tonga that led to bloodshed. In preparing for the fight, the natives collected stones in their canoes and pulled down branches of trees to fashion spears. Their weapons were made ready, as if a full-scale battle were to ensue. To the British seamen, an attack seemed so imminent they put sails over the cabin windows to protect them from the hail of stones. Marines were sent to shore to protect the astronomers and some sought refuge in the ships. Gilbert offered a vivid account, "one morning we perceived a number of Canoes full of people well armed coming into the cove ... from which we naturally supposed they intended to jointly attack us. (We) sent some men armed upon the rock to protect the Observatories ... (Captain Cook) was unwilling to fire at them until they began to attack. ... At last we discovered it to be a quarrel betwixt the two parties, and that the dispute was the right of trading with us." After several "threatening gestures and long harangues," the argument subsided and both parties began to trade.

The same hostilities were repeated the next day. Gilbert said, "We were all in expectation that they were coming to an action as one party stood up, shoke their weapons at the other, and made every motion for fighting; by way of a challenge ... singing at the same time and beating their paddles against their Canoes for the space of half an hour." As on the previous day, after each side alternated their ominous threats four or five times on each side, both finally sat down and paddled away. This "engagement of tongues," as Samwell called it, seemed a better way to resolve differences, and less costly to the male population, than practiced in European wars.[10]

Later the Nootka did allow the newcomers to approach the ships but only under their watchful eye. Trade was always supervised to ensure the English did not pit one tribe against the other, particularly for the sea otter skins that attracted so much attention with the English. Cook also believed the Nootka men resold English goods to the other tribes. To Cook this seemed yet another example of their uncanny trade practices, worthy of the commercial brilliance of the merchants of Fleet Street.

Cook was operating with the mistaken belief that, since the Vizcaino and Drake voyages two centuries ago, no Europeans had been in this area of the coast. He knew Russians were in Alaska but he was not aware that the advancing Russian merchant fleet had caused the Spanish to occupy Alta California in the preceding decade. He noticed that the Nootka people had adzes and knives made of iron blades and he speculated on how iron might have reached the area. He assumed it came from trading with people under the influence of the Spanish in California or the Russians in Alaska. There were also two silver tablespoons, carved with small images, that a man was wearing as an ornament around his neck. Clerke saw some similar spoons in Rio de Janeiro, so he assumed they were made in a Spanish or Portuguese colony in America. Gilbert guessed they originated with the Spaniards in California, and had been handed through a series of transactions to this place, "as we could not learn that any ships had been here before."

In fact a Spanish ship had been to Nootka, for just a few days, four years earlier. One of the key figures in the extension of Spanish power up the west coast was José de Gálvez. He first arrived in New Spain, or Mexico, in 1765—before Cook started his first voyage. Gálvez was charged by King Carlos III to reform the administration of his Mexican colony, a polite way to demand greater profits for the crown. Soon Gálvez became so alarmed about reports of Russians creeping down the coast to California that he pushed Spanish rule to the north. He enlisted Junipero Serra, leader of the Franciscan missions in Baja California, to establish missions in Alta California. The Spanish assumed settlements of Christianized Indians would repel Russian efforts to colonize the coast.

So two ships under separate command were sent from Mexican ports in the Spring of 1769 and two overland expeditions followed. Serra and Gaspar de Portola, military governor of the Californias, led the second expedition. Both ships were so overcome by scurvy that they lay disabled in San Diego harbor when the first overland element arrived on May 14. Portola and Serra arrived six weeks later. The situation was so desperate that Serra stayed behind while Portola went on to search for Vizcaino's port of Monterey.

On Sunday, July 16, 1769, Serra founded Mission San Diego de Alcala. But the Indians resisted conversion and, when a fight ensued, Serra retreated to the protective walls of the mission. The next spring a ship from Mexico arrived with food, supplies and men, rescuing the besieged settlement. Serra then sailed to Monterey, where a second mission was established on June 3, 1770. In the following years Father Serra was a dominant influence in the colony.

By the time he died at Mission Carmel in 1784, nine missions and four presidios were established from San Diego to San Francisco.[11]

Not satisfied with these meager colonies, Gálvez and Viceroy Bucareli of Mexico commissioned secret explorations to take possession of lands north of California. In 1773 a newly built vessel, named the *Santiago*, was placed under the command of Juan Pérez, who sailed from Mexico on January 24, 1774. The captain first discharged supplies to the beleaguered colonies, then set out to sea, returning in the southern capes of Alaska, just north of the Queen Charlotte Islands. Three Haida canoes approached, then a lively trade developed, as the Spanish acquired sea otter skins for knives, bits of metal and old clothes.

Further south, the ship anchored at Nootka Sound. Like Cook's approach to Nootka, Pérez was greeted by hundreds of people in dugout canoes, intent on trade. But a strong wind came up, and Pérez had to leave without anchoring. He was there less than two days, in August 1774. The only remarkable result was that the Spanish left the two tablespoons behind, perhaps the first introduction of metal to this society. As Pérez returned from Nootka, scurvy broke out, and winds, rain and seas prevented investigations along the coast before the expedition entered Monterey Bay. Pérez never took possession of any land for the King, but he also did not find any Russians, which must have comforted his superiors.[12]

Disappointed with the Pérez expedition, Viceroy Bucareli dispatched the *Santiago* on another mission the following year, this time with Bruno Heceta in command. Pérez came along as Heceta's pilot. The expedition included two other ships recently constructed in the Mexican shipyards, the *San Carlos* and the modest 36-foot schooner *Sonora*, under the command of Juan Francisco de Bodega y Quadra. The three ships sailed from Mexico on March

16, 1775 with a dual mission of supplying the fledgling California colonies and exploring lands along the coast. The *San Carlos* stopped in California, and later made the historic first maritime entry into San Francisco Bay.

But the other two vessels sailed on. After leaving Monterey, the ships were separated in coastal shoals near the mouth of Washington's Quinault River. As the crew of the *Santiago* began trade with the local inhabitants, six men off the *Sonora* were ambushed by natives on a watering mission and killed. Bodega retreated from shore, the small swivel gun in the bow of his small vessel the only protection from advancing war canoes. Heceta rejected his pleas for a counter attack or any reprisals. Instead, discouraged by advancing scurvy, Heceta abandoned the *Sonora* and retreated with the *Santiago* to Monterey,

Although short on water and rations, Bodega set course in his tiny craft to the northwest. In three weeks he came upon Mt. Edgecumbe near modern day Sitka, Alaska. Coasting to the south, he came into an inlet he called Bucareli Bay. He spent several days in fruitless search for the Strait of Anian and Russian outposts in the area. Historians speculate this foray may have caused an outbreak of smallpox in the area, which is said to have killed a substantial part of the Tlingit population of western Prince of Wales Island. Leaving the bay, the small craft tacked northward for a week, reaching the latitude of Lituya Bay, before winds, high seas, depleted rations, and scurvy forced a retreat. Five weeks later Bodega reached Heceta at Monterey Bay, and together they returned to Mexico. While Pérez died of scurvy along the way, the viceroy gladly received the favorable reports of the captains, confident that Spanish claims to the north were intact; there were no signs of Russians as far north as coastal Alaska.[13]

It is unlikely that Cook was aware of much of this. The Spanish were notorious for keeping secrets, particularly about their prize in California. But some information had reached England about these voyages prior to Cook's departure in July 1776. In the *Annual Register* for May 29, 1776, Cook and the Admiralty learned much about these secretive voyages and the establishment of presidios and missions along the way.

> Several Spanish frigates having been sent from Acapulco to make discoveries and propagate the gospel among the Indians to the north of California; in the month of July, 1774, they navigated as high upon the coast as the latitude 58 degrees 20 minutes, six degrees above Cape Blanco. Having discovered several good ports, and navigable rivers, upon the west coast of this great continent they established in one of the largest ports a garrison and called the for "Presidio of San Carlos"; and besides left a mission at every port where the inhabitants were to be found. The Indians they here met with are said to be a docile sort of people, agreeable in their countenances, honest in their traffic and neat in their dress, but at the same time idolatrous to the highest degree, having never before had any intercourse with Europeans.[14]

The Spanish were aware that Cook was sailing to the Northwest Coast and they did not take kindly to it. Unlike the French and Americans, who from a safe distance commended Cook's achievements, the Spanish saw the third voyage as an incursion on the "Spanish Lake," their exclusive coastal domain since the time of the papal decree. After the expedition of 1775 the Viceroy sent the journals of the Pérez, Heceta, and Bodega expeditions to Madrid, where they were received with muted acclaim.

The only response from Madrid was to inform the Mexicans that Cook was about to sail to the Northwest coast. Gálvez and Viceroy Bucareli went to work immediately, hoping to mount an expedition to intercept Cook. Two new ships were constructed in Mexico and Peru. All the captains of the prior voyages were then assembled to compile a comprehensive coastal map and plan a new expedition. But the vessels left a year late, sailing from San Blas, Mexico on February 11, 1779—mere days before Cook's death at the hands of the people of Hawaii. While one vessel stalled in the area of southern Alaska, Commander Ignacio Arteaga and the indomitable Bodega reached Prince William Sound and Afognak Island (north of Kodiak Island) by early August. Their discoveries were kept secret and, by virtue of missing Cook by a year, they safely returned to Mexico assuming he did not reach the coast.[15]

But Cook had reached the coast in 1778 and spent most of April on the stormy, rain-soaked Pacific shores of what is now western Canada. At Nootka, after three weeks of near constant rain, the weather cleared. Cook had spent most of this time supervising the work of the ships' rigging, so he had little contact with the local people except as he observed trading from the ships or on the nearby shore where the ships were being repaired. In the final week, he took time out to join his midshipmen in the exploration of the sound. Cook rarely left his flagship, so this special outing was important to both Cook and the morale of his men.

Two boats and a crew of midshipmen surveyed thirty miles of shoreline. They crossed the Sound to its western point and stopped in the village of Yuquot, which still exists, where Cook observed the interaction of families, especially the women. This was the first time he saw many women on the trip, as they were rarely observed trading at the ships. They were smoking herring, which Cook called sardines, a messy business. It was not a pleasant sight to the visitors. Cook later wrote, "The women were dirtier & more loathsome & despicable looking Figures than the Men they were never cloathed in Skins or adorned with ornaments of any kind. They Hair full of filth hung over their Faces in clots, in short a woman could not present herself to us under a more disagreeable form than these did."

At one point Cook came upon a party of young women, who quickly dressed themselves with their "best cloaths" and "sung us a song which was far from being harsh or disagreeable." He thought the Nootka were offering their daughters and sisters for prostitution, but scholars have suggested that he misunderstood and that the women proffered were servants or slaves. King recognized that the Nootka had slaves, presumably captives taken in battle, and was surprised when they occasionally tried to sell women and children to the English.[16]

Cook stayed in Yuquot only a short time, as he wanted to survey the Sound with his midshipmen. James Trevenen, one of those midshipman, recorded their exhausting labors, and Cook's mercurial demeanor:

> We were fond of such excursions, altho' the labour of them was very great as, not only this kind of duty, was more agreeable than the humdrum routine on board ships, but as it gave us an opportunity of viewing the different people & countries, and as another very principal consideration we were sure of having plenty to eat and drink, which was not always the case on board the Ship on our usual allowance. Capt. Cooke also on these occasions, would

sometimes relax from his almost constant severity of disposition, & condescend now and then, to converse familiarly with us. But it was only for the time, as soon as we entered the ships, he became again the despot.[17]

The midshipmen certainly had cause to consider Cook a despot, as he was as firm with his young trainee officers as he was with ordinary seamen. And as we have seen, on the third voyage Cook was tired and unhappy. The stress of three intense voyages had gotten the best of him.

By the end of the four-week stay Cook or members of his crew probably had visited five villages. King speculated that the three larger villages each had 700 residents, and probably a total of 2600 inhabitants in the area. Very little distinction in rank was detected amongst the people, with the exception of a nearly foundational division between slaves and freemen. Slaves were war captives from another Northwest Coastal tribe, so not kinfolk. Each slave was the property of its captor and would perform drudge labor or humiliating work. There was no formal government, just the rule of chiefs in each of the independent tribal communities and each of the villages was mutually hostile. But warfare was muted, more threatening than actual hostility. To the British, the Nootka appeared to have little need for religion. The English assumed they were "Idolaters," given to the worship of carved images found in conspicuous place in their houses, as well as masked dancing, potlatches and similar tribal celebrations.[18]

John Rickman offered a charming summary of the expedition's encounter with the people of Nootka Sound, a genial and trouble free encounter by all accounts. "When we first arrived in the Sound, the rough countenance of the men seemed to promise no very agreeable entertainment during our stay," he wrote, "but when they saw our distress, and they we only meant to repair our ships, so far from giving us any disturbance, they gave us every assistance in their power; they supplied us regularly with fish and, when they found that our men liked oil, they brought it in bladders, and exchanged it for whatever they pleased to give for it." Even though the British and Nootkans could only communicate through sign language, trade between them was brisk, unlike any other experience between the sailors and other native people on the voyage. In the end Rickman said the English crewmen left with over 300 "sea beaver" skins on board.[19]

The constructive adventures in Nootka Sound were brought to a close on April 26, 1778, when the ships sailed out, serenaded by the local people one last time. Cook was especially fond of the chief, who was the last to depart the ships. "(A chief) who had sometimes before attached himself to me was one of the last who left us," Cook explained. "Before he went I made him up a small present and in return he presented me with a Beaver skin of greater value ... (then) the Cloak he had on. And as I was desirous he should be no sufferer by his friendship and generosity to me, I made him a present of a New Broad Sword with a brass hilt which made him happy as a prince."

In offering this exchange, and noting it in his journal, Cook seemed to return to his well-honed diplomatic skills of the first and second voyages. The chief was probably Maquinna, one of the most prominent figures of the later history of Nootka Sound, particularly during Vancouver's return in 1792. The Nootkans continued singing, and their canoes accompanied the ships nearly to the open ocean. But their melodies were soon drowned out by the howl of the wind and the mounting waves, as the ships left the serenity and safety of protected moorage and sailed into another hurricane.[20]

The Mowachaht have handed down over the years a number of recollections about the visit of Cook to Yuquot. Today they remember that Cook was desperate and, thanks to the local people, he found a safe anchorage and shelter for his ships. Another memory, recorded in 1970, places Chief Maquinna in the central role:

> The Indians didn't know what on earth it was when his ship came into the Harbour ... So the Chief, Chief Maquinna, he sent out his warriors ... they went out to the ship and they thought it was a fish come alive into people. They were taking a good look at those white people on the deck there. One white man had a real hooked nose, you know. And one of the men was saying to this other guy 'See, see ... he must have been a dog salmon, that guy he's got a hooked nose.' The other guy was looking at him and a man came out of the galley and he was a hunchback, and the other one said 'Yes! We're right, we're right. Those people, they must have been fish. They've come back alive ... Look at that one, he's a humpback [salmon].'[21]

After leaving Nootka, Cook found more sea otter in Prince William Sound and, after his death, his crew discovered these pelts could be sold to the Russians in Kamchatka and the Chinese in Canton for as much as £200 each, such that a few pelts could fetch the same price as a small-sized ship. The publication of the events of the voyage on the return to England, with reports of the remarkable value of this seeming unending supply of fur from the coast, led to numerous trading expeditions to the Northwest Coast in the 1780s, with significant impacts to the local people and the animals they hunted. Between the years of 1789-1796, the Spaniards built a military post near Cook's anchorage in Nootka Sound and observed the people closely. An international incident affected the area in the time of Vancouver's visit and soon Europeans abandoned the place. Seven years later, in 1803 the Nootka attacked the ship *Boston* in the area. Twenty-five of the twenty-seven crewmembers were killed. The two survivors were kept as slaves and feared for their death almost daily before escaping. After that, as the supply of pelts was exhausted, and the inner reaches of Vancouver Island discovered, the Nootka people were left free of European interference until the colonization of British Columbia in the nineteenth century.[22]

Cook's visit to Nootka nonetheless was the first substantial European visit between the fledgling European outposts of California and Alaska. It set in motion the imperial ambitions of the European community that lead to commercial and colonial domination and dispossession of this last uncharted portion of the Northwest Coast.

-Chapter 5-

Southern Alaska

It was a summer of storms. As the ships left Nootka, the wind quickly shifted from the north to the southeast. Soon a frightful storm was upon the them, with high waves, winds and a drenching rain. Clerke called it "a perfect hurricane." By nightfall the gale was tearing at the rigging, as the vessels pitched in the seas. The weather was so hostile that even at daybreak they could not see the length of their ships through the fog, mist and screaming winds. The weather was "dark and rainy."[1] They could only navigate by compass and sheer will, not by coastal features.

Cook wrote that the need to make up lost time outweighed any other consideration, so he pressed on, unwilling to return to Nootka to wait out the storm. Trevenen found this to be the common practice of the brazen English. He wrote:

> It was Captn Cook's constant maxim and practice never to wait in port for a fair wind, but to go to Sea & look for one, & it is much more the characteristic of English seamen than of any others. A Dutchman never stirs out of port till the wind is settled. The Dutchman acts upon a safe plan, the Englishman on a bold one, the consequence is that the latter may be sometimes lost by his rashness, but in general he may make 3 voyages to the other's 2 .... [2]

But Cook also decided it was too risky to sail near shore, so the ships followed the direction of the storm well out to sea, missing any chance to glimpse the shoreline. With few sails furled, they continued north, parallel to what Cook guessed was the trend in the coast. The ships rolled and pitched like never before as they waited out the storm.

John Ledyard wrote, "...before 12 that [first] night, the wind veered from NNW to ESE and was succeeded by a sudden and impetuous gale of wind that threw us into the utmost confusion from its unexpected approach and our unprepared situation to receive it." The gale lasted "with very little intermission" for nearly a week. After the first night the ships lost sight of each other for two days, and "we concluded from our own distresses some irreparable misfortune had attended her."[3]

To add to their misery and gloom, in the early afternoon of the second day *Resolution* sprung a leak, which Cook reported, "alarmed us not a little." They could hear and see the water rush in, and watched casks float in the fish room as the ship was violently tossed in the stormy seas. In a matter of hours the stern of the ship was full of water, requiring all hands at the pumps. They struggled to stay afloat as thousands of gallons of water poured into the damaged hull. On the entire voyage the crew had never been so worried about their safety. For two days the flooding persisted, nearly engulfing the ships and everyone aboard, until they finally gained the upper hand.[4]

Midshipman George Gilbert wrote of the frightening situation:

> "We had no sooner got out of the Sound, but the same evening a very hard gale came on directly off the land, attended with the most severe squalles we had yet experienced, which drove us quite off the coast. The ship very

unfortunately too at this time sprung a leak in her starboard buttock acasioned (sic) by the violence of the gale which obliged us to stand to the North and to keep her upon that Tack. The fish and spirit rooms were intirely filled with water, which rendered our situation rather alarming, as knowing the ships was much decayed in her after parts. The people were now put to two watches and kept constantly employed at the hand pumps and bailing with buckets, yet! could scarce keep the leak under. In this disagreeable situation we remained for two days after which the gale abated; and the weather coming to moderate, we made no more water than we could keep clear with one pump.[5]

The storm finally passed after a week's fury. There were no injuries, just weary agitation about the deplorable condition of the ships, especially the *Resolution*. In a week at sea they had passed a good part of the coast, six degrees in latitude, and all without any sight of land. The Admiralty's instructions told them not to waste time exploring inlets or rivers until they reached 65° latitude. Apparently there was nothing to benefit the British nation south of the Arctic, but they could not have imagined that two terrible storms would prevent viewing the coast this long.

It was the early morning of April 30 when the storm abated. Cook had the two vessels edge back to the coast, "regretting very much that I could not do it sooner, especially as we were passing the place where the Geographers have placed the pretended Strait of Admiral de Fonte." Cook confirmed his disbelief of the much heralded passage in the ship's log, "For my own part, I give no credit to such vague and improbable stories, that carry their own confutation along with them, nevertheless I was very desirous of keeping the Coast aboard in order to clear up this point beyond dispute; but it would have been highly imprudent in me to have ingaged with the land in such exceeding tempestuous weather, or to have lost the advantage of a fair wind by waiting for better weather."[6]

Cook had missed the entrance to the Columbia River and the Strait of Juan de Fuca during the earlier storms along the Oregon and Washington coastline. With this storm he missed the northern part of Vancouver Island, the Queen Charlotte Islands, and Prince of Wales Island. The Admiralty had not expected anything south of the Arctic, presumably because they reasoned a passage connecting the Pacific to Hudson's Bay could not be this far south. But thanks to all the storms the expedition could not have proven it. Only after the return of George Dixon in 1785 could the British confirm there was no passageway to the east and realized the complex tapestry of islands, bays, inlets and fjords along the Southern Alaska coast.

Cook turned back to the coast on May 1, making the first Alaskan landfall in the late evening in the latitude of modern day Sitka. The landscape was so vast and varied they were taken aback. It was beyond the scale of human comprehension. The sun broke out, and a round, snow-capped mountain appeared. He called it "Mt. Edgecumbe," after George Edgecumbe, commander of the Plymouth dockyard, and later British admiral. The point of land jutting out from the mountain was called Cape Edgecumbe. "Mount Edgecumbe far out-tops all the other hills and is wholly covered with snow," he wrote, "but the lower ones bordering the sea are free from it and covered with wood."[7]

John Gore, first lieutenant on the *Resolution*, kept a separate map that he filled with more romantic names.

"The land is high and hilly." he wrote, "Much snow on the hills, some low land on the coast and much wood and many appearances of inlets." After the frightening storm, Gore was captivated by the countryside and unlimited visibility. He found Mount Edgecumbe "beautifully capped with snow," so he called it "Mount Beautiful."[8]

The Alaska coast was even more rugged than the topography of Nootka, a wild and tremendous tapestry of high mountains, deep valleys and rocky shores. It was a stark and dramatic terrain, teaming with wildlife. Steep, dense woodlands of spruce, hemlock and cedar surrounded each body of water. Cook and his companions frequently saw whales, seals, sea otters, and especially bird life. The next day they came upon a series of inlets that finally disclosed the island maze they were passing. The largest body of water, which seemed to connect through several arms deep in the continent, was named "Cross Sound," so named because the day was marked Holy Cross on their calendar. This naming was unusual for Cook. Unlike the Spanish and Russians, he avoided place names with religious significance. The expedition was still ten degrees south of 65° latitude, so no exploration occurred to the east; instead the voyagers continued along the coast.

Calm seas and sunny skies prevailed, in sharp contrast to the dismal weather experienced since arriving on the coast. Beyond Cross Sound a sharp, jagged, snow-encrusted peak loomed over a ridge parallel to the shoreline. So Cook rebuffed his stormy Cape Foulweather in Oregon by calling this lofty peak "Mount Fairweather." Measuring 15,300 feet, the mountain retains this name today. It was an idyllic scene. Whales, sea otters and seals were everywhere in the water, and eagles occasionally soared overhead. The usually understated Clerke, who had been on all three of Cook's voyages in the Pacific, was so taken by this part of Alaska he wrote "I never in my Life before, in any Climate whatever, saw for such a length of time, the Air so perfectly serene; the Sea so perfectly smooth, and the Weather altogether so perfectly pleasant ... the happy influence of the pure Atmosphere, was apparent in every Countenance."[9]

Cook was aware the expedition was now in the area of Russian influence, so he began to refer to maps he carried that were supposed to come from first hand observations of the Russian voyagers who had explored the region. In the late afternoon of May 5, he observed a monstrous snow-covered mountain above the horizon, probably 120 miles away. Recalling the farthest eastward reach of Bering's voyage to this area in 1741, Cook assumed this was Bering's Mt. St. Elias.[10] There are a series of even higher peaks behind Mt. St. Elias, but since St. Elias itself rises to over 18,000 feet out of the sea, it was the most impressive peak, dominating the surrounding landscape.

Soon they arrived at a bay near the base of this snowy summit. By comparing the description written by Bering, they assumed he had anchored here. Consequently the region was named "Bering Bay." Today it is known as Yakutat Bay. One peak in this range that shares Alaska's border with Canada was later given the name Mt. Cook, commemorating this voyage. Another is Mt. Vancouver, in honor of Clerke's midshipman, who later charted all the coastal features of the western shoreline of North America.

The Russian Empire seemed an unlikely competitor in the North Pacific when Czar Peter the Great came to power in the late 17th century. Russians were not seafarers, but Peter insisted that his country embrace western civilization by creating a modern navy. He chose the Dane, Vitus Bering, to take on the responsibility of learning about Russia's proximity to America. Bering's assignment was daunting. It required an appalling 6,000 mile march across the top of the Asian continent from St. Petersburg to the Pacific shoreline of the Kamchatka Peninsula. Once he reached the Pacific he was required to build ships from uncured timber felled in local forests. Indeed, overcoming the hardships of Siberian travel and fulfilling the immeasurable logistics of Bering's two overland trips far overshadow his accomplishments at sea.

In his first expedition, after three and a half years en route, in July, 1728, Bering sailed northeast from Kamchatka in the *St. Gavril*, a undersized vessel just 60 feet long, barely large enough to be called a ship at all. In constant rain and fog, he rarely saw the Siberian coastline, and never Alaska, although the two continents come together at a point where they are separated by just over fifty miles. Bering passed by the coast of Alaska without a clue. Later, when his ship encountered ice floes, he hastily retreated.[11] On his return to the Russian capital in St. Petersburg, the reception was mixed. He had certainly completed the most notable exploring expedition of the Empire to that time, but there was criticism for his timidity in the ice. So he brazenly proposed a second expedition to seek out Europeans in America.

This was no modest proposal. His first expedition used one hundred men; the second would require more than three thousand. His plans were burdened with assignments to find the northern reach of Siberian rivers and make contact with Imperial Japan. But eight years later, on June 4, 1741, the *St. Peter*, under the command of Captain Commander Vitus Bering, and the *St. Paul*, under the command of Captain Aleksei Chirikov, sailed from Kamchatka for America. The ships coasted to the southeast to search in vain for the imagined Juan de Gama Land. As they did, Captain Chirikov's vessel was driven away in a storm. They sailed in futile circles, unable to regain contact, finally continuing toward America on separate voyages.

Six weeks after leaving Siberia, Chirikov's vessel reached the west side of Prince of Wales Island at Cape Addington, near Dixon Entrance in southeast Alaska. Chirikov found the shoreline steep and rocky, and he could not find a safe harbor. Sailing to the north, after three days the ships entered a large bay south of Sitka, on Baranof Island, where mystery enshrouded the expedition. The mate and ten of the crew were sent to shore on a simple watering mission. The ship's crew watched them row out of sight around a headland, but no landing signal was given and they never returned. After five days of waiting, crewmen spotted a fire on shore, so a carpenter and caulker were sent to the same place in the remaining shore boat, assuming the first crew was simply beached and in need of repairs. They followed the same route, but like the first party, they made no sound or signal, and were never seen again.

Chirikov and his remaining men were distraught. Over a dozen of his men and the only shore boats were now lost with no possibility they would return. The Russians waited precious days for some sign, but no signal came. Two Indian canoes finally came out, but after shouting something unintelligible, they paddled out of sight. Chirikov was certain these people had killed his men, or held them captive, but being thousands of miles from home, with limited water supplies, he abandoned any attempt to rescue the lost sailors and left for Kamchatka.

Later, when Russians came to dominate the area, they sought the fate of these men. Little was found. Most scholars today assume that a tidal rip caused the loss of the crews, not a native encounter. On his return, Chirikov sailed in a near fatal battle with fog, headwinds, scurvy and thirst. At Adak Island seven natives came out in kayaks, offering fresh water, but they did not board. As the voyage concluded, the sailors drew short of water, and then fell to scurvy, too sick to handle the boat. Even Chirikov expected to die. But the expedition sighted Kamchatka on October 8 and two days later sailed into port.[12]

As the *St. Paul* made its first landfall in southern Alaska, Bering's *St. Peter* was several hundred miles to the north, sailing in cloudy, drizzly weather in the Gulf of Alaska. Just after noon on July 17, a high, snow-covered volcano appeared out of the haze. Since this was St. Elias day, Bering named it Mt. St. Elias. In the evening the fog lifted and the entire Alaskan landscape opened. The ship's company was elated, but Bering was not. In his journal, the impatient German naturalist, Georg Steller wrote that the captain accepted the discovery "very indifferently and without particular pleasure ... he even shrugged his shoulders while looking at the land." Although he must have known this was his crowning life achievement, Bering was already fearful of the return to Kamchatka through the vast ocean, its rain, fog and winds.[13]

Coasting to the north, the *St. Peter* found Kayak Island, where they sought fresh water. Bering sent both of his boats to shore. The larger was charged to Fleet Master Kitrov, who investigated the inner bay. As he filled the water casks for the return voyage, his crew found some empty wooden huts with carved wooden boards, suggesting the Americans were quite civilized. The house had a fireplace, a bark basket, and a wooden spade. They also found a whetstone for sharpening, so assumed the people had metal implements.

The smaller vessel was sent on a watering mission to Kayak Island with Steller, who upon reaching shore began one of the briefest, yet most well known of all the scientific expeditions of his day. He was on land just ten hours where he spent his time feverishly collecting plants and tracing evidence of human habitation. He correctly surmised these people were related to the natives of Kamchatka and speculated on their ancestral crossing. He wanted to stay longer, but Bering decided to sail with the onset of a fair wind, even though the watering effort was not complete. This would prove to be a fatal decision. At the time, however, it did little more than shorten Steller's time on the island.[14]

Bering set his return course in fog, rain and wind. Within a month, scurvy broke out and he paid for his hasty departure. Now he was forced north to find fresh water in the Shumagin Islands, named for the first of his crew to die from scurvy, who was buried there. Two native people unexpectedly paddled into view in their kayak, offering whale meat for cloth and iron. On shore, a larger group seized a Siberian interpreter and a boat. The Russians fired their muskets in the air to disperse the crowd and abandoned the watering effort. It was September. They had barely retraced one-third of the route across the Pacific. Despite Steller's ministrations of shore weeds, many of the crew were now doomed from scurvy. In fact, Bering himself was so overcome he gave up command to Sven Waxell. When they arrived in the area of Adak Island, a terrible storm drove them so far southeast that it took nearly a month to regain their position en route to Kamchatka.[15]

The log of the ship reported the growing drama of sickness and death. In the heavy seas of autumn scurvy claimed another life nearly every day. Exhausted, the crew approached an unknown island that they took for Siberia. The tides drove the ship mercilessly onto a reef where it was shattered. The island was uninhabited. Only driftwood could be found to build shelters and fuel fires. This was a grim prospect that began a winter on a miserable island. A hollowed-out berm was built for Bering but, too frail and weak, he could not recover. Suffering hallucinations, he refused the company or ministrations of his own men. Sand rolled down the sides of his hole, covering most of his body in a premature grave. On December 8, 1741, after most of the survivors had regained their health, he died. A driftwood cross was erected, and the forsaken place was named Bering Island.[16]

The winter on Bering Island was not so desperate as the final days of the voyage, although there were blizzards and high winds. The survivors built rudimentary shelters from driftwood and pieces of the broken ship. Slowly the men regained their health, making forays into the far reaches of the island. They found plenty of sea otters, on which they subsisted. They killed far more than they could eat, as they knew the skins were of high value in the Orient. In the Spring, they dismantled the wrecked *St. Peter* and in two months built a single decked hooker with a draft of just five feet, no larger than a single-masted shore boat. In early August 45 men wedged themselves in the modest craft and sailed away. The small vessel was so laden with crewmen and pelts that the freeboard was only a few inches above water. A storm would have swamped them, with the loss of all hands, but the journey was uneventful. They reached Kamchatka two weeks later.[17]

The tragedy that befell the Second Kamchatka Expedition far overshadowed its accomplishments. But two achievements, though probably unsuspected at the time, mark the expedition's success. First, Steller's brief foray on Kayak Island, and his later visits ashore on Bering Island during the return to Kamchatka, gave new and valuable information about the flora and fauna of the North

Pacific. Second, the crew brought hundreds of sea otter pelts back from Bering Island, setting in motion a new compulsion among the Russian fur hunters to conquer the adjacent islands and their inhabitants.

For James Cook, the record of the voyages had even greater significance, as they were translated to Russian maps he carried into Alaskan waters. Bering and many of his officers did not return from Alaska, but the survivors offered the awaiting mapmakers their insights about new lands they discovered east of Siberia. Although the imagined Juan de Gama Land was eliminated, speculative geographers were hard at work conceiving the connection of these new lands to the Spanish New World colonies. Soon these speculations were recorded on the maps of the day.

Cook carried two of these maps: first, an account of Bering's voyages by Gerhard Fredrich Müller, a historian from the Russian Academy of Sciences, second a map that described the more recent Russian voyages in the Arctic by Jacob von Stählin. Although Müller's map depicts with reasonable accuracy the tracks of Bering and Chirikov, it also shows a great bulge in the North American continent stretching back to Asia. Stählin's version was the newer report, supposedly updated by the recent activity of the fledgling Russian fur industry and two modest expeditions conducted for the Russian Navy by Lt. Ivan Sindt (1764-67) and captains Peter Krenitsyn and Mikhail Levashev (1766-69). Sindt claimed he found a new chain of islands to the north of the Aleutians, but he vastly distorted his voyage accomplishments, as his ship did not venture much past the Pacific coastline of the Kamchatka Peninsula. The Krenitsyn-Levashev expedition at least reached America. After shipwreck, mutiny and serious bouts with scurvy, Krenitsyn and Levashev finally reached Unalaska and nearby Unimak Island in 1768. Repelled by hostile Aleuts, they quickly retreated to Kamchatka.[18]

Both voyages did little to expand geographic knowledge of the Bering Sea or the Alaska mainland, but Stählin's map reported their movements in earnest, offering a depiction of Alaska as a large island between the North American and Asian continents. Of greatest importance, this map showed Sindt's "new northern archipelago," with many other islands and a wide passage into Arctic waters between Alaska and North America, making it appear that the Arctic was relatively accessible from Southern Alaska.[19] Given today's knowledge, both maps were nonsense, steeped in lore and imagination, with a bit of wishful thinking. A simple comparison shows the two maps had nothing in common, but the Admiralty delivered them to Cook assuming they would provide him accurate landmarks and clear sailing to the Arctic.

As it turned out Cook found the maps hopelessly inaccurate. When his voyage unfolded, they caused Cook constant aggravation, and little help, making it difficult to accurately place himself at any point in comparison to the routes traversed by Bering and Chirikov. It would have been better for Cook if he had left them at home. At least Müller's map told Cook the plain truth, that the only way to the Arctic Ocean was through the Bering Strait, and that coastal Alaska would expand to the west, even southwest, before he could enter the open sea and reach Arctic Ice.

In honor of Bering's accomplishments, Cook decided at one point to affix Bering's name to a bay on the Gulf of Alaska where Bering had anchored. But it was hard for him to tell where to place the name. Cook concluded, "… the account of that Voyage is so very much abridged and the Chart so extremely inaccurate, that it is hardly possible by either the one or the other, or both together, to find out any place that that navigator either saw or touched at all. I am by no means certain that the Bay to which I have given his

Name is the place where he anchored, nor do I know that Mount St. Elias is the same as the one to which he gave that name and as to Cape St. Elias I can form no judgment where it lies."[20]

To the north, after passing Mt. St. Elias, Cook was disappointed to find the coastline trending first to the west, then to the southwest. His directive was to follow the coast to the Arctic so each additional day they fell away from northern latitudes the success of the mission was threatened. He had the latest maps, but the Stählin version said there were islands and passageways separating Alaska from North America, with a strait that would take him almost due north to the Arctic. He did find a large bay to the west of Mt. St. Elias, which he called Icy Bay. But there was no passageway to the north.

To his regret the Müller map seemed to be more accurate. On it the continental arc bulged to the west, almost to Asia. Even so, Cook could do little more than follow the trend in the coast, making slow progress in calm, mostly westerly winds. James King, second lieutenant of the *Resolution*, wrote how all the officers were on deck comparing the Stählin and Müller maps to the landscape and topography that unfolded in front of them. "We are kept in a constant suspense," he wrote, particularly as the maps were time and again proven wrong.[21]

But the weather had finally improved. "We are forwarding our business in tracing the Coast, but our breeze enables us to get on but very leisurely," Clerke wrote.[22] The *Resolution* was leaking again after the weeklong battering out of Nootka, and in the slight breeze they hoisted out the shore boats so the carpenters could work on the leak. But these were temporary repairs; she needed to be careened and recaulked. The sailors encountered and attempted to land at a low cape they named Cape Suckling. It was named after Captain Maurice Suckling, the uncle of famed naval officer Lord Nelson. As the party came near a sheltered bay on the north side of the cape, the winds shifted to the south, driving them away from shore to a small island Cook called "Kaye's Island," (now called Kayak Island) after a personal friend from Yorkshire, an esteemed English reverend who was chaplain to King George.

Cook came ashore simply to reconnoiter the region to find a place to repair *Resolution*. This was his first time ashore in Alaska, and his excursion was frustrated by a difficult traverse, even though he found the trees stunted and small. It was so thick with underbrush and hilly that he retreated after two hours, so he saw little of the island. At the foot of a tree he left a bottle with a paper in it, naming the ships and the date of discovery, and enclosing a few of His Majesty's coins. Dated in 1772, they were apparently given to Cook by the Reverend Dr. Kaye for this purpose.[23]

Cook was especially taken with the southwest point of the island, with a naked rock promontory that appeared from a distance to be a ruined medieval castle, noting it as a significant coastal feature for mariners traversing this part of Alaska. Cook had landed on the same small island, now called Kayak Island, where Bering first stopped in 1741. Ironically, the point of first contact in the vast Alaskan coastline for the two captains, separated by 37 years, was on the opposite shores of the same desolate island!

After returning to his ships, Cook sailed around the island and observed a new part of the Alaska mainland. He first saw Controller Bay, on the mainland north of the island. Sailing to the west, he passed the Copper River delta and modern-day Cordova. But the ships were probably too far offshore to notice the expanse of the outlet of one of Alaska's largest rivers. By May 12 they came to a peninsula they called Cape Hinchinbrook. Cape Suckling, Controller Bay, and Cape Hinchinbrook are all names that continue in use today. Although Cook was not aware of it, Cape Hinchinbrook was the western extremity of an island, which was later called Hinchinbrook Island.[24] The shipping lane for modern day oil tankers exiting Prince William Sound is Hinchinbrook Entrance.

This part of the continent was bearing to the southwest, so if the Russian maps on board had any validity, the Captain expected to turn back north at any moment. Soon such an entry appeared, the first one observed since Nootka. The southward inclination of the coastline, Cook reasoned, was "... a direction so contrary to the Modern Charts, founded upon the late Russian discoveries, that we had reason to expect that by the inlet before us we should find a passage to the North, and that the land to the West and SW was nothing but a group of islands." That gave hope of finding the grand passageway to the east. Cook also needed to repair his ship, as a storm was brewing. "Besides the wind was now SE and we were threatened with both a fog and a storm and I wanted to get into some place to stop the leak before we incountered a nother gale."

They entered a large bay in this westward reach of land that Cook called "Sandwich Sound" after the First Lord of the Admiralty, naming another geographical feature in honor of the First Lord's worldly accomplishments. Unfortunately for him, Cook's name did not last. Upon the expedition's return to England, the Admiralty at the First Lord's request changed Cook's charts to honor King George's son, Prince William Henry. This body of water has been known ever since as Prince William Sound.

Today Prince William Sound is treasured as one of Alaska's leading wilderness charms. Viewed from above, it is a mixture of ocean, land and glaciers with a spectacular maze of islands, channels and bays scattered throughout. Glaciers have worked on these lands for millennia, forming a mountainous and jumbled coast, gouging channels with depths resembling man-made canals. Dense forests of spruce, hemlock and cedar blanket the lower slopes, which then rise from the rocky coast to huge snow-capped and glacier-clad mountains above. Massive waterfalls pervade the landscape. Some falls rival the more celebrated examples in Yosemite and Yellowstone, spilling vast amounts of water between steep and barren cliffs to the shores below.

On May 12, coasting around Cape Hinchinbrook, Cook found an anchorage. Gore, Gilbert and others were sent to shore to find water and other fresh provisions, "in hopes of shooting something for the pot or spit." "But he had hardly gotten there," Cook wrote, "before about twenty Indians made their appearance in two large Canoes on which he thought proper to return to the Ships and they followed him." Gilbert wrote of the incident, "We had no idea from the appearance of the Country, it being entirely covered with snow, that there were any Inhabitants here, till our people that were upon the beach ... saw two large Canoes full of men making towards them... The Natives came off within about a cables length of the ships (about 600 feet) and paddled around them three or four times singing and hallowing all the time very loud but we could not entice them to come alongside..." [25]

These were the first Alaskans seen on the voyage. While they offered the same friendly greeting, standing with arms crossed in their small craft, much distinguished them from the people at Nootka. One man held out a white garment, which they interpreted as a sign of friendship, and another stood up in the canoe, quite naked, for almost a quarter of an hour with arms stretched out like a cross and motionless. Their canoes were not made of wood, like the Nootkans, but were more slender, made of sealskin stretched over a wooden frame. As friendly as they were, these natives would not come on board the ships.

After gifts were exchanged, the ships sailed again, finding a better anchorage at a place Cook called Snug Corner Cove. They anchored there on May 16, in this deep inlet on the eastern side of the Sound. The leak in the *Resolution* had to be repaired, so in this safe, snug cove new sheathing was placed over the leak. This was a difficult proposition, since two to three feet of snow still lay on shore. The crew could not careen the vessel, so instead they "heeled over" at anchor in the near shore, listing her to the point where the normal waterline could be exposed for repair. The sailors found the oakum gone from many of the seams at the water line, explaining their near catastrophe. Gilbert wrote that the seams between the boards were inches apart in some places, "in two days we repaired this defect being obliged to put two and half inch rope along the seams which were too wide for caulking..."[26]

The expedition was fortunate to be in such a harbor. No sooner had they arrived than the weather turned to rain, then violent squalls in a thick fog, which continued after dark in what Cook called an "exceedingly stormy night." Indeed, it continued to be a summer of storms.

Here the crew met several dozen local people, who came to the ships despite the nasty weather. They came all night and, after a time, some ventured on board. "Amongst those that came on board was a good looking middle-aged man who was afterward found to be the Chief," Cook wrote. "He was cloathed in a dress of sea otter's skin and on his head a Cap as is worn by the people of King George's Sound, Ornamented with sky-blue glass beads. Any sort of beads appeared to be in high estimation with these people, and they readily gave finer sea otter skins in exchange for them. These people were also desirous of iron, but they ... rejected small pieces. Consequently they got but little from us; iron having, by this time, become rather a scarce article." Samwell reported "one of our Gentlemen bought as many Sea Beaver [otter] Skins for half a dozen blue Beads as sold afterwards for 40£ at Kamchatka."

These people reminded Cook of Greenland Eskimos that some members of his crew had observed in Canada years earlier. He had a copy of the *History of Greenland*, an illustrated book with chapters offering "a Description of the Country and its Inhabitants." Written by a Moravian missionary, David Crantz, it was published in 1767. Cook enthusiastically wrote about the people of the Sound in relation to the book. Certain he had found Eskimos so far from Greenland, he speculated on their possible water-borne connections. Ledyard, who had seen Eskimos, was certain. "The inhabitants seem to be a distinct tribe from those at George's Sound, and bear a very striking resemblance if not an exact one to the Esquimaux. ...Their skin canoes, their double-bladed paddles, their dress and other appearances of less note are the same as on the coast of Labrador and in Hudson's Bay."[27]

He was half-right. The inhabitants of Prince William Sound were related to Eskimos, but they had arrived in migrations that took centuries and certainly not by navigating a great-unfound waterway. The natives wore sealskin clothing, not furs, and were adorned with tattoos and unsightly bone labrets protruding from their faces, usually from their lower lips. At first the crewmen thought the people had two mouths. "Some both men and women," wrote Cook, "have the under lip slit quite through horizontally, and so large as to admit the tongue which I have seen them thrust through, which happened to be the case when it was first discovered by one of the Seamen, who called out there was a man with two mouths." Ornaments were placed in the opening, giving the Europeans the impression they had two rows of teeth, thus impeding their speech.

James King's observations are particularly insightful, since he had observed Eskimos during his service in Newfoundland. "The single canoe," he wrote, "was precisely the shape & size of what I have seen among the Eskimaux." Like the others, he also noticed the "striking difference in their Colour, in their Canoes, implements & their turn of mind" from the people of Nootka Sound.[28]

Cook felt the people had seen Russians before, since they exhibited a certain litany for initiating trade, but this was probably just the result of the well-honed trade with other native people along the coast. The procedure was first to proffer symbols of friendship, sticks with eagle feathers or wings tied to them, then to offer to trade. Fresh food and sea otter skins were traded and the crew made off with many skins for the price of simple beads.

The local vessels were sleek kayaks and larger, skin-clad oomiaks. Ellis explained:

> Their canoes were constructed upon a different plan from those of King George's Sound, they were much broader and apparently more commodious. They consisted of a frame, which was covered with skin of some large fish, brought over the sides, and was then braced very tight, and fastened in the inside of the canoe: their paddles were roughly made, were very light and differently shaped from the last, not ending in that long point.[29]

They also had mittens made of bear paws, and high-crowned conical straw caps, as well as hats or helmets fashioned in wood to mimic a seal's head.

Cook discovered these people also had larcenous traits like other places in the Pacific. During the first night in the cove, after three hours on *Resolution*, some of the natives boarded the *Discovery*. When they found the crew absent from the main deck, either asleep or at breakfast, they assumed the ship and its goods were free for the taking. They started pilfering anything they could find, but at the alarm of the ship's watch the boat's crew chased them off with drawn cutlasses. The local residents were apparently impressed with the size of European knives, as they only had modest ones bartered from the Russians.

Samwell watched the landing party explain their defeat to the waiting chiefs. "Having been defeated in their Intentions they soon left that Ship;" he explained. "As they were going away some of their Chiefs who had not been in the Ship enquir'd the reason why they had failed in putting their Design in Execution, on which they made signs that we had Knives as long as their Arms & much longer than their own, & the Chiefs seemed to allow that it was a pretty reasonable argument for their Retreat."

Fortunately, the residents of Prince William Sound never knew of firearms. "I have not the least doubt that their visiting us so early in the morning was with a view to plunder, on supposition that they would find us all asleep," Cook explained. "However, after all these tricks, we had the good fortune to leave them as ignorant of firearms as we found them. They neither saw, nor heard, a musket fired." They did have iron, however. "They had several spears, which were all headed with iron;" Ellis wrote, "their knives were near eighteen inches long, and shaped something like a hanger, these they wore round their necks. From the circumstance of the beads and iron, we thought it probable that they might by some means or other have connections with the Russians, who have extended trade an immense way."[30]

Cook and his crew took care to describe these people and the differences between them and the Nootkans. "These people are not of the same Nation as those who Inhabit

King George's Sound," he stated with some certainty, "both their language and features are widely different." He was especially taken with their kayaks, and the way they kept rain and sea water out of them when underway.

> They are small of stature, but thick set good looking people, ... and the women are more delicate. ... Their frocks are made of the Skins of different animals, reaching generally to the ankles, all of which they wore with the fur side out. When it rains they put over this another frock, ingeniously made from the intestines of whales or some other large animal. It is made to draw tight around the neck, its sleeves reach to the wrists, around which they are tied with a string, and its skirts, when they are in their canoes, are drawn over the rim of the hole in which they sit, so that no water can enter, and at the same time it keeps the men entirely dry, for no water can penetrate it.[31]

They were excellent craftsmen and well-groomed, "always clean and decent without grease or dirt," which was a stark contrast with the people of Nootka Sound. "Everything they have is ingeniously made, as if they were furnished with the most complete tool chest. Their sewing, plaiting, and small work on little bags may be put in competition with the most delicate manufactures found in any part of the known world." Cook felt they had accomplished a great deal by surviving this harsh climate. "Considering the otherwise uncivilized or rude state in which these people are, their northern situation amidst a country perpetually covered with snow, and the wretched materials they have to work with, their invention and dexterity in all manual work is equal to that of any nation."

The facial ornaments worn by the people repulsed the English seamen. "... they had a slit between their lower lip and chin through which they could put their tongue, that gave them the appearance of having a double mouth," Rickman wrote in disgust, "Add to this the ornaments they wore in their noses and ears, of tin and copper, and no figures upon earth could be more grotesque."[32]

Both Webber and Ellis feverishly drew of the landscape in Snug Corner Cove showing its ice, mountains, coastal rocks, forests, and the ships dwarfed at anchor with local native people looking on. They also drew portraits of the people in full costume, with the unsightly ornaments protruding from their lips. The result is what some have called the finest drawings from any port, composed of ships, kayaks and a hostile and forbidden landscape, as well as intricate, delicate drawings of the native people.

There are four major Alaska Native cultures: the Tlingit and Haida on the southeast coast, the circumpolar Eskimo (Inuit and Yupik), the interior and coastal Athabascan Indians, and the Aleut. In the course of his voyage in Alaska that summer, Cook came in contact with all but those from the southeast coast and frequently did not distinguish the differences. Modern scholars believe the people Cook observed in Prince William Sound were Pacific Eskimo, from the coastal branch of the Alutiiq nation, also known as the Pacific Yupik or Sugpiaq. The Alutiiq, a southern, coastal branch of the Alaskan Yupik, ranged from Prince William Sound to the Kenai Peninsula, the Alaska Peninsula, and Kodiak Island.

Along with the people who lived on the southern shores of the Kenai Peninsula, the people Cook encountered represented a small population that spoke the Chugach or coastal dialect. They shared the coastal Chugach range of mountains that separated them from the Dena'ina Athabascans to the north. In contrast, the Koniag dialect was spoken on the Alaska Peninsula and on Kodiak Island. The Alutiiq migration to Prince William Sound is still not firmly established, but it is presumed to run from common connections in western Alaska, as the Alutiiq language is similar to that spoken by the Yupik in the Alaskan areas around Bethel and Dillingham. There is even evidence suggesting they have cultural ties to the Russian people of the Chukchi Sea beyond northwestern Alaska.

The Alutiiq lived a traditional coastal lifestyle, subsisting primarily on ocean resources of salmon, halibut and whale, as well as berries and land mammals such as caribou, moose and bear. Before European contact with Russian fur traders and the occasional European exploring expedition, many Alutiiq lived in semi-subterranean homes. They often traded and intermarried with the Aleuts of the Aleutian Islands, the Central Yupik, Dena'ina Athabascans, and even the Eyak and Tlingit to the east. Like other Alaskan native people, they were generally a peaceable people. They have rich oral histories that tell of sensitive and powerful spirits of animals and natural forces, in addition to battles fought over territory and resources.[33]

In response to Bering's voyage, Russian traders first came by ship in the 1740s in search of sea otters and other furs. Alutiiq warriors drove away many early Russian expeditions, but in 1784, Grigorii Ivanovich Shelikhov conquered the people of Kodiak Island and built a Russian outpost at Three Saints Bay, one of the oldest European settlements on the Northwest coast. Alutiiq people were forced to work for the Russian fur companies; some intermarried with the few Russians who lived in Alaska. Men hunted sea otters and women sewed clothing and gathered food but under Russian rule little time was left to meet basic needs in the villages. Hunger and death from smallpox and other new diseases prevailed. The Chugach people in Prince William Sound generally were spared. In the early 1800's Russian priests and fur traders convinced some of the smaller tribes to resettle at the Russian Fort Alexandrovsky, the present site of Nanwalek, formerly English Bay on lower Cook Inlet.[34]

Over time, life in the Russian colonies became less harsh. The local people often adopted Russian customs, language and Orthodox religion. People of mixed Russian and Alutiiq heritage became the backbone of life in Russian America. Some even served as teachers, managers and clergy. Today the Alutiiq still live in coastal fishing communities, where they work in all aspects of the modern economy, while still maintaining the cultural value of their traditions and subsistence lifestyle.

Before leaving the Sound and the Alutiiq, Cook was obliged to explore to the north to see if he could find the great passageway to Europe. Sign language had persuaded some of his men that the local people thought there was a broad passageway to the north. "They gave us to understand that there were two ways to the sea," Cook wrote, "the one South by which we came in here, the other North, which latter would take us two days and nights before we came into the open sea. Their method of communicating this intelligence was by turning round with their hands closed and opening them only in the directions of the passages."

Although far short of the parallel at which they were to begin investigating, Cook knew that retreating to Cape Hinchinbrook would lead them to a coastline that trended to the southwest, further away from their objective. So the investment of a few hours or days might be their salvation. If there was any truth in the Russian maps he carried there would be islands and openings in the offing to the north. Yet in a matter of hours they were forced to anchor, observing sunken rocks and reefs, and suffering from a failing wind. In the north the land seemed to close in, and the flood tide moved from the south. Cook discharged the shore boats for further investigation.

John Gore and Henry Roberts, master's mate on the *Resolution*, were sent to examine the northern arm of the sea, probably entering modern-day Valdez Arm before retreating. Gore reported he saw "the entrance of an arm which he was of the opinion extended a long way to the northeast, and that probably by it a passage might be found." Roberts was less enthused, advising Cook "they saw the head or end of this arm." William Bligh took another crew east, and returned with a similar report. They decided no passageway existed to the north in this area. The only matter of consequence was that they found and named Bligh Island, later assigned to the nearby Bligh Reef, on which an oil tanker, the *Exxon Valdez*, would famously ground some 200 years later.[35]

Other arms of the Sound reached to the west. Ever the optimist, Gore wanted to press on to these distant inlets, but Cook declined, speculating that it was unlikely any channel or strait could extend 1560 miles (520 leagues) to the east to connect with any part of Baffin's or Hudson's Bay. Rather than get entangled in the shoals of a narrowing inlet, Cook now resolved to investigate to the west. Gore said there was still "deep water and bold shores" to the north,[36] but Cook was not convinced. He discounted chances of finding another route to the open sea except that by which they arrived, so further northward exploration ceased.

The Russian maps indicated there would be a maze of islands to the west, and they could regain the route north using a westerly approach. "As the wind came favorable for getting out to sea," Cook wrote, "I resolved to spend no more time in searching for a passage in a place that promised so little success. I besides, considered, that if the land on the west should prove to be islands agreeable to the late Russian discoveries, we could not fail of getting far enough to the north and that in good time, provided it was not spent in searching places where a passage was not only doubtful but improbable."

So the next morning, on Monday, May 18, at 3 a.m., at first light in these northern shores, the ships weighed anchor and retreated south, returning the identical way they came into the place. The storm that plagued them in Snug Corner Cove had passed so they returned to the south slowly, picking their way through rocks and small islands. Whales, seals and otters were in abundance. "We saw an incredible number of whales and seals sporting round us," Ellis wrote, "from whence we concluded that we were nearly out of the Sound, and not far from the sea." Eagles and other waterfowl soared overhead.[37] It was an idyllic encounter with Prince William Sound, but for Cook it was just eight days wasted repairing a leak in his broken flagship and charting the eastern portion of the Sound.

As they exited the Sound they passed far to the west of Cape Hinchinbrook and another, larger island even further to the west that protects the entrance to the Sound. Cook named that larger island Montagu Island, as Montagu was Lord Sandwich's family name. Chart makers later added a final "e" and the largest island in Prince William Sound still bears the name Montague Island. The channel where he exited the Sound is now Montague Strait. Across from Montague Island is Green Island, which was given the name by Cook because it was already free of snow early in the season.

Gore remained unconvinced that there was no passageway. On entering the Sound he named a point of land "Cape Hold with Hope," anticipating a safe passage home and a share of Parliament's £20,000 reward. Now his shipmates were certain Prince William Sound was a great cul-de-sac. But Gore was not, claiming he had seen "Deep Water and Bold Shores." So as they abandoned the Sound he decided to name a cape on Montague Island "Cape Lost Hope."[38] In his mind further exploration would have yielded the great prize and their quick return to Europe.

-Chapter 6-

Turnagain River

Leaving Snug Corner Cove, Cook's expedition coasted southwest in fair winds along the Kenai Peninsula, past the rugged fjords and glaciers that now make up Kenai Fjords National Park. The peninsula ended abruptly at a headland called Cape Elizabeth, which Cook named after Princess Elizabeth, whose birthday was on May 21. At first Cook thought Cape Elizabeth was the corner marking the easternmost point of land on the Alaska coast. He expected to turn the corner and sail unimpeded in a vast ocean to the north. But soon snow clad peaks appeared in the distance to the southwest, beyond the vast body of water. Discouraged, he guessed the continent continued to the west.

Cook wrote that this was probably the place Bering called Cape St. Hermogenes, or at least that was how it appeared on the Müller map. But before an investigation could begin, a strong gale arose, driving the vessels far south. As the sailors attempted to regain the lost ground they saw land that seemed to connect the cape to the west. Cook called it Cape Douglas, after Canon Douglas of Windsor, the editor of Cook's second voyage journal. A nearby spit was called Point Banks, after Joseph Banks, the esteemed naturalist who traveled with Cook on the first voyage. Many of these names are still in use as the prominent features of the outlet of Cook Inlet. As the winds abated, the ships tacked back to the north. As they passed the intervening land, they found it was instead a series of islands, all devoid of vegetation. They were aptly called the Barren Islands.

The gap of open water ahead of them stretching to the horizon in the north was fifty or sixty miles across. Most of the crew was convinced this was the great passageway to the Arctic, possibly even back to Europe. Cook and Bligh were not so certain, but decided it bore further exploration. "I was fully persuaded that we should find no passage," Cook later wrote, but the other officers were buoyant, assuming this was the end of the American continent and the beginning of a great inland sea.[1]

The irrepressible Gore offered optimistic place names on his own map: Hope's Return, Mount Welcome, Land of Good Prospect.[2] He was convinced this channel would lead to open water in the north, presumably connecting with the channel he was not permitted to explore in Prince William Sound. If Stählin's map was at all accurate, they had now entered the wide passage that would lead them to Arctic waters between Alaska and North America.

Like Cook, Clerke was ambivalent about whether to proceed:

> We are still in the same predicament as yesterday in respect to our Western Gale. Here's a fine spacious opening, which this wind will not enable us to examine: as the Season now advances so fast, shou'd we leave a passage to the N'ward behind us, it wou'd be a most unfortunate incident; or on the other hand shou'd we get engaged in an extensive Sound, and after searching its various crooks & corners, find ourselves under the necessity of returning, from whence we came, it might have a most unhappy effect upon this Seasons operations.[3]

The explorers were supposed to sail for the Arctic and not lose time exploring rivers along the way. They were still four degrees short of the 65° latitude goal set by the Admiralty, but Cook and Clerke were unsure whether they were in a river or a northern sea. So at the end of May they entered this stretch of water and sailed north. As they did, enveloping fog and shifting winds hampered their progress. The inlet's tides were very strong, sometimes rising and falling 20 feet or simply racing by. This tidal movement caused the ships to drift south on the current, so an anchor was set with each tide to prevent losing ground. They crept forward, sailing with the flood and anchoring with the ebb.

At daybreak on May 26th, the horizon was still unbroken in the northeast, but to the west a chain of islands seemed to close that side of the inlet. A "conical figure of very considerable height" was seen on the nearest island. Since it was St. Augustine's Day, Cook called the volcano Mt. St. Augustine. The landscape on each side of the inlet was unimpressive. "The land which surrounded this bay was high, and had a barren aspect;" Ellis observed, "the bottom was in many places clothed with trees, but they were apparently stinted in their growth; the middle and tops of the hills had not a shrub of any kind upon them, and seemed to be little else than solid rock. The snow lay but in small quantities, owing perhaps to the winds which at times blow here very violently."[4]

Cook was now convinced he was not in a channel leading to the Arctic.

> We clearly saw that what we had taken for islands were the summits of Mountains that were every where connected by lower land, which the haziness of the horizon had prevented us from seeing at a greater distance. This land was everywhere covered with Snow from the

summits of the hills down to the very sea beach, and had every other appearance of being part of a great Continent, so that I was fully persuaided that we should find no passage by this inlet and my persevering in it was more to satisfy other people than to confirm my own opinion.[5]

Cook pressed on only to convince the others, especially the optimistic Gore, his second in command. Still, Gore and the others watched with anticipation, expecting at any moment to exit a strait as Magellan did as he entered the Pacific at the tip of South America. Many of the others agreed with Gore. Second Lieutenant Rickman wrote on May 27 "we found the river to widen ... We were once more flattered with having found the passage." On May 29 Gore wrote "Came to Sail plying with the Tide of the Northward in the Gulf River or Streight, the Latter I hope." As late as May 30 midshipman Edward Riou still thought the tidal rip came from an open northern sea, "A fine Even swell from N'ward, which is still in our favor of this place being an opening." Gore called the eastern shore "Nancy's Foreland," after a favorite female acquaintance, and the western shore "Gore's Head." Cook did not adopt these names, and the apparently unromantic Vancouver later called them simply the East Foreland and West Foreland.[6]

The fog thickened, then lifted, but the wind remained from the north. Without warning it would occasionally rise to a gale. With the contrary winds and tides, the ships crept up the inlet, anchoring against the ebb tide. Once *Resolution* lost an anchor and spent a fruitless afternoon attempting to recover it. On the eastern shore Cook saw two columns of smoke from fires, the first sign of inhabitants, so he called it "Smokey Cape." Later he turned the ships to sail in that direction, spending their first night at a place still called Anchor Point.

Day after day the explorers made little progress. Off Doubtful (now Kalgin) Island, the ships picked up a southerly breeze at last. With each hour north, the water was weighed and even tasted. It was less saline, a sure sign of fresh water. Its light weight also seemed conclusive. Cook wrote, "in so much that I was convinced that we were in a large River and Not a Strait that would communicate with the Northern Seas. But as we had proceeded so far I was desireous of having stronger proofs and therefore weighed with the next flood and plyed higher up or rather drove up with the tide for we had but little wind." He later wrote of "evident proofs of being in a Great River; such as low shores, very thick and Muddy water, large trees and all manner of dirt and rubbish floating up and down with the tide."

It was a treacherous channel and a "prodigious" tide. Seaweed, sludge and tree trunks floated in the tides and hidden shoals constantly had to be avoided. Later visibility improved in the north and what were thought to be distant islands were actually mountaintops deep in the continent. As the vessels reached the island now called Fire Island on the last day of the month, the sailors were impressed by the snow-capped peaks in the distance. But the near shore landscape suggested they were at an end, as the channel now divided into two smaller arms, one running east, the other northeast. Only Gore seemed unsure.[7]

Despite the slow progress, the sailors rarely glimpsed evidence of local people along the shore. But as they came to the end of the large channel, a group of about forty natives approached. "...five canoes, two large and three small, with several of the natives, who had for some time been endeavoring to overtake us, came under our stern;" Ellis wrote, "in each of the large canoes were sixteen or seventeen people, in the small ones two. We purchased very little of them, as their visit seemed to be the effect of

111

curiosity, and they were not willing to trade. Their dress was made of the skins of small animals sewed together, and furnished with sleeves."

The ships anchored six miles off the west shore, just to the south of Fire Island, in the deepest part of the channel. Bligh was sent in a shore boat to examine the northeast arm, known today as the Knik Arm. After landing, he found currants and other berries on the island, already edible by late May. He then sailed north, returning after midnight to report a deep and navigable river for ten or twelve miles between ridges of mountains. One cannot tell if it was the Matanuska or Knik River. He told of a spectacular landscape, as he probably saw the Alaska Range, looming over 100 miles to the north. Mt. McKinley or Denali, the highest peak in North America, is a part of this range. But there was no inland sea, "the land to all appearance joined on all sides." Cook summarized Bligh's excursion:

> At 2 oclock in the Morning [the 1st of June] the Master returned and reported that he had found the Inlet or rather river contracted to the breadth of one league by low land on each side, through which it took a northerly direction. He proceeded three leagues up this narrow part which he found navigable for the largest Ships. ... While the Ebb or stream run down the Water was perfectly fresh, but after the flood made it brackish and towards high-water very much so even as high up as he was. He landed on an island which lies between this branch and the eastern one, on which he found some Current berry bushes with the fruit already set, and some other fruit trees and bushes unknown

to him. ...to the Northward of where he was, there was a nother seperation in the Eastern chain of Mountains ... these two ridges as they extended to the North inclined more and more towards each other ... All hopes of a passage was now given up.[8]

The eastern arm was larger, but contrary winds and the lamentable tides prevented Cook from advancing the *Resolution* or the *Discovery* up the channel. So King was dispatched with two shore boats up the arm, but he made no headway against the tide and was recalled. For anyone familiar with the tides in Turnagain Arm, the fact that Cook's expedition journeyed this far up the inlet in such small ships, facing the second highest tide in the world in adverse winds, is a testament to English determination and seamanship.

Thinking the [shore] boats might [make headway], I sent two under command of Lieutenant King, to examine the tides, and make such other observations as might give us some insight into the nature of the River. At 10 oclock finding the Ebb tide made I anchored in 10 fathoms of water over a gravelly bottom; and finding the Tide too strong for the boats to make head against it I made the signal for them to return on board, before they had got half way to the entrance of the River they were sent to examine, which River was named Turnagain, and bore for us S 80° E 3 leagues distant. ... On the north side of this River it again begins and stretches out from the foot of the Mountains down to the banks of the great River, so that before the River Turnagain it forms a large bay, on the South side of which we were now at Anchor. ... After we had entered the bay the flood set strong into the River Turnagain, and Ebb came out with still greater force and the Water fell upon a perpendicular, which we lay at anchor 20 feet: these circumstances convinced me that no passage was to be expected by this River no more than by the Main branch. But as the water during the Ebb, tho very considerably fresher than the Ocean, had a strong degree of saltness, it is but reasonable to suppose that both these branches are Navigable much farther than we examined them; and that by means of this River and its several branches a very extensive inland communication lies open.[9]

Cook was frustrated they could make no progress, so lamentably called it "River Turnagain," a name that continues today as "Turnagain Arm." Clerke said it was "a fine spacious river, but a cursed unfortunate one to us." Ellis said it probably connected back to Prince William Sound. But there was no more exploring to be done, and Cook abandoned the search.[10] It was left for the later survey of George Vancouver to determine the full reach of the two branches of water that faced Cook that day.

Before departing Cook sent King again in the boats to a nearby point of land to take possession of the area for the British crown. Before the crewmen could come ashore a dozen natives halted their progress, fearful of the sailors' intentions. The English laid down their muskets and the natives dropped their spears, only to hide them in nearby bushes. The two groups then began to trade. The local people offered some salmon and two dogs in exchange for some iron. Fearing some mischief, the British decided to demonstrate the firepower of the English muskets with the dogs. John Law, surgeon on the *Discovery*, seized one acquired in trade and "took it down to the boat and shot it dead in their sight," Cook reported, "which seemed to surprise them very much." Trevenen later wrote that this was not "wanton cruelty," since Law was "a very amiable character," but the dog was simply shot to show the local people the superiority of British firearms "to prevent any evil intentions they might form." Clerke had a less complicated explanation. "They had an abundance of dogs … some of which (we) bought to regale upon, as a fresh Meal, and a very good one it is…"

The ritual claiming British possession occurred on June 1, 1778. It was similar to the one performed on Kayak Island, a routine performed for centuries by Europeans in new lands. The shore party displayed the flag, turned the turf, buried a bottle with some coins and papers, and drank some port wine to the health of the king. The natives observed with a touch of wonder and amusement. Midshipman Gilbert explained, "We … took possession of the Country in the name of His Britannic Majesty. About a dozen of the Natives were present and behaved very friendly but had no idea what we were doing."[11] King offered a full description of the rather elaborate ceremony:

> I made our folks remain on the beach, & as they beckoned me to come to them, I went, & they placed a Skin on the Grass for me to sit down upon; but their fears returned on seeing Mr. Bailey & the Doctor follow me; but however as they & I made motions that we had no arms about us, they remaind quiet; they were very civil in their Manner, yet suspicious; a few trifling presents were made & receiv'd; they

prest me to go alone somewhere with them, but their refusing to let any one Accompany me was a sufficient reason for my not chusing to rely on their good faith. After some time we returnd to our Party & performd the Ceremony of taking Possession, by hoisting the Colours &c; & drinking his Majestys health in good English Porter, by us, as well as by three of the Natives who repeated what we said; (& what we did not expect) were fond of the Liquor; they had also the empty Bottles; we contriv'd to place a bottle that the Captn had given us (with a Parchment Scroll in it) not in a conspicuous place, for that the Natives would find, but under some rocks by the Side of a Stuntd tree, where if it escapes the Indians, in many ages since it may Puzle Antiquarians.[12]

Today residents periodically return to the site, called Point Possession, looking for the buried bottles. But despite King's efforts to hide the booty, it is likely the local observers dug up the bottles and coins soon after their departure. In any event, no bottle has ever been found, so it truly has, in King's words, puzzled the antiquarians! The promontory is still called Point Possession on the northern tip of the Kenai Peninsula. King was not impressed with the conditions on shore, as the soil was wet and marshy, with a few stunted spruce trees. Although King may not have been impressed with the area, modern scholars believe it had been inhabited for at least a century before the English arrived and it continues to be used in the summer and fall to collect subsistence resources by the Dena'ina descendents of the area.

Dena'ina oral history recalls this first encounter with Europeans. In these recollections, as many as forty people from the local village were present for the ceremony. When they first saw Cook's men coming, they thought it might mean war, so they hastily armed themselves with spears and other weapons before confronting the English as they landed on shore. The story then turns friendly, as the English were able to convey sociable purposes. The natives ended up giving the British sailors a porcupine or a deer, and the English buried a jar of coins with the proclamation of ownership. In later years, after the Europeans had left the area, the children of the village would remove a jar or can they found floating in the water near the beach for their elders to look for remnants of Cook's visit.[13]

Cook observed that a lucrative fur trade could be established with the inhabitants in the region. He suspected that Great Britain could not participate unless the unfound passage directly back to Europe was discovered. Cook was, of course, prophetic. The Russians soon came to dominate these lands and engaged the local people, often as slaves or with paltry pay, hunting the fur to its virtual extinction. Although a useful passage to Europe was never found, British seamen (some who sailed with Cook) returned to take advantage of the fur trade on the coast. When English and even Spanish traders arrived in Prince William Sound and Cook Inlet in the late 1780s, the Russian strength in the region was already firmly established and, by the end of the century, the Russian America Company held a monopoly.[14]

Cook and the other crew members were so consumed with the prospects of finding a great northern sea that they wrote little about the people they encountered. However, on at least two occasions while they advanced up the inlet, the indigenous inhabitants came out to the ships in groups of two or three canoes. In each case the reception was friendly. As the local people arrived at the ships they would display a leather frock on a long pole, a sign of their peaceful intentions. They would offer fresh salmon and halibut in exchange for old clothes, beads, and small pieces of iron.

After he turned his attention to the open sea, Cook described the people of the area with more care. At Point Possession, he reflected on King's narrative of the encounter on shore. About twenty natives made their appearance with their arms extended, which seemed to be to the local expression of a peaceable disposition. They had with them fresh salmon and several dogs, and they exchanged the offerings "for such trifles as we had to give them." Several salmon and halibut were procured; most of it was fresh, recently split and ready for drying.

Cook and Gore thought these people resembled those who inhabited Prince William Sound, but they were probably incorrect. They also assumed they had not come in contact with Russians, as they were clothed in sea otter skins, which they speculated the Russians would have taken in trade. Yet they possessed iron implements, especially knives, suggesting they obtained them from native neighbors who had engaged in communication and trade with the Russians.[15]

Samwell seemed to better understand the differences between these people and those just observed in Prince William Sound. He instead likened them to the people of Nootka Sound, and commented extensively on their appearance, facial ornaments, clothing, and means of transport:

> The Inhabitants in general are a good looking people of a light copper Complexion & about the middle Size; if we compare them with those of King George's Sound they are in their Persons very clean, tho' like them daub

their Faces with red Oaker and Soot, they also wore one Sort of Caps exactly like those of that past of the Coast ... They thrust Feathers & sometimes Stones through the Gristle that divides the Nostrils. They make a large Hole in their under lips about an inch in length more or less in which they wear various Ornaments, some are made of bone & others of Stone. ... Their Cloathing consists of the Fur of the Sea Beaver & Seal Skins & those of other Animals made into Frocks, over which they have when they go upon the Water a kind of quilted Frock made of the Gutts and bladders of Fish, which keep out the wet exceeding well ... Their Canoes are of two sorts, one large & open capable of holding 30 or 40 people, the other small & covered & never carrying above one or two Persons. The large & Open Canoes are made of a slight frame ... covered with Seal Skin closely sewed together, they are from 20 to 40 feet long ... they will carry great Weights and they hardly make any Water, being much superior in both these respects to wooden Canoes.[16]

The American John Ledyard, who had prior experience with American Indians on the Atlantic Coast, also claimed these were the same people as those of the Sound, but he noticed their language was like that of Plains Indians. "The inhabitants are the same as those we left in Sandwich Sound," he wrote. "We called them the New Eskimaux: they were also possessed of a little iron, and some European beads. It is remarkable that we distinctly heard pronounced words ... which I very well remember to have heard pronounced by the American Indians from the frontiers of the northern American States. They have here as well as the other parts of the coast we had hitherto explored a plenty and variety of rich furs, which they exchanged with us upon the same terms we had hitherto practiced."[17]

While Cook and Ledyard correctly attributed traits of the Inuit Eskimo to the Alutiiq residents of Prince William Sound, they were incorrect in thinking the people of Cook Inlet were Eskimos as well. They were, however, Dena'ina Athabascans, related to the Athabascans who occupied Interior Alaska and Canada. The earliest evidence of Athabascan occupation dates to the end of the last ice age, about 12,000 years ago. The earliest cultural remains in interior Alaska, as on the coast, are chipped stone blade complexes about 10,000 years old. Ledyard noticed subtle differences in their language, so he might have understood their relationship to the Navajos or Apaches in what is now the southwestern United States.

The Athabascans believe they have evolved in Alaska, where they developed eleven distinct languages. Their subsistence is based on hunting and fishing, supplemented by berries and edible plants. The major game animals are caribou and moose, and salmon is a primary food resource. Waterfowl are taken during spring and fall migrations.

The Athabascans started as a mostly nomadic people without tribal organization. People lived in small family groups that were often on the move. Eventually they developed permanent homes and communities, tracing their ancestors through their mothers and grandmothers, rather than through the men. The Dena'ina had access to the sea, and its abundant resources, so they tended to be more sedentary than other Athabascans and developed a more structured clan system. The people spent their winters in permanent camps that became villages. Their winter homes were hemispherical in construction, and were covered with moose or caribou hides. They were well known for multi-faceted use of the birch tree. The birch not only provided house frames, but the branches also served them to make snowshoes, utensils, containers, and canoes. They also perfected a storage technique to preserve late-run salmon in "cold storage" pits that pre-dated modern refrigeration by centuries.

In the summers they moved to temporary fish camps along the rivers, streams, and coasts teeming with abundant resources, especially salmon, which return annually in great numbers to the present day. The clan system helped to provide the means for orderly labor during the intensive fishing period that was overseen by a "qeshqa" or chief, most often male, but sometimes female. Evidence shows that more than 160 such camps and settlements dotted the entire Cook Inlet basin.[18]

Linguistic and archeological evidence suggests that the Dena'ina were expanding their territory at the time of European contact. They had lived in Upper Cook Inlet for at least 1,500 to 2,000 years, and were established along the Kenai Peninsula and Kachemak Bay in southern Cook Inlet by 1000 A.D. There were four branches of the Dena'ina: on the Kenai Peninsula, the area of Upper Cook Inlet north of Anchorage, and the coastal and inland areas on the western side of the Cook Inlet that includes parts of Lake Clark and Iliamna Lake. Of these, the ancestors of the Kenaitze Indian tribe on the Kenai Peninsula were probably the people who came out to Cook's vessels as he sailed in the inlet, as well as those who observed King's efforts at Point Possession. This is confirmed by Anderson, Cook's surgeon, who reported 11 Dena'ina words from the brief encounter.

Cook was correct in speculating that the Dena'ina he met probably had no direct contact with Europeans. However, further exploration of Cook Inlet in subsequent years increased that contact markedly. Navigators visited and traded with the coastal Dena'ina and the Russians established settlements and trading posts along the Kenai Peninsula as part of their fur trading activities. The two Russian companies that arrived in Cook Inlet were the Lebedev-Lashtokin Company and the Shelikhov Company. The Lebedev Company set up its first trading post called St. George at Kasilof in 1787. Four years later, in 1791, it established St. Nicolas in Kenai. The Shelikhov Company had set up a post at Fort Alexandrovsky (English Bay) in 1784 and a ship building site at Resurrection Bay in 1791, at the location of modern-day Seward.

Because the two companies were competitors, the employees and managers of each tried to get exclusive trade with all the natives in the area. They used threats and the kidnapping of people associated with the opposite post. Modern scholars have confirmed hundreds of violent acts against the people as some 200 Russians attempted to control the lives, and fur harvesting practices, of probably 4,000 to 6,000 Dena'ina throughout all of Cook Inlet. This period of unfair dealings and mismanagement came to crisis when the local people rose up against the Russian Fort at modern-day Kenai, at the outlet of the Kenai River, at the Battle of Kenai in 1797. All 25 Russians who lived at the fort were slaughtered, as well as about 100 Dena'ina who were under the control of the Fort's manager.

The Russians occupied this fort, Redoubt St. Nicholas, for many years. On May 10, 1794, Captain George Vancouver paid an official visit to the fort, which he reported was about 120 square yards and surrounded by a paling about 12 feet high. The fort was occupied by about 36 Russians under the command of Stepan Zaikoff, who at that time was away on a visit to Prince William Sound. The Russians had two main buildings: a large hall that served as a dormitory and mess hall, and a small house for the commander. At least twenty other small huts were used for storing supplies, for teaching the local people the Russian language and religion, and as residences for people committed to the fort's operations.

Although the Kenai Peninsula continued to serve Russian interests, the Battle of Kenai had a significant impact in Russian-American history. When the battle was reported to Russian authorities, the warring companies were forced to merge to prevent further violence and streamline collection of furs and tribute. In 1798 the Lebedev Company was driven out of Alaska and the Shelikhov Company, renamed the Russian-American company under Baranov, took over. However, as the furs of the region depleted, most of the company's operations moved further east to Sitka, and the Cook Inlet region was mostly abandoned.[19]

It is likely that the battle gave the Dena'ina 80 more years of sovereignty before the arrival of Americans after the purchase of Alaska from the Russians in 1867. After American occupation, however, epidemic diseases vastly reduced the Dena'ina population. Nonetheless, today the Dena'ina still live throughout Southcentral Alaska at Kenai, Knik, Tyonek, Eklutna, Nondalton, Lime Village, Stoney River, Pedro Bay, Iliamna, and Anchorage.

After his venture into the Inlet, Cook turned to the south and quickly regained the open sea. Anchoring and weighing alternately every six hours, he was now able to use the wind and tide to his ships' advantage. Mt. Iliamna, a lofty volcano dominating the western shore, gave off a plume of steam, "white smoke, but no fire." In their zeal to exit the inlet the navigators misjudged the entry into one of the shoals in mid channel, grounding the *Resolution*. No damage occurred and the ship floated off with the next flood tide. The *Discovery* nearly had the same result on a shoal later called the "Snare." Finally the ships safely returned to the open sea in little more than three days. Modern pilots report that the tide can run at up to eight knots in the area of the East and West Forelands at full tide, explaining the predicament of these early explorers.

Cook and Clerke were so discouraged by the loss of a week charting this inland sea that they did not bother to name it. "If the discovery of this River should prove of use, either to the present or future ages," Cook wrote, "the time spent in exploring it ought to be the less regretted, but to us who had a much greater object in View it was an essential loss; the season was advancing apace..."[20] Cook had found the site of the future Municipality of Anchorage, the largest city north of Vancouver, Canada, on the west coast of North America. Local residents take pride in knowing that Cook was among the first Europeans to visit the region, now with the largest population of all the places he visited that summer, but few are aware that Cook despised the place. He spent eleven valuable days in this needless pursuit of the channel, which embittered him for the time still required for his urgent quest to find the Arctic. Ironically, the British Admiralty later named it after the Captain.

After Cook was underway west of Kodiak Island, he offered a more positive outlook on his journey through the inlet in the voyage log:

> It is now sixteen days since we came in sight of the land before us, which time has been spent to very little purpose, and is the more to be regretted as the wind has been favourable the most of the time for ranging the Coast to the South or SW and would probably have carried

us to its extremity in that direction. I was induced, very much against my own opinion and judgment, to pursue the Course I did, as it was the opinion of some of the Officers that we should certainly find a passage to the North, and the late pretended Discoveries of the Russians tended to confirm it. Had we succeeded, a good deal of time would certainly have been saved but as we did not, nothing but a trifling point in Geography has been determined, and a River discovered that probably opens a very extensive communication with the Inland parts, and the climate seemed to be as favorable for a settlement as any part of the world under the same degree of latitude.[21]

Residents of Anchorage today would not want to hear that Cook considered their home "nothing but a trifling point in Geography." But he was certainly prophetic about the area's climate. Today, this region is home to well over half of Alaska's population.

It is illogical that Cook would not name the great passageway, the largest inland passage found on the coast that year. He simply referred to it as a river. Later, when reflecting on his accomplishments that season, he left a blank space in his journal, planning to give it a name at a later time. Maybe he was looking for the contribution of other crewmen, and they all had ideas. King was unimaginative, calling it the "Great River." Predictably, Gore called it the "Gulf of Good Hope." But William Bayly, astronomer on *Discovery*, captured the captain's sentiments—he called it "Seduction River." William Ellis applied the name River Turnagain to the whole inlet, presumably with the same disgust.

After the expedition returned to England, Sandwich decided the great river should carry Cook's name. It was an important tribute for the recently deceased captain, though naming it for him bore considerable irony, given that Cook lamented the time spent exploring it. There is only one other geographical feature in all of the three voyages that bears Cook's name, Cook Strait, between New Zealand's North and South Island. It was also named for Cook by the Admiralty, not by Cook himself.[22]

George Vancouver, who sailed with Cook on *Discovery*, returned in April, 1794, to make the definitive survey of the inlet. His monumental 5-year expedition charted the coastline from Kodiak to San Diego. The Admiralty required that Vancouver resurvey Cook's River, as the armchair geographers did not agree with Cook, so speculated this might be the outlet of the Mackenzie River. In entering the inlet, a wisp of volcanic steam rose from one of the loftiest peaks, probably Mt. Iliamna. The vista of snow-capped mountains was even more awe-inspiring on Vancouver's expedition because they arrived while winter weather still gripped the land. Snow fell frequently and temperatures reached 7° F. Ice floes drifted in the ebb and flow of the tide, crashing into the sides of the ships.

After landing in the estuary off Eagle River for water, Vancouver repositioned his ships near Fire Island, as Cook had done 18 years earlier. Joseph Whidbey left with two shore boats on April 28 to explore the eastern arm that Cook named "Turnagain River," and in two days he returned to report that it was "no longer entitled to the name of a river."

Vancouver and his biologist, Archibald Menzies, then surveyed the northern branch of the river in a yawl and small cutter. Vancouver found the shoals in the middle of the arm were dry at low tide, and that the two shores came together. They waited for high tide, as Vancouver wanted to end all the speculation, "I resolved to continue our researches as far as it might be found navigable for the boats." The shores gradually inclined to one another, and soon they sighted the end of Knik Arm.

They landed near the end of an arm and climbed a small hillock to look to the north, viewing the tall peaks of the Alaska Range in the distance. "[We] had a good view of the Banks & sandy shoals which seemed to extend across the inlet about 3 or 4 miles above the ship, & backd one another to the very head of the arm," Menzies wrote. "Our station at this time was little more than a league above where Capt Cooks boats returnd, & had they come up this far what a satisfactory view they would have had of the termination of this great inlet, where they could behold the impossibility of navigating it higher up, & consequently preventing the indulging of those chimeral speculations concerning its spacious & unbounded extent." Menzies later wrote that the inlet should be called "by the name of Cook's Gulph, as it no more resembles a river than any other great Inlet on this coast."

Having proved this inlet was not the estuary of a great river, Vancouver decided to substitute the name "Cook's Inlet" for "Cook's River," frustrated that Cook had been so careless. He wrote "This terminated this very extensive opening on the coast of North West America, to which, had the great and first discoverer of it, whose name it bears, dedicated one day more to its further examination, he would have spared the theoretical navigators, who have followed him in their closets, the task of ingeniously ascribing to this arm of the ocean a channel, through which the north-west passage existing according to their doctrines might ultimately be discovered."[23]

Cook's party coasted again in contrary winds down the inlet, then to the west, deeper into the Pacific. Gore was finally silent. The imagined passageway to Europe, if it existed at all, had not been found. Cook felt the theoretical geographers had played an ugly trick on his expedition, a theme many adopted. King wrote of these frustrations as they sailed to the west.

> It may be asked why we tried and Afterwards perserver'd so long in this Inlet; to those who have heard the Russian Accounts since Beerings time of these parts and who chose to place even the smallest confidence in a Map of their late discoveries publish'd under the eye of Dr. Matty, must allow, that it was highly probably if not certain that a good deal of what Beering supposed to be continent was broken into Islands (which even now if it proves so in part, we may yet not be too late) in which case it might have appeared strange not to have tried all large openings, and certainly would have been said, that every one we did leave unsearch'd was a Passage, which would have led us to our Wishes.[24]

Capt. James Cook
of the Endeavour.

Portrait of Captain James Cook. Artist Hodges traveled around the world with Cook on his second voyage. This painting was discovered in Ireland at a country auction in 1986, then restored and sold to the National Maritime Museum in Greenwich. There are five surviving portraits of Cook painted from life and this is regarded as the finest, showing the strength of the commander's presence and resolve. David Cordingly, The Discovery of a Lost Portrait of Captain Cook, in David Cordingly, ed., Capt. James Cook, Navigator, National Maritime Museum, 1988, pp. 108-09. Original oil painting on canvas by William Hodges, circa 1775 © National Maritime Museum, London

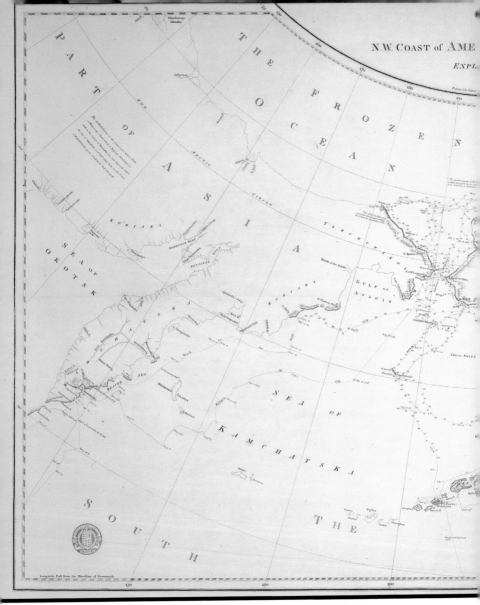

Chart of the NW Coast of America and NE Coast of Asia. This chart was prepared by Captain James King, second lieutenant, and Lieutenant Henry Roberts, master's mate aboard *Resolution* to show the track of Cook's Voyage in the North Pacific and the first reasonably accurate outline of the Northwest coast, including Alaska. Since it added the

topographical detail of Samuel Hearne's unrelated journey through Northern Canada in 1771-2 and several Alaskan place names not given by Cook (e.g. Cook's River) it was separately published and not part of the official voyage account. The Hearne detail was shown too far to the northwest. Engraving by W. Palmer and published by William Faden, 1784 © British Library, London

Portrait of Captain James Cook. This full-length representation shows Cook in captain's uniform with a telescope in his left hand and his hat in the right. It was prepared during the third voyage, probably in 1777. Mrs. Cook complained it made the captain look "too severe." Beaglehole, Life of Cook, p. 695. Original oil painting on canvas by John Webber, circa 1780 © Museum of New Zealand Te Papa Tongarewa, Wellington

A View in Ship Cove. The *Resolution* lies at anchor at right, stern forward at Nootka Sound, western Vancouver Island, surrounded by native craft. A chief with an imposing headdress stands in one of the canoes in the middle foreground offering a carved figure. Several other natives are standing in other canoes with arms outstretched in the traditional local greeting. Original drawing in pen, wash and watercolor by John Webber, April 1778 © British Library, London

A View in Ship Cove. Artists John Webber and William Ellis, also a surgeon's mate, drew from the same location with far different results that reflect both their talents and impressions of the cove. The *Resolution* and the *Discovery* are shown at anchor and under repair, with the observation tents erected nearby. Original drawing in pen and watercolor, attributed to William Ellis, April 1778 © National Library of Australia

A Sea Otter. The Russians had already discovered the considerable value of sea otter pelts, "soft gold." Cook's crew sold Nootka fur in Macao for a considerable sum. This spurred European and American traders to swarm the coast in search for more pelts, nearly wiping out the sea otter population in the decades that followed. Original drawing in pen, wash and watercolor by John Webber, April 1778 © National Library of Australia

A Woman of Nootka Sound. This woman of Nootka Sound, Vancouver Island wears a cedar bark rain cape with a sea otter fur collar and a basket hat decorated with whale hunting scenes. Original drawing in pen, ink and grey wash by John Webber, April 1778 © 2006 Harvard University, Peabody Museum

A Native Prepared for Hunting. A full-length figure of a Nootka Sound man in a heavy fur cloak fastened over his shoulders, carrying a bow in his right hand and a quiver slung over his shoulders. He wears a nose ring and has a basket hat with a bulbous top depicting a whaling scene. Original drawing in pen, ink and watercolor by John Webber, April 1778 © 2006 Harvard University, Peabody Museum

An Inside View of the Natives' Habitations. A large home found by Cook and his party in the village of Yuquot, which Cook, Clerke and Webber visited on April 22, 1778. Five people are seated on a platform on the left with four others, including a child, around an open fire in the center. Four more people, including another child, observe from the right. Fish hang from the poles near the roof and the back wall is adorned by two large carved wooden images. Original drawing in pen, ink and watercolor by John Webber, April 1778 © 2006 Harvard University, Peabody Museum

A View of the Habitations in Nootka Sound, Vancouver Island. Local people clad in skins stand in groups on the beach, some speaking with English sailors. There are local canoes on the beach and flat-roofed cedar houses beyond. Around the houses are racks for drying salmon. This is also the village of Yuquot that the English visited on April 22, 1778. This drawing was prepared for the third voyage publication after artist John Webber's return to England. Original drawing in pen, wash and watercolor, by John Webber, circa 1781-83 © Dixson Library, State Library of New South Wales, Sydney

Mount Edgecumbe, Kruzof Island, West Coast of America. After a devastating storm that kept the expedition away from shore for an extended period, on May 1, 1778 the crew observed their first Alaskan feature in the latitude of modern day Sitka. The dormant volcano was named after the commander of the Plymouth dockyard and later British admiral. Original drawing in pencil and wash, with traces of watercolor, by John Webber, May 1778 © British Library, London

A Woman of Prince William Sound. This is a field sketch drawn on the spot by Webber in front of the subject. It was used for more refined watercolor drawings prepared later on the voyage. She wears a close-fitting skin jacket and two bone ornaments through the septum, with beads attached in strings to the lower lip and from the ears. Original drawing in pencil, chalk and sepia by John Webber, May 1778 © Anchorage Museum at Rasmuson Center, Anchorage, Alaska

A Man of Prince William Sound. He wears a conical basket hat with chinstrap decorated with geometrical designs and glass beads around the rim. He is dressed in a sealskin frock and wears a nose ornament beaded at each end. Original drawing in pen and ink, grey and red wash by John Webber, May 1778 © 2006 Harvard University, Peabody Museum

A View of Snug Corner Cove, in Prince Williams Sound.

A View of Snug Corner Cove, Prince William Sound.
The *Resolution* and the *Discovery* are shown at anchor in the
eastern Sound on May 16, 1778, surrounded by a stunning
array of towering ice-covered peaks. Two large canoes filled
with natives approach the ships from the left, with a smaller

kayak with two natives paddling on the right. This drawing was prepared for the third voyage publication after Webber's return to England. Original drawing in pen, wash and water-color, by John Webber, circa 1781-83 © Dixson Library, State Library of New South Wales

Chart of Cook's River in the N. W. part of America. Despite his propensity to name most of the principal landmarks he saw, the Admiralty named "Cooks River" (later called "Cook Inlet" by Vancouver) and substituted "Prince William Sound" for Cook's name after the expedition returned to England. These two names were first used in this official engraved chart for the area, a region that frustrated Cook in his effort to find a northwest passage through the American continent to Europe. Engraved Chart from the Publication of Cook's Third Voyage, 1784, © Anchorage Museum at Rasmuson Center, Anchorage, Alaska

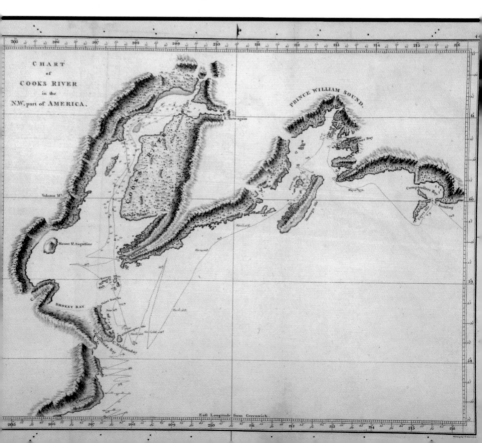

A Man of Turnagain River, Prince William Sound.
Although identified by Webber to be a man of Prince William
Sound, this half-length portrait is probably a resident of
Point Possession in Cook Inlet dressed in an elaborate coat
of skins with pendant feathers beneath his chest. He wears
a long, slightly curved bone ornament through his nose. His
lower lip has been perforated and holds three beaded pen-
dants. Original drawing in pen, wash and watercolor by John
Webber, May-June 1778 © 2006 Harvard University, Peabody
Museum

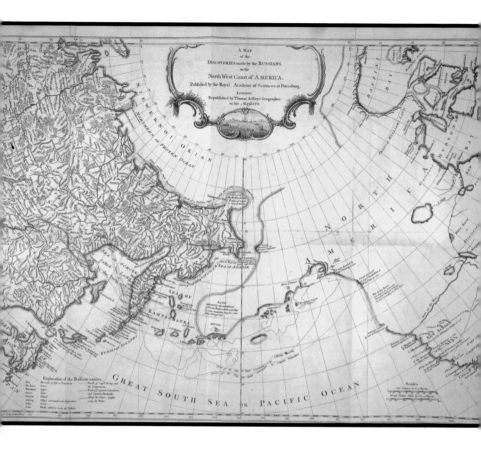

Voyages from Asia to America. The Admiralty gave Cook this Russian map prepared by G.F. Müller to assist in his search for the Northwest Passage. It depicts the Bering/Chirikov voyage tracks with some accuracy, showing the northwest coast of America bulging toward Kamchatka with a 500-mile wide channel between Siberia and northwest Alaska. The English version was printed by Thomas Jeffreys in 1761 © British Library, London

Stählin's Map of the Russian Discoveries in An Account of the New Northern Archipelago. This second Russian map was of more recent vintage and was to supplement Müller's Map with more up to date information about Russian discoveries in the North Pacific. Despite the fanciful depiction of many non-existent islands, the Admiralty assumed it was correct, so instructed Cook to search for the imagined northwest passage by sailing north from the Oregon coast. The English version was published by Dr. Maty (Secretary of the Royal Society) and C. Heydinger in 1774 © British Library, London

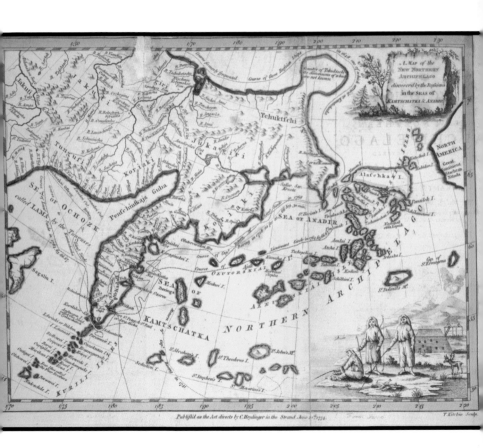

Schumagin's Isles, near Turnagain River, on the NW Coast of America. This is a "coastal view" field study, one of many prepared by Webber and Ellis to feature major landmarks during the expedition's running survey of the coastline.

The Shumagin Islands, west of Kodiak Island, were named by Vitus Bering after the first of his crew to die of scurvy in 1741. Original drawing in ink and watercolor over pencil by William Ellis, June 1778 © Alaska State Museum, Juneau, Alaska

Shooting Sea Horses. The expedition was in frequent contact with herds of "sea horses" or walrus while coasting along the ice pack. Cook had them killed and eaten by the crew, insisting they consume fresh provisions to prevent scurvy. The captain found this "marine beef" to be "as sweet as Marmalade." Most of the crew disagreed, finding the taste "disgustfull," more like "train oil." Original drawing in pen and watercolor by John Webber, August 1778 © University of Washington, Seattle, Suzzallo Library, Edward W. Allen Collection

The *Resolution* beating through the Ice, with the *Discovery* in the most eminent danger in the distance. This is probably drawn to show the harrowing brush with catastrophe near Icy Cape on August 18, 1778, when the ships were almost surrounded by the pack ice and the shore. "Our situation was now more and more critical," Cook wrote. "We were in shoald water upon a lee shore and the main body of ice in sight to windward driving upon us." Original softground hand colored etching, tinted in brown and grey wash, by John Webber, 1792 © National Library of Australia

A White Bear. Polar bears were first observed in the second summer in the Bering Sea icepack. Two of the bears were killed and eaten by the crew, who found the taste "fishy" but preferable to walrus or the salted pork brought from Hawaii. Original drawing in pen, ink, and wash by John Webber, July 1779 © National Library of Australia

Inhabitants of Norton Sound and Their Habitations.
The people of Norton Sound were encountered briefly on
the return from the Arctic. A small family is shown with the
woman carrying her child in a frock on her shoulder in a
customary fashion. A log hut and canoe are shown in the
background. This drawing was prepared for the third voyage publication after Webber's return to England. Original
drawing in pen, wash and watercolor, by John Webber, circa
1781-83 © Dixson Library, State Library of New South Wales,
Sydney

A Portrait of a Woman of Oonalaska. This as a preparatory sketch, probably drawn on the spot in front of the subject, leading to more refined watercolor drawings aboard the ship for the published account. She wears a close-fitting sealskin coat with her hair tied in the back. There are tattoo lines across both cheeks, as well as nose and chin ornaments and a perforated lower lip. Original drawing in pencil and charcoal by John Webber, July 1778 © Museum of the Aleutians, Unalaska, Alaska

A Portrait of a Man of Oonalaska. A half-length portrait of an Aleut man wearing an eyeshade or visor. A small ivory carving of a human is fastened to the crest. He wears an ornament through the nose and another beneath the lower lip, as well as a seal gut frock with a hood drawn around the neck. This drawing was prepared for the third voyage publication after Webber's return to England. Original drawing in pen, wash and watercolor, by John Webber, circa 1781-83 © Dixson Library, State Library of New South Wales, Sydney

Inside a House in Oonalaska. The Aleut homes were sunk partially underground and covered with earth "to a considerable thickness." The only entrance was at the top. There are five people seated and two children standing in conversation. Around the walls are shelves with baskets, mats, fish and other provisions. Original drawing in pen and ink by John Webber, July 1778 © 2006 Harvard University, Peabody Museum

Natives of Oonalaska and their Habitations. Webber drew the Aleut village at English Bay, near present day Dutch Harbor, with several local residents and the local landscape in view. The scene includes several of the partially sunken homes used by the people, as well as kayaks on racks. Original drawing in pen and ink on sepia washed paper by John Webber, July 1778 © 2006 Harvard University, Peabody Museum

Natives in Unalaska in their kayaks. This drawing depicts natives and their canoes from two separate but closely related Western Alaska cultures, showing the differences in styles of canoe and clothing then in use. The drawing at the top is a kayak used by Aleuts at Unalaska; the lower drawing is a Yupik canoe from the area of Cape Newenham, on the Alaska mainland in the northern part of Bristol Bay. Original drawing in pen and watercolor by John Webber, July 1778 © University of Washington, Seattle, Suzzallo Library, Edward W. Allen Collection

A View of Kealakekua Bay. A view prepared from shore with the *Resolution* and the *Discovery* at anchor surrounded by native craft. The large double-hulled canoes with upright lateen sails bore the Hawaiian chief Terre'oboo in his visits to the English ships. Over 1,000 canoes and 10,000 local people swarmed the bay when the ships first arrived on January 17, 1779. This drawing was prepared for the third voyage publication after Webber's return to England. Original drawing in pen, wash and watercolor, by John Webber, circa 1781-83 © Dixson Library, State Library of New South Wales, Sydney

The Death of Captain Cook. There were many pictorial accounts of Cook's death prepared in the years after the event, but only John Webber was in Hawaii at the time. He was not an eyewitness, but his drawing closely follows the first-hand accounts. Cook is about to be stabbed in the back while Lt. Phillips, who has fallen to the ground, fires at an assailant. Cook is holding his hand up to the marines, presumably to tell them to stop firing, but it is too late. This drawing was prepared for the third voyage publication after Webber's return to England. Original drawing in pen, wash and watercolor, by John Webber, circa 1781-83 © Mitchell Library, State Library of New South Wales, Sydney

XXXV

The Narta, or Sledge for Burdens in Kamtchatka.
The use of dog sleds was common in Siberia for travel and hauling freight at the time of Cook's expedition. Lt. King and his expedition used dog sleds to cross the Kamchatka Peninsula to reach Major von Behm in Bolsheretsk on the Sea of Okhotsk. Native summer and winter habitations are depicted in the background, as well as a volcano that was active during the expedition's first visit to Siberia, April-June 1779. Original softground hand colored etching, tinted in brown and grey wash, by John Webber, 1789 © Anchorage Museum at Rasmuson Center, Anchorage, Alaska

The Inside of a Winter Habitation (in Kamchatka).
This drawing portrays a native Kamchatka winter home observed during the expedition's first visit to Siberia, April-June 1779. It shows cooking, local dress and the care of an infant. Two large posts support the structure and a dog is seen licking from a trough in the background. Original drawing in pen, wash and watercolor by John Webber, May 1779
© National Library of Australia

A view of the Town & Harbour of St Peter and St Paul in Kamtschatka.

A View of the Town and Harbour of St. Peter and St. Paul (Petropavlovsk). The view looks east toward the entrance of Avacha Bay, with the tiny village shown on a sandy peninsula with raised native summer huts ("balagans") and Russian log homes. This drawing was prepared for the

third voyage publication after Webber's return to England.
Original drawing in pen, wash and watercolor, by John
Webber, circa 1781-83 © Dixson Library, State Library of New
South Wales

Balagans or Summer Habitations with the method of Drying Fish at St. Peter & Paul Kamtchatka. This drawing was prepared during the expedition's second visit to Siberia, August-October 1779. It features huts with conical roofs, called "balagans," used by the native people during the summer months. A woman is cooking with a kettle suspended from a tripod of poles. Original softground hand colored etching, tinted in brown and grey wash, by John Webber, 1792 © Anchorage Museum at Ramuson Center, Anchorage, Alaska

~Chapter 7~

The Arctic Sea

Nearly three months had passed since the expedition first sighted the West Coast of North America. Carrying Russian maps suggesting a direct route from New Albion to the Arctic, they instead found an impenetrable continent, trending first to the west, then the southwest. As the breadth of Alaska became more apparent, the imagined northwest passage seemed all the more improbable. The explorers had investigated the two most promising openings in the Alaska coast, Prince William Sound and Cook Inlet, but both were dead ends. The whole crew, even the unflappable Gore, was discouraged.

Leaving Cook Inlet on June 6, 1778, they continued south. The expedition could only follow the coast in near-continuous rain, and in what seemed an endless line of barren cliffs guarded by submerged rock and shrouded in banks of swirling fog. Cook lamented, "We had almost constant Misty weather with drizzling rain so that we seldom had sight of the Coast." The landscape, when he could see it through the dense fog, rain and snow, stretched out for miles, descending from snow capped mountains into the rock-filled breakers of the sea. He could not be certain of the ships' position as the clouds obscured the sun, so navigation was slow and painstaking, with deadly shoals and capricious winds. These dreary conditions plagued them all the way to the Arctic. No wonder the speculative geographers had so much to say about Bering's voyage, as both Bering and Chirikov found the same frightful conditions along this coast in 1741, leaving much to the imagination.

A broad opening soon appeared to the west. After failing to find inland seas in earlier attempts, Cook decided against taking it. He reasoned, "In standing in for this Coast, we crossed the mouth of the ... bay and saw land all round the bottom of it, so that either the land is connected or else the points lock in one behind another; but I am more inclinable to think the former, and that the land East of the bay is a part of the Continent." So Cook passed Shelikof Strait, which would have taken him between the Alaskan continent and Kodiak Island. Troubled before by such tantalizing openings in the coast, he took the more circuitous route south of Kodiak Island. As he sailed south he must have been discouraged by his progress. The Admiralty wanted him at 65° north latitude in June. On the first day of June he was at 61° 30' in Cook Inlet. By the end of the month, nine weeks from Nootka Sound, they were at 53°, almost back to the latitude of Vancouver Island, before the Alaska coastline permitted them to turn north again.

Rounding the Kodiak Island landmass, the sailors had favorable winds, but the "air raw and cold." On June 11, off Cape Kaguyak on the southern coast, they saw two round hills they called "Twoheaded Point," with peaks of 1,700 and 1,800 feet. Cook wrote, "This part of the Coast is composed of high hills and deep Vallies, some of the latter are pretty extensive and in some parts the tops of hills were seen beyond those which form the Coast. It was but little incumbered with snow, but had a very barren appearance; not a tree or bush was to be seen upon it, most parts seemed to be covered with a Mossy substance that gave it a brownish hue." It was so early in the summer Cook probably saw tundra grasses which just appeared after a winter in snow.[1]

By Sunday, June 14, they had passed Kodiak Island and found two or three rocky inlets they named Trinity

Islands. This is now called Cape Trinity, the southwestern point on Kodiak Island. Cook most likely did not see the actual cape, but his name was assigned by later mapmakers to the true cape. Now the land trended north for the first time since leaving Cook Inlet. The ships passed Shelikof Strait and drew near to the Alaska shore. The strait was never mapped or reconnoitered at either end, even though much wider than Cook Inlet. It was simply unknown to them, as the weather required that they frequently stand away from the coast that they could not see. Cook explained, "...seeing no land and the gale increasing with a thick fog and rain, I steered WNW under such sail as we could haul the wind with; for I was very well apprised of the danger running before a strong gale in a thick fog, exposed to us."

Clerke was tiring of the dreary conditions, this summer of storms. It was always too windy, or too foggy, to make reasonable time, not to mention how unnerving it was to sail blindly ahead, knowing at any moment they could be shipwrecked on this isolated, broken and rocky shoreline enshrouded in constant mists. He wrote "We have now a very staggering Gale, which, if it lasts any term of time, will give a very pleasing change to the aspect of our affairs; the Atmosphere at present is rather too hazy and thick to run freely in, but the Season presses on and we must not stand for trifles."[2]

Periodically the fog would clear enough to expose their precarious position among the rocks and crags of this windy shore. In the early morning hours of June 16, the fog lifted long enough for a momentary view of rocky islands before the ships again "fell in with the fog." These pinnacle rocks were dubbed "Foggy Island," assuming this was the same place given that name by Bering. But it was difficult to know accurately, since in their separate voyages both Bering and Cook encountered only miserable enshrouded weather. In 1794, during his final year charting the Alaska coast, Vancouver solved the mystery when he realized that Cook and Bering had actually given two different clusters of rocks the same name. So he renamed Cook's "Foggy Island" the Chirikov Islands, to commemorate the often-overlooked captain of Bering's consort.[3]

The next day the expedition came to the Shumagin Islands. In 1741 they had been named by Bering after the first of his crew to die of scurvy, who was buried there. The weather was unusually clear and pleasant, affording the first use of the sextant in over two weeks. Cook noted the coastal topography was rocky and the inland rugged. "For some distance to the SW of that Cape this Country is more broken or rugged than any part we had yet seen," he wrote, "both with respect to the hills themselves, and the Coast which seemed full of creeks or small inlets. ... Every part had a very barren appearance, and was covered with snow from the summits of the high[e]st hill down to a very small distance from the Sea-Coast."

Cook stayed north of the islands in the channel against the Alaska Peninsula. The *Discovery*, which was two miles back, suddenly fired three guns. The officers of *Resolution* were "a good deal alarmed," according to Cook. They assumed there was some accident, or that the vessel had sprung a leak. Instead, Clerke was signaling that he met up with natives who had been paddling in three or four kayaks under his vessel's stern.

Clerke wrote, "an Indian in one of them made many signs, took off his cap and bowed after the manner of Europeans." They threw the leader a rope "to which he fastened a small thin wood case or box." The box seemed to be some kind of musical instrument, but on closer inspection they found a piece of paper folded inside, with Russian writing. As there was no one on either vessel who could read Russian, the writing elicited all manner of speculation. It had the date of 1778, but the body of the note seemed to refer instead to the year 1776. Clerke speculated there were Russians on the near shore who had been shipwrecked and, seeing the British vessels pass, sent natives to plead for rescue. He wanted to investigate, but Cook felt otherwise. Cook was certain any Russian in distress would accompany the natives, so he assumed this was just "a note of information left by some Russian trader who had lately been in these parts, to be delivered to the next that came." The natives simply erred in giving the note to the British, as they would not have known these Europeans were not Russian hunters.[4]

King wrote "... most of our people were of opinion that some Russian Sailors had been Shipwreck'd here, & that they had taken this method, on seeing us pass by, to inform us of their situation, but if so it was most extraordinary that they did not come out themselves." He knew it would be impossible to find shipwrecked sailors in such a vast area, concluding "we however enquired no farther about the matter, nor would our time & situation allow us to have made further enquiries."[5]

Cook was right. Bayly later reported "we afterwards learned that [the writing] was a receipt for Tribute paid to the Russians," that is, a simple Russian acknowledgement for tribute paid in furs. Presumably the natives wanted Cook to know they had already paid their obligations to the Czar, and did not want to pay again! The chief consequence of the letter was that the English knew they were finally in the realm of Russian fur traders and they should be watchful of other Europeans. Bayly wrote, "This seems to be the farthest East that the Russians trade along the Coast of America."[6]

But soon the Russians pressed further to the east. At the same time Cook's expedition left England in 1776, Grigor Ivanovich Shelikhov arrived in Kamchatka to enter the sea otter trade. He fell in with prosperous merchants and, in 1783, outfitted three ships at Okhotsk to begin the largest Russian commercial venture up to that time. In a year, he stood in a bay off the southeast coast of Kodiak, which he named "Three Saints Bay" after his ship. Here he decided to build the first permanent settlement in Alaska.[7] Until then, the closest settlement to the south was the tiny Spanish presidio and mission in San Francisco, founded just eight years before.

Summer solstice arrived as Cook and his men continued along the coast to the west, reaching the westernmost tip of the Alaska Peninsula. They were still sailing blind along a coastline that even today ships find treacherous, with all too frequent groundings despite modern radar and navigational instruments. It is a testament to the judgment and skill of the great navigator that his ships traveled through unscathed. Between clouds and rain they observed two conical peaks on nearby islands, one of which "continually threw out a vast column of black smoke." This was probably Shishaldin Volcano, nearly 10,000 feet in elevation. Cook simply called it "Volcano" but Gore was more effusive. "This Mountain from its Top Emits Large Collums of Smoak, hence I distinguish it by the Name of Smoaker." It is no wonder a Russian name was ultimately given to the peak.

Cook rarely wrote of his passionate devotion to the diet of his crew and his regular effort to freshen their supplies. The sailors often hunted for shore birds, fished from the boats, traded for fresh supplies with local people, and collected shore grasses for salads. But on this solstice day Cook describes a remarkable episode of halibut fishing, even by modern Alaskan standards. After leaving the area of the volcano, the ships were soon becalmed off the mainland. In a few hours "our people caught upward of a hundred Halibut, some of which weighed 100 lb and none less than 20, which proved very great refreshing to us."

In the midst of what must have been a frenzied scene a single native in a small kayak appeared. Like the contact two days earlier, this Alaskan was the model of courtesy and good manners, removing his cap and bowing to the ships in the manner of Europeans. He wore green cloth pants and a black jacket over his seal gut shirt, showing some influence from nearby Russians. He had nothing to barter, except a few fishhooks, which the English eagerly purchased as they continued their halibut fishery. Although the native's lip was perforated in the Alaskan custom, his size and features resembled the people of the Hawaiian Islands. As a result, the English concluded he might have Polynesian extraction, and attempted to speak with him in languages from the South Pacific. Their efforts were fruitless. With the trade concluded, the wind came up and the kayaker returned to shore.[8]

For several more days Cook coasted with following winds and fog along the coast, rarely observing land. On the 25th the skies cleared and Shishaldin Volcano came out behind them in stark relief, with other mountains to the east and west, "and all the Mainland under them much plainer than at any time before." At last Cook observed a break in the monotonous coast, and saw a passageway through to the north. "...there appeared a large opening for which I steered, till be raised land beyond it; which land, although we did not see it join to the Continent, made a passage through the opening rather doubtfull." Again, the uncertainty of coastal topography caused him to hesitate, pressing to the west instead of proceeding north. This was a major blunder, as the days ahead would confirm. He had failed to locate a passage at Prince William Sound and in Cook Inlet. So like the opening at Shelikof Strait, he passed another apparent entrance at Unimak Pass, which is the first passage north at the end of the Alaska Peninsula.

"It [was] doubtfull whether the land we saw to the SW were Islands or Continent," he reasoned, "and if the latter then the opening would be a deep bay or inlet into which, if we entered with an Easterly tide we could not so easily get out. Not caring therefore to trust too much to appearances, I steered to the Southward ..." Not only did this caution prove to add several more days to the journey north, it also led them to near disaster as they entered the next fog bank to the west.

It was daybreak on the 26th when they skirted Unimak Pass and held their westerly course. Again, there was heavy weather and mist and dreadful silence on the fog-shrouded deck. "Daylight availed us little as the Weather was so thick that we could not see a hundred yards before us," but as the wind moderated Cook raised more sails and gained speed. No sooner had they let the wind take the ships than the crash of nearby breakers surrounded them. There was no way out, so again they hastily brought their ships to a halt, anchoring until the weather cleared.

"The sound of breakers had been the sound of salvation," Cook wrote. The ships had been rushing head long for the shore. In an instant they would have been crushed, shipwrecked in a place with little hope for rescue or salvation. They made the best of the unplanned anchorage, as they were suddenly in a cove where the landing was easy and grasses abundant. "I sent a boat to see what the shore produced," and it was plentiful. There was "tolerable good grass and several other small plants, one of which was like Parsley and ate very well either in soups or as a Sallad."[9] The master mariner seemed to always know how to make the best of a difficult situation.

The good luck continued. The following day the wind turned south and moderated, and the fog dispersed.

A channel guided them north, away from the dangers of the evening's anchorage. In places it was less than a mile wide, surrounded by huge peaks. Cook was uncertain, but proceeded north, as he did not want to press his luck sailing in fog along the rocky Aleutian coastline. His choice was a good one. The channel is known today as Unalga Pass, a narrow, tidally influenced canal that separates Unalaska and Unalga islands. It is not as wide as Unimak Pass, which Cook bypassed two days earlier. Its tides were less predictable, but as fast as Cook Inlet. The *Discovery* was nearly swamped the following morning as it exited the passage. Nonetheless, it offered the necessary opening to finally get them north.

The British adventurers later learned the land to the west was Unalaska Island, then the center of the fledgling Russian fur empire. As they sailed through Unalga Pass, they spotted many of the local people and their habitations. The first people since Tahiti who were in contact with Europeans, their manners and dress were more agreeable to Cook's Euro-centric tastes. "A few now and then came off to the Ships and bartered a few trifling things with out people," he offered, "but never remained above a quarter of an hour at one time. On the contrary they rather seemed shy, and yet seemed to be no strangers to Vessels in some degree like ours, and had acquired a degree of politeness uncommon to Indians." Edgar reported "...these are the first set of Indians we met with which are not in the least addicted to thieving ..." [10]

After the two English ships exited the channel more natives came aboard, bartering fishing hooks and other implements for tobacco. One young man fell out of his kayak and into the water as he came on board. While the ship's crew rescued him from the water, his companions took his kayak to shore, stranding him aboard. "The youth was thus left alone and without his Canoe, came into the Ship and down into my Cabbin on the first invitation and without shewing the least restrai[n]t or uneasiness," Cook reported. "His dress was an upper Garment like a Shirt, made of the large gut of some sea animal, probably the Whale, and an under garment of the same shape, made of birds skins dressed with the feathers on and neatly sewed together." Cook offered him dry clothing "in which he dressed himself with as much ease as I could have done." This behavior convinced the captain that these people were no strangers to Europeans or their customs and that they had a peaceable demeanor unlike any he had previously encountered in the North or South Pacific.

It was now early July. Thick fogs and contrary winds prevented the departure of the ships, so they turned into a protected harbor on the north side of the island, which the local people called "Samgoonoodha."[11] As a result of Cook's visit, the Russians later called it English Bay. They lingered just a day and, as with earlier encounters on the island, the English reported that all contacts were pleasant, and the people good natured, clean and respectful. Cook would return to Unalaska after three months in the north for a three-week stay. It would be his longest stop in Alaska and his last before his ill-fated return to Hawaii.

All now seemed open to the Arctic and Cook suspected he would gain the Admiralty's assigned 65° latitude and the Arctic Sea in short order. He was still required to inspect coastal features along the way, referring to the Russian maps as he did. He turned east, sailing with a following wind along the northern boundary of the Alaska Peninsula in a broad, open sea. According to Müller's map, he was now sailing over land; Stählin had him darting between islands. On July 10 the continent took an abrupt turn north and Cook anchored in the estuary now called Kvichak Bay.

He wrote of a deep, shallow bay between distant peaks and named the winding river draining the region "River Bristol," after the third Earl of Bristol, who lived west of London in the town of the same name. Bristol is now the largest city in southwest England, with a population of about half a million.

The expedition was anchored at the outlet of either the modern-day Kvichak or Naknek Rivers. They apparently arrived at the peak of the annual salmon run that frequently chokes the rivers and bays of the region, as Cook was astounded by the number of fish in the bay. "It must abound with Salmon," Cook wrote, "as we saw many leaping in the Sea before it and some were found in the Maw of Cod we caught." Later mapmakers replaced Cook's name for the river, using the local names. But he also assigned the name "Bristol Bay" to the entire thousand-mile coast of Southwestern Alaska. His friend, Augustus John Hervey, third Earl of Bristol, was now immortalized in both hemispheres, as Cook had previously named the Hervey Islands in the South Pacific during the second voyage.[12]

Leaving Bristol Bay they sailed to the northwest, following the land in intermittent fog and mist. In the early morning of July 16 the fog cleared and, to their amazement, they had nearly run into a promontory Cook named "Cape Newenham," after an Irish friend. This cape, still known today by this same name, is the defining coastal feature marking the northern extent of Bristol Bay. The usually understated Clerke found the place depressing, "a damn'd unhappy part of the World, for the Country appears just as destitute as a Country can be, and the surrounding Seas are scarcely navigable for the numberless Shoals."

Cook sent Lt. Williamson to take possession of the land at the cape, the first such official act since departing

Cook Inlet. "Soon after Mr. Williamson returned and reported that he had landed on the point, climbed the highest hill" Cook wrote, "... he had a sight of the coast to the North and the farthest point he could see in that direction bore nearly North. He took possession for the Country in His Majestys name, left a bottle in which was inscribed on a piece of paper the Ships names &cta and named the promontory *Cape Newenham*." Williamson described the land in stark terms. The hills were barren, and there were no trees or shrubs, just open Alaskan tundra. He claimed to see "a doe and a fawn," but more likely, the animals were moose or caribou.

The vessels continued to follow the Alaska coast to the north but found themselves ensnared in the shoals of Kuskokwim Bay and the vast delta of the Yukon River. Each way they turned they were mired in mud. Both ships sent scouting parties to look for channels to take them north, but without success. Cook was impatient with the loss of time and urgently felt the need to press north, so he abandoned the coast, retreating all the way back to Cape Newenham. In frustration, the farthest point north was jokingly called "Shoald Ness," their own monster of shallows and shoals.

Because of constant flats, the ships frequently ran in just five feet of water, which slowed their return to Cape Newenham. On the 21st they came across two dozen local Yupik people in kayaks. Cook reported the encounter as yet another brief trading session with a local populace:

> While we lay here Twenty seven men of the Country, each in a Canoe, came off to the Ships which they approached with great caution hollowing and opening their arms as they advanced, which we understood was to

express their peaceable intentions. At length
some ventured near enough to receive some
trifles that were thrown them; this incouraged
the rest to venture along side and a traffick
presently commenced between our people and
them. ... They seems to be the same sort of
people we had lately met with, wore the same
kind of ornaments in their lips and noses; but
were far more dirty and not so well clothed.
... The most of them had their hair shaved or
cut short off, except a few locks behind or on
one side; for a covering for the head they wore
a hood of skin, and a bonnet which appeared
to be of wood. ... By this dress it should seem
that they some times go naked, even in this
high latitude, for they hardly wear it under their
other cloathing.[13]

While many of the crew assumed these were the same
people first met in Unalaska, they were not. These were
Yupiks, not Aleuts, who are related to the people Cook
met in Prince William Sound. The Yupik or, in the Central
Alaskan language, Yup'ik, are indigenous people who live
along the coast of western Alaska, especially on the Yukon-
Kuskokwim delta and along the Kuskokwim River. They
are Eskimo and are related to the Inuit. This was probably
the first contact of Yupiks with Europeans, who were
not yet under the influence of Russians like the Aleuts in
Unalaska. Clerke wrote that the Natives were captivated
by the woven cloths from Tahiti they had on board, but
he found that their trading skills were poorly developed.
"They were rather loose in their mode of traffick," he wrote,
"the Goddess of Justice appeared by no means to be the
Deity of their Adorations."[14]

From this point the weather again deteriorated badly. Fog, rain, adverse winds, all plagued efforts to find a new course to the north. So the expedition went out to sea in order to inspect the coastline from afar. In so doing they came across an island in the middle of Bering Strait, hundreds of miles from the coast. Cook called it "Anderson's Island," after the ship's surgeon and naturalist, who died that afternoon after a lingering bout of tuberculosis. Both Clerke and Anderson had contracted tuberculosis in England before the start of the voyage. Although Clerke remained well enough to continue in command of *Discovery*, Anderson declined steadily after he came in contact with the fog and cold of the North Pacific. Cook and crew alike were fond of Anderson, and were devastated by the loss of the surgeon, the first to die on the voyage. "Mr. Anderson my Surgeon," Cook wrote, "who had been lingering under a consumption for more than twelve Months, expired between 3 and 4 this after noon. He was a Sensible Young Man, an agreeable companion, well skilld in his profession, and had acquired much knowledge in other Sciences."[15] This was Bering's St. Matthew Island.

They had now passed the Kuskokwim and Yukon River deltas far to sea and assumed it was safe to edge back to the Alaska mainland. On August 4 they again reached the coast, entering Norton Sound, named to honor Sir Fletcher Norton, the speaker of the House of Commons. This bay surrounds the modern-day city of Nome, the largest community in Western Alaska and terminus of the annual Iditarod Sled Dog Race. Residents of the area might be troubled to know that Fletcher was not held in high regard in England and that Cook gave this area his name out of a sense of national obligation, probably without knowing the man personally. One contemporary characterized him as a "shrewd and unprincipled man, of good abilities and offensive manners." He had a violent temper and "lack of discretion" that did not serve him well, but he was knighted by the king in 1762, and held the post of speaker for nearly three years.

By August 8th the ships reached a high cape to the east, which Cook correctly surmised was the westernmost point of the mainland of North America. He called it "Cape Prince of Wales."[16] The area had only been briefly observed a century ago by the legendary, if not mythical, Siberian adventurer Semen Dezhnev, who discovered the strait that separated Asia from America. Dezhnev's voyage is a matter of some speculation among scholars today, as it preceded Bering by a century and is based on documents discovered by Gerhard Müller, the Russian academician whose fanciful map frustrated Cook. Dezhnev most likely existed, and probably was one of the few survivors of a party of 90 cossacks, traders and hunters who were the first Europeans to sail between the continents at Bering Strait in 1648. Whether anyone in the party observed Alaska, given the notorious summer fogs in the strait, is a matter of conjecture.[17]

Cook's expedition then advanced across the narrow inlet of the Bering Strait to the Russian coast, presumably to verify they had reached Asia, and to compute the distance between Alaska and Russia at that point. Midway in the journey they observed two high, rocky islands known today as the Diomede Islands. Here Russia and Alaska are separated only by little more than two miles in these two isolated but inhabited islands in the central Bering Sea.

By August 10 the expedition had reached Eastern Siberia and anchored in the large opening Cook called St. Lawrence Bay. There was a small community of local people, the Chukchi of Eastern Siberia. On Cook's first approach these people were fearful:

As we were standing into this place we perceived on the North shore an Indian Village, and some people whom the sight of Ships seem to have thrown into some confution or fear, as we could see some running inland with burdthens on their backs. ... I went with three Armed boats, accompanied by some of the Officers, and found 40 or 50 Men each armed with a Spontoon Bow and Arrows drawn up on a rising ground on which the village stood. ... I followed them alone without anything in my hand, and by signs and actions got them to stop and receive some trifles. ... They seemed very fearfull and causious, making signs for no more of our people to come up ... as I advanced they retreated backwards.[18]

Cook seemed to throw caution to the wind, always his policy on first meeting a strange and potentially hostile people in earlier voyages in the South Pacific. While he had some lapses in these standards earlier on the third voyage, with disastrous results that would be revisited in Hawaii, he seemed in true form in Siberia. Samwell described the remarkable scene, as Cook waded into a hostile group of 60 Natives alone:

...about 60 Indians armed with Bows & arrows and long spears pointed with iron drew up in a body on the rising ground to oppose him. ...Capn Cook having drawn up his Men in proper Order advanced alone towards the Indians, making signs of Friendship & holding some Necklaces & other Trinkets in his Hand as a present to them, on which an old man came to meet him. ... a Line which they had drawn across from one Jaw bone of a whale stuck in the ground to another & which seemed to have been set up as a boundary between them & our People was now taken down, on which several of our People advanced to them.[19]

With remarkable patience and the use of sign language, Cook convinced them of his peaceable intentions and trade commenced in the manner repeated on so many occasions throughout the Pacific. The English lingered for three hours. Cook wrote at length of the clothing, kayaks and weaponry of these people, correctly concluding they were different from the Alaskans he had seen at Unalaska and Cape Newenham. He noted the differences between the summer houses, lifted on stilts out of the marshes, and winter habitations buried in the ground, and recorded the operation of dogs and dogsleds, which he had not observed in Alaska. He concluded this was the land of the "Tchuktschians" or Chukchi, first encountered by Bering in 1728. [20]

The Chukchi are the largest Native nation (about 15,000) on the Asian side of the North Pacific. At present, they populate a huge area that reaches from Bering Strait to the Kolyma River valley deep in inland Siberia and extends along both the Arctic and Pacific coasts of northeast Asia. The name was given to them by the Russians, which comes from the Chukchi word Chauchu ("rich in reindeer"). Reindeermen use this word to distinguish themselves from coastal folk, who are usually called Anqallyt ("the sea people"). Although an indigenous Siberian people, the Chukchi apparently came to Bering Strait later than the Eskimos. Anthropologists trace their origin to the ancient residents of interior and coastal Siberia, around the northern Okhotsk Sea, about a thousand miles from Bering Strait. Their closest kin are the Koryak people of northern Kamchatka, with whom the Chukchi share similarities in language, beliefs, and historical traditions.[21]

Leaving the realm of the Chukchi after this short visit, Cook once again dismissed the troublesome Russian maps supposed to be the product of Bering's voyage. Stählin had placed a series of imagined islands in the area that he thought separated the Asia and American continents. The largest was called "Alaschka" in this exact place, dividing Russia from a distant American mainland. "I must have concluded Mr. Staehlins Map and account to be either exceeding erroneous even in latitude or else a mere fiction..." Cook wrote, noting instead the close proximity of the two continents at this point.

The expedition now returned east, leaving Siberia for Alaska. Cook was finally at 65° north latitude and able to begin looking for the Admiralty's imagined passage to Europe. King shared the sentiments of the crew, "All our Sanguine hopes begin to revive, & we are already begin to compute the distance of our Situation from known parts of Baffins Bay." Here Vitus Bering timidly turned around on his first expedition in 1728 but Cook continued, even though he rarely saw the coastline thanks to continuing poor weather and cold. Since the crew had no visual reference they measured the water depths to avoid grounding, sailing on in the mists. The fog would lift occasionally to afford a glimpse of the shore and they saw low-lying coastal plains devoid of vegetation, with distant hills. "The whole was free from Snow," Cook wrote "and to appearance destitute of Wood." But they sailed on without anything in view, just a few hundred yards of water surrounding their tiny wooden ships. It was a risky enterprise, to be sure, and no wonder that Bering retreated in similar circumstances on his first voyage through the area a half century earlier.

On August 16, in 68° north latitude, the ships were finally above the Arctic Circle. Cook first saw walrus, several flocks of birds, and sea ice. He had spent much of the second voyage in and out of the ice approaching Antarctica, and the northern horizon had an unmistakable brightness that warned they would be at the ice pack soon. "We perceived a brightness in the Northern horizon like that reflected from ice, commonly called the blink," he reported "it was little noticed from the supposition that it was improbable we should meet with ice so soon, and yet the sharpness of the air and Gloomyness of the Weather for two or three days past seemed to indicate some sudden change."[22]

They reached the ice pack as they neared 71° north latitude just two days later. Suddenly winter was upon the ships. "... the weather began to grow piercing cold," Rickman wrote, "The frost set in so hard that the running rigging was soon loaded with ice and rendered almost impossible to make the sheafs or blocks traverse without the assistance of six men to do the work of one." The day before had been warm and pleasant, but there was a sudden change in the weather such that in the middle of August "the ice was seen hanging at our hair, our noses, and even at the men's finger's ends. It came to the point that hot soup would freeze on the seamen's tables before they could gulp it down.[23]

The ice rose up in sheer cliffs directly from the sea dashing any hopes of a quick passage home and the glory of Parliament's prize. Seeing ice this early surprised the crew, because here they were still south of the latitudes of northern Norway, the island of Spitsbergen, and Baffin Bay in the North Atlantic, all of which are free of pack ice in the summer. "We were at the time in 20 fathoms Water, close to the edge of the ice which was as compact as a Wall and seemed to be ten or twelve feet high at least, but farther North it appeared much higher, its surface was extremely rugged and here and there were pools of Water." The weather cleared so they could see land 3-4 miles to the east, which Cook dubbed "Icy Cape," a significant coastal feature that still bears the name. This cape is southwest of modern-day Barrow, the northernmost community in Alaska. The most northern feature of land in Alaska named by Cook, it was the northernmost point on the voyage.

Suddenly Cook found the *Resolution* embayed in shallow water, nearing shore where the ice held fast. With the wind at his back, the ice pack was descending to shore. *Discovery* was a mile astern, too far away in the intermittent fogs, so Cook tacked toward shore and his own potential doom to maintain contact with Clerke. They now risked grounding in a vise grip between ice and rock, with no possibility of retreat. Cook optimistically reported the dire situation in the log:

> Our situation was now more and more critical; we were in shoald water upon a lee shore and the main body of the ice in sight to windward driving down upon us. It was evident, if we remained much longer between it and the land it would force us ashore unless it should happen to take the ground before us; it seemed nearly if not quite to join to the land to leeward and the only direction that was open was to the SW. ... I made the Signal for the Discovery to tack and tacked me self at the same time.

Cook had sailed hundreds of days in Antarctic ice on his second voyage. He maintained constant sight of his consort and kept a wary eye for a route of escape. But now, in his third day in the Arctic, his ships were separated and both were nearly ensnared in pack ice. "This was what I expected and most feared, and was not a little alarming" he wrote in the log, "for we must be inevitably forced ashore, if we could get without the Ice, and we had but a bad prospect as the wind was right in out teeth; the only change we had was the ice taking the ground before us, for we had no reason to expect a harbour on so flat and shallow a coast as this."[24]

In their zeal to find an ice-free route along the coast, the two ships were almost trapped with no way out. It was a terrible blunder. Alaskans today know the ice pack frequently moves far off shore at this time of year, exposing open water leading past Point Barrow to the Canadian Arctic. Fortunately the pack ice was solid that year. Had they been able to follow the coast any further north, changing winds would have almost certainly ensnared them, blocking any hope of retreat.

Another century would pass before seamen with sturdier craft and substantial provisions finally completed this coastal passage and achieved the Admiralty's directive of finding the northwest passage, such as it is. Dozens of ships made the attempt, usually starting in the east and working their way west, and always with the same disastrous result. Sir John Franklin led the most celebrated voyage of doom in 1845. When his expedition failed to return, a number of relief expeditions and search parties explored the Canadian Arctic in the middle of the nineteenth century, resulting in final charting of the passage west. Only in 1906 was the Norwegian explorer Roald Amundsen able to complete a three-year voyage that achieved this objective. Amundsen, who left Norway just in time to escape creditors seeking to stop the expedition, sailed in the converted 47-ton herring boat *Gjøa*. At the end of this trip, he walked into the city of Eagle, Alaska, and sent a telegram announcing his success. The first single-season passage was not accomplished until 1944. Then the Canadian ship *St. Roch*, a Royal Canadian

Mounted Police schooner commanded by Henry Larsen, made it through from west to east, completing the voyage from Vancouver to Halifax, Canada.[25]

Cook and his modest ships were no match for an Arctic passage. He was fortunate that the pack ice stood firm against the Alaska shore and did not ensnare him like so many explorers who followed him. Instead Cook now worked his way east, away from the coast, always testing the ice pack for openings, working in a zigzag fashion in an effort to break through the impenetrable ice pack. But after the near grounding, his forays were more cautious, recalling the precautions of his Antarctic journey. On August 18 Cook and his crew were nearer the North Pole than any previous expedition, reaching 70° 44' north latitude. In January 1774, on the second voyage, the seamen had come even closer to the South Pole, at 71° 10' south latitude.[26]

As the vessels ran alongside the ice, the crew frequently came in contact with walrus or "sea horses," as Cook called them. On August 19 they came upon a large herd, and killed several for fresh meat. The ships were short on supplies and the fear of scurvy among the crew was great. But it was difficult to kill these lumbering beasts. While it seemed they were asleep, one was apparently always alert enough to signal an alarm if danger approached. As the hunters came closer, the warning was given and the entire herd would splash into the water. Even if the hunters were lucky to shoot one, the herd would come together to protect their fallen comrade, at least until his body sunk below the surface. And if the wounded animal was young, they would have to contend with the angry mother, who would attack without regard for her own safety. King was disturbed by all this mayhem, calling it a "cruel sport."

The taste of walrus was awful, particularly to the crew, and the novelty of eating "sea beef" was short-lived. Cook and Clerke found the taste pleasant and made certain every crewman had his fill, given the importance of fresh provisions to their diet. Cook said the fat was "as sweet as Marmalade." He wrote "...we had got on board the Resolution Nine of these Animals ..., so that we were not a little disappointed, especially some of the Seamen who for the Novelty of the thing, had been feasting their eyes for some days past... we lived upon them so long as they lasted and there were few on board who did not prefer it to salt meat." Later he called the walrus "marine beef." Clerke was equally effusive. "For my own part," he wrote, "I declare I think them pleasant and good eating; and they doubtless must be infinitely more nutritive and salutary than any salt Provision we can possibly have in store, or I believe any in the World."[27]

But most of the crew disagreed. They found the taste acrid, however prepared. Midshipman George Gilbert described the awful taste and the remarkable means of preparation:

> ... the flesh disgustfull as it was we eat thro extreme hunger ... the quality of which will be best described in the several preparations it went through before it was possible to eat it; in the first place we let it hang up for one day that the blood might drain from it, which would continue to drop for four or five days, when permitted to remain so long but that our hunger would not allow of at first; after that we towed it overboard for 12 hours then boil'd it four hours and the next day cut it into stakes and fry'd it; and even then it was too rank both in smell and taste to make use of except with plenty of peper and salt and these two articles were very scarce amoungst us ...[28]

On his return to England, Trevenen refuted Cook's accolades for walrus eating after reading Cook's statements in the voyage journal. He said most of the crew only ate walrus because the officers required they kept a fresh diet and because the stores of salt beef were sealed until the walrus was fully consumed. Trevenen wrote:

> Captain Cook here speaks entirely from his own taste which was, surely, the coarsest that ever mortal was endured with. ...I am pretty confident that there was not an Officer or Seaman in the Ship that would not pronounce the fat to resemble train-oil instead of marrow. Indeed, on being melted it became train-oil. It is true that almost every one ate the flesh at first, but that was only because they were rapaciously hungry, having been fed on nought but Salt Meat for several months past. ... many who absolutely could not eat the sea horses, because it produced purgings & vomitings, were reduced to live on their scanty allowances of bread, till at last the discontents rose to such complaints & murmurings that he restored the salt meat.[29]

While the taste of the walrus was disputed, their ungainly majesty caught the attention of captain and crew. Cook spent pages describing them in earnest resulting in the most significant entries in the otherwise uneventful days against the Arctic ice pack. He wrote:

> They lay in herds of many hundred upon the ice, huddling one over the other like swine, and roar or bray very loud, so that in the night or foggy weather they gave us notice of the ice

long before we could see it. We never found the whole herd asleep, some were always upon the watch, these, on the approach of the boar, would wake those next to them and these the others, so that the whole herd would be aware presently. But they were seldom in a hurry to get away till after they had been once fire[d] at, then they would tumble one over the other into the sea in the utmost confusion ... They did not appear to us to be that dangerous ..., not even when attacked, they are rather so more to appearance than reality; Vast numbers of them would follow and come close up to the boats. The female will defend the young one to the very last at the expence of her life whether in the water or on the ice; not will the young quit the dam though she be dead so that if you kill one you are sure of the other.[30]

Cook had a copy of a natural history volume on board and suspected these were the "Arctick Walrus" described in the book. But these were so much larger than the book described, the size of horses, so he chose instead a corrupted Russian name to call them a "sea horse." He reported a modest-sized adult walrus reached over 9 feet in length from snout to tail, and weighed nearly half a ton. Clerke later reported that the *Discovery* had hauled in one walrus that weighed 1145 pounds.

Corporal John Ledyard offered a unique perspective on the animals:

The loose fields of ice are covered with numerous herds of sea horses who repose themselves upon them, after they have completed their excursions in the water in pursuit of their food, which is fish and such marine productions as they find at the bottom of the water. They are a large unwieldly sluggish animal weighing some of them nine hundred and some eleven hundred weight. Their legs are very short and terminate in a webed membrane, with which they swim very swift and are very active in the water though exceeding clumsy out of that element. They are amphibious and between a quadrupede and a fish, their heads are somewhat like those of a dog, without ears...; they have a thick skin like that of a horse (and) ... they are exceeding fat, and will produce more than a barrel of oil.

Ledyard thought it was "an ill reward for their labor" when Cook commanded the crew to eat walrus rather than their usual rations of salt beef. "The people at first murmured," Ledyard wrote, "and at last eat it through mere vexation; and trying to see who would eat most of it in order to consume it the sooner, some of the people rather overdid the matter, which produced some laughable circumstances..."[31]

Other sea and bird life were noted in this part of the journey, but none captivated the sailors quite like the walrus. Whales were periodically seen between ice floes, and flocks of birds soared overhead. The crew called them ducks or geese, but modern scholars assume they were Scoters, Pacific Harlequin, Pacific Golden Plover, Long-tailed Jaeger, Pacific Fulmar, European Wheatear and the Bluethroat.

Three days after near catastrophe, the fog cleared away and offered Cook an expansive view of the entire

Alaska coast from a safe distance off shore. Here he named his final Alaska coastal feature, Cape Lisburne, which he observed in the southern horizon. He also saw that the ice that had nearly ensnared him now extended further south, so he assumed that the season was late and winter was approaching. He was certain that if he had arrived earlier he would have made better progress to the north, so vowed to return earlier the next year. That fateful decision, which must have been very unwelcome news for the crew, was carried out the following year without Cook.

As they sailed west Cook noted deteriorating weather, "as we advanced to the west, ... with the northerly wind the air was raw, sharp and cold; and we had thick fogs sunshine, showers of snow and sleet by turns." Ice was building in the masts, just as in Antarctica, to the point where the sheer weight of the ice might topple the ships. The late summer sun did little to melt the ice in the rare moments when it was seen. The captain continued to observe the walrus and the ebb and flow of the ice and snow, speculating on the size and age of the ice pack.

On August 29 two islands were observed, then the rocky cape signaling the ships had reached the Asian coastline. It appeared no different from northern Alaska. "The Weather at this time was very hazey with drizzling rain," Cook wrote, "but soon after it cleared ... so that we had a pretty good View of the Coast which in every respect is like that of America, that is low land next the Sea with elevated land farther back. It was perfectly distitude of Wood and even Snow, but was probably covered with a Mossy substance..." This was second time they had reached Siberia, but this time they only observed the barren, flat tundra of the far northern reaches of continent.

Cook wanted to press further west against the Siberian coastline, maybe wistfully thinking they could find a passage over the top of Russia. But he instead turned south. "The season was now so very far advanced and the time when the frost is expected to set in so near at hand," he advised, "that I did not think it consistant with prudence to make any farther attempts to find a passage this year in any direction so little was the prospect of succeeding." He was troubled by the weight of ice in the ships' masts and the need to find water and wood to continue the expedition. "My attention was now directed towards finding some place where we could Wood and Water, and in the considering of how I should spend the Winter, so as to make some improvement to the Geography and Navigation and at the same time be in a condition to return to the North in further search of a Passage the ensuing summer."[32]

King wrote that Cook announced his decision to the entire crew, with the postscript, that they would return the next year. "The Captn inform'd the Ships company that he should leave the Ice as fast as he could," King wrote, "& that the next year should come up amongst it again, he advised … as the only method to enable us to perform Effectually the service we are sent upon. Those who have been amongst Ice, in the dread of being enclosed in it, & in so late a season's, can be the best judge of the general joy this news gave." The next summer they would try again. They turned south on Saturday, August 29, 1778.

-Chapter 8-

English Bay Unalaska

The decision to turn south was inevitable and welcomed by officers and crew alike. Although only in the final days of August, temperatures were now dipping into the twenties at night "so that the Water and the Water Vessels on deck were frequently covered with a sheet of ice." With Cook's decision, the ships quickly turned southeast along the Siberian coast, heading to Bering Strait. In two days they passed East Cape, the easternmost point of Asia. Miserable weather plagued them. "...the thick Snow showers which succeeded one another pretty fast and settled upon the land, hid great part of the coast at this time from our sight. Soon after Sun whose face we had not seen for near five days, broke out at the intervals between the showers and in some measure free'd the coast of the fog, so that we had a sight of it and found the whole connected."[1]

Cook, still confounded by the Russian maps he carried, attempted to place Stählin's island of Alaschka somewhere in the geography he now observed. He considered the northerly routes he chose and how the island might still exist. He planned his return from a different angle to find what was supposed to be this prominent geographic feature. "The more I was convinced of being up the *Asia* Coast the more I was at a loss to reconcile Mr. Staehlens Map of the New Northern Archipelago with my observations," he wrote, "and I had no way to account for the great difference, but by supposing I had mistook some part of the island of *Alaschka* for the American Continent and missed the Channel that separates them." He decided he needed to clear up this geographic mystery on his way south.

On September 3 the ships passed St. Lawrence Bay where they met the Chukchi people on the way north. They did not land, but continued south for another two days, reaching 64° north latitude. Then they veered sharply east, back toward Alaska, as Cook assumed another thrust below the strait might lead him to Alaschka. Having crossed Bering Strait at its narrowest point, he attempted again to find these imagined islands further south. On September 5 he observed Bering's St. Lawrence Island, but as he sailed back to Alaska there were no other islands. "If any part of what I had supposed to be America coast was the island of *Alaschka* it was that now before us and that I had missed the Channell between it and the Main." He had now made landfall in America again, presumably now seriously doubting whether Stählin's archipelago existed at all.

The landfall was in Norton Sound, in the area of modern-day Nome. The ships traversed an easterly course in the shoals along the north shore. Cook was fairly certain he was on the American continent but still speculated whether this might be the island of *Alaschka*. They coasted along the shore looking for evidence of an island. Needing wood and water, Cook sent off shore parties nearly every day, but only found driftwood, and no water. Occasionally natives would appear on shore, and even in canoes near to the vessels, but they always disappeared without making contact.

On Monday, September 14, the ships approached a vegetated area with small spruce trees. Cook sent King ashore to verify whether the land "belonged to an island or the America Continent," but King found nothing but a small river behind some sand banks, suggesting it was the continent. The irritable Bligh complained this was all a waste of time, certain the lands surrounding Norton Sound were just a part of the American continent and not an imagined island. A large amount of water and wood was taken on along with spruce boughs to brew some beer. Later in the day a few natives came to the ships in their canoes and bartered some dried salmon "for such trifles as our people had to give them."[2]

The first significant contact with the local people came the next day when nine men in separate kayaks came to the *Resolution*. These were Eskimo people, probably the Yupik met on the route north. They did not seem interested in trade, just curious about the ship. They sang a chant while seated in their kayaks while one of their number beat upon a drum and another "made a thousand antic Motions with his hands and body," part of some elaborate ceremony that fascinated the crew. "Their cloathing which were mostly of Dear skins were made after the same fashion and they observed the custom of boring and fixing Ornaments to the under lip," Cook observed.

The sailors soon saw some huts on the shoreline, probably the summer houses of the kayakers, and several parties were sent ashore to investigate. The officers reported that they found an inhabited village further inland and "treated them with civility." Meanwhile, the crew shot birds and collected fresh provisions, returning by midday with pails of fresh grasses, as well as currants and other berries and dozens of Spruce Grouse. Late in the afternoon, after completing his customary maritime measurements on board, Cook also went ashore. He wandered through abandoned summer dwellings and observed "The Dwellings of these people are seated upon the Sea coast close to the beach, ...they are simply a sloaping roof without any side wall, composed of logs and covered with grass and earth. The floor is also laid with logs, the entrance is at one end, the fire place just within it and a small hole is made near the door to let out the smoke."[3]

After a week in Norton Sound, Cook was convinced this was no island, but part of the American continent. "Having now fully satisfied myself that Mr. Staehlin's Map must be erroneous and not mine," he explained, "it was high time to think of leaving these Northern parts." Cook knew he should retire to a place further south where his men could rest yet remain active. He decided that he would leave the North Pacific and return to Hawaii, a fateful decision for him. "*Petropavlowska* and *Kamtschatka* did not appear to me a place where I could procure refreshments for the people and a small supply of Provisions for so large a number of men," he reasoned, " and besides I [had] the great dislike ... to lay inactive for Six or Seven Months, which must have been the case had I wintered in any of these Northern parts." [4] So he decided to leave for Hawaii.

Before he left Norton Sound, he resolved to complete the survey of the Alaska coastline. In July he was unable to chart the area between Norton Sound and Bristol Bay, so sought to extend his survey south, to fill in the missing link. But in a few hours he was again in the dangerous muddy shallows of the Yukon Flats, often scraping the ship hulls in as little as three fathoms of water. One point of land named was named "Point Shallow Water," a name that has since disappeared. The ships finally left the coast on September 19, as "we could no longer Navigate with any degree of safety." Cook concluded all these muddy shoals and shallows were part of an outlet to a great river and that they were no place for larger vessels. As he left continental Alaska for good, the area between 60° and 63° north latitude remained "intirely unexplored."

On September 20, as they sailed west, Cook found an island separated a fair distance from Bering's St. Lawrence

Island. In his previous voyage north on July 29, he had found and named Anderson's Island, which he surmised was west of this point. He speculated this was yet a third island in the central Bering Sea, and called it Clerke's Island. Cook concluded they were finally in the island maze so inartfully drafted on the Stählin map.

He was incorrect. In fact the three islands he observed were just different parts of the same island, St. Lawrence Island, a broad expanse that extends a hundred miles across the central Bering Sea. This inaccuracy is one of the great geographic mysteries of Cook's third voyage, as Cook did not further investigate the sighting of three islands in such close proximity. But he was at the end of a long year of exploration and his attention was drawn away from geographical investigations to the prospects of a warm and relaxing winter anchorage. In any event, the official voyage atlas contains this error, showing the ships' track running between the two islands where there is really dry land!

Bligh was certain the cartographers had it wrong. While setting out on his second breadfruit voyage in 1791, he complained to Burney, who was also on the voyage. "I wish also particularly to take Notice of an Error in a map published with C. Cooks works last voyage," he wrote, "...is placed down an island not existing. It is called Andersons Island laid down to the eastward of Clerks Island, whereas the east part of the latter was the land seen, although it is made another island of..." Bligh was apparently infuriated by the error, a commentary on his own difficult and cantankerous personality. He went on, "This unaccountable error arose only from sheer ignorance not knowing how to investigate the fact, & it is a disgrace to us as Navigators to lay down what does not exist." [5]

Bligh was later placed in command of the British Hydrographic Office and went so far as to write a critical note on Robert's manuscript chart of the voyage, opposite the name of "Anderson's Island." He wrote "Here is a gross mistake, for Anderson's Id & the east end of Clerke's Id is one in the same land & how they have blundered to lay them down as two I cannot conceive." He then signed his name. He placed the same comment on the engraved chart in the office's published account of Cook's third voyage.[6]

Bligh was correct. It is remarkable that with the spotty reputation he enjoyed after the ill-fated *Bounty* breadfruit mutiny, he would openly criticize the work of the renowned Captain Cook, England's greatest navigator. There is, after all, some justification for this mistake. The decision to name three islands came as a result of four separate sightings, one at a distance, and the others in hail, fog and snow. The final sighting came in the teeth of a growing storm where there was little time to investigate. And the sightings came on three separate days, first in July, then again in early and late September. But even Bligh was only partly correct. He assumed this combined Anderson-Clerke island was different from St. Lawrence Island, and in fact they are all the same.

Cook did not spend much time in the area as an awful storm soon arose. With little warning sleet, snow and terrible winds were upon them, and in a few hours the gale brought waves over the ships' decks. In 1741 Bering incurred the wrath of a similar storm, losing more than a month as he was driven away from Kamchatka on his return home. That storm was a major cause for his shipwreck and later death on Bering Island. Cook knew such fall storms could also be his undoing. It was almost inevitable when, in the second day of the storm, the *Resolution* sprung a leak. The leak "filled the Spirit room with Water before it was discovered; ...and was so considerable as to keep one pump continually going and some hands bailing." Unlike Bering's month-long storm, however, this gale relented after four days.

Clerke wrote in his typical understatement at the height of the storm, "We have a very heavy Sea from the Southward this Forenoon, which tumbles us about confoundedly." Two days later he was simply glad they had left the Yukon shoals in this sudden fury. "This afternoon the Gale and Swell continuing," Clerke wrote, "we are happy at the prospect of a clear Sea around us. I think we have reason to congratulate ourselves that [the gale] did not attack us during our 5 or 6 fathom business, when we were at the same time engaged with the Land; we should then have found it a confounded awkward amusement, now we can howl it out cheerfully." The storm blew over in a few days, and they headed for Unalaska, reaching the safety of English Bay on Friday afternoon, October 2, three months to the day after leaving it to sail north.[7]

The expedition's three-week stay in Unalaska bore a striking resemblance to the four weeks in Nootka Sound. Beaten and weary, the crew spent much of its time repairing the vessels while Cook and the other officers took celestial readings and observed the people on shore. Cook called the harbor "Samgoonoodha," after the name given by the local people. It was the Russians who later called it English Bay. As soon as they landed the carpenters went to work on both ships, ripping off the outer sheathing to expose seams that were "so open it was no wonder that so much water found its way into the ship." As the crews recaulked the seams, the holds of the ships were cleared and cleaned and more ballast hauled aboard.

Most of the stores of vegetables and other provisions were spoiled on the journey north, so they were thrown overboard and replaced by a bountiful harvest of local berries and salmon. The men purchased what they could not gather, but soon fishing was a favorite occupation. Salmon and dolly varden (called "Salmon trout") were plentiful.

Their favorite was halibut, and they caught many, one that Cook said weighed 254 pounds. A fishing boat was sent out each morning and seldom returned with fewer than eight to ten halibut, "sufficient to serve all hands." In time, the storehouse was filled to capacity. "Thus we not only procured a supply of fish for present consumption," Cook brimmed, "but had some to carry to sea with us, and was some saving to our Provisions, which was the object of no small importance."[8]

Unlike Nootka, the local Aleut people were already under the influence of Europeans, the Russian fur hunters or "promyshlenniki." The occupation of all the Aleutian Islands west of Unalaska had progressed rapidly since the day Bering's crew returned to Kamchatka in 1742 with their treasure of sea otter furs. The fur hunters were descendants of the daring Cossack hunters and nomads who conquered the steppes of the Russian east, including Siberia, and after seeing the resplendent sea otter furs, conceived of high risk expeditions to bring more of these furs to the markets of the Orient.

As early as 1743, the Cossack Emelian Bassov headed to Bering Island in a small koche, or tiny wooden ship the size of a small schooner. Spending a winter ashore, he turned the island into a virtual killing ground, returning to Kamchatka the following spring with 1,200 sea otter and 4,000 fur seal pelts. In the next few years he made other voyages, all wildly successful, and others soon followed. As each island's treasure of furs was wiped out, the crews searched further east along the Aleutian chain. Each venture was like the conquest of Siberia. After a brief fight, Aleut leaders were held hostage so that native hunters were forced to enter the water in kayaks to kill as many sea otters as possible. The Russian government insisted that the island inhabitants be treated with care, but there was no government presence or oversight. So these encounters often turned to violence, with the most notable coming in the few years before Cook's arrival during the conquest of Unalaska. In the first twelve years alone, 22 fur gathering expeditions were undertaken and millions of rubles in furs were returned. During this exploitation, the *promyshlenniks* discovered Copper Island and the Near Islands and obtained sufficient maritime experience to pursue fur-gathering voyages further away from Siberia.[9]

Cook's expedition was in regular contact with the Aleuts after the English arrived, but they did not see any Russians. At the end of the first week, Clerke received a salmon cake and a note from one of the local people. The note was in Russian, which none of the English could read, so Cook sent the American marine, John Ledyard, to find the authors. His orders were to gain further information and, above all, avoid conflict. "If he met any Russians, … to endeavor to make them understand that we were English, Friends, and Allies."

Ledyard accompanied three natives, with no provisions except presents of brandy and bread. He was unarmed. The first day they reached a small village of 30 huts in the interior of the island, about 15 miles from English Bay. Ledyard must have been a curious figure in the little community, "The whole village was out to see us," he reported, "and men, women and children crowded about me." He shared his bread and spirits, and the villagers offered dried fish. He spent the night sleeping in animal skins in their modest home. At daylight Ledyard's party was off again, a continuation of the forced march across the island. In the late afternoon they came to a large bay. The guide took all the baggage and went off in his kayak into the bay, leaving Ledyard to follow on foot around the edge. He feared he had been abandoned, but then two men came across the bay in a skin canoe "after the Esquimaux plan with two hole to accommodate two setters." There seemed no place for Ledyard, so he was "thrust into the space between the holes extended at length upon my back and wholly excluded from seeing the way I went."

After an hour stowed inside the kayak the voyagers landed on the opposite shore. "I saw some lights and a number of huts like those I left in the morning. As we approached one of them a door opened, and discovered a lamp, by which to my joy and surprise I discovered that the two men who held me by each arm were two Europeans, fair and comely, and concluded from their appearance they were Russians. ... As soon as I was rendered warm and comfortable," he explained, "a table was set before me with a lamp upon it; all the Russians in the house set down round me, and the bottles of spirits, tobacco, snuff, and whatever ... I presented to the company (as if from) Commodore Cook, who was an Englishmen." The Russians in turn explained they were the subjects of the Empress Catherine.

With the formalities completed, Ledyard was given fresh clothes and his hosts brought out food for a feast. They had boiled whale, broiled salmon and rye bread fried in oil for dinner. "They were very fond of the rum," Ledyard surmised. After dinner the Russians led the Aleuts in the village in prayers "after a manner of the Greek Church." After a comfortable night's rest, the American was put through an unanticipated test. His hosts escorted him to a steam bath, well known among natives of the region. "Several Indians were heating some water in a large copper cauldron over a furnace, the heat of which, and the steam which evaporated from the hot water, rendered the hutt which was very tight extremely hot and suffocating." After nearly fainting from the heat and stifling conditions in the small space, Ledyard recovered enough to consume a breakfast of smoked salmon and biscuit.

The following day Ledyard returned with three Russians, now in a much larger skin boat with 12 oars and several native rowers, retracing his steps to the waiting Captain Cook. He was gone five days. "The satisfaction this discovery gave Cook," Ledyard wrote smugly, "and the honor that rebounded to me may be easily imagined, and the several conjectures respecting the appearance of a foreign intercourse rectified and confirmed."[10]

Communication between the Russians and English was crude. Cook wrote of Ledyard's journey and description of the nearby Russian base. They had erected a few dwellings, some storehouses for fur and a small church in an established Aleut village. They also had a 50-ton sloop that coasted between the islands to collect furs. The Russians had all left Kamchatka several years earlier on a five-year assignment to the islands. They had brought some native people with them from Kamchatka, by Clerke's estimate there were 60 Russians and 60 from Kamchatka, but most of the native people in the surrounding villages were Aleuts. Both Cook and Clerke observed that there appeared to be an intermingling of cultures, including the apparent intermarriage of Russians, Kamchadals and Aleuts, and even the Russians seemed to wear clothing in the local custom.

King was told there were two groups of Russians in the islands, extending from Kamchatka to Unalaska, who worked for the merchants of Okhotsk on the Russian mainland. In addition to the group at Unalaska, there were about 100 others in the islands to the west, with no more than five vessels in total, all about the same size as the one Ledyard observed at the Russian village. There were eight to ten small villages of 50 to 100 persons in the general area of Unalaska, he was told, and many more in the far reach of the islands toward Russia.[11]

The Russians knew of the Bering voyage. The oldest of the three sailors with Ledyard said he sailed as a young man with Bering, wintering on Bering Island. When asked about local geography, the Russians were familiar with the Aleutian chain of islands but knew nothing of the Stähdlin map. "They seem to have a thorough knowledge of the attempts that had been made by their Country men to Navigate the Frozen Sea," Cook reported, "and the discoveries that had been made in this, [but] had not the least idea of what part of the World Mr. Staehlins Map referred to when leaid before them."

Several days later, while Cook and Webber were visiting a nearby village, the principal Russian factor for the region, Gerasim Grigorovich Ismailov, came ashore in the company of twenty or thirty Aleut hunters in kayaks. He was a man of great importance with extensive knowledge of local geography. Although they did not share a common language, he and Cook spent hours sharing rum and brandy, and poring over Russian maps and Cook's own discoveries. Cook "felt no small Mortification in not being able to converse with him any other way than by signs assisted by figures and other Characters which however was a very great help." Cook and the Admiralty blundered by failing to take anyone who could speak or read the Russian language on the expedition.

Cook learned a great deal about the geography of the Russian coastline to Japan and the far reach of the Aleutian Islands to the west, as the Russian allowed him to copy liberally from two of their charts onto Cook's more comprehensive chart of the North Pacific. The Russians knew little about the continent to the east, "It appeared by Chart as well as by the testimony of Ismyloff and the others that this is as far as the Russians have discovered and extended themselves sence Behrings time," Cook wrote, "they all said no Russian had been where the Indians gave Captn Clerke the note." Like the three hunters, Ismailov scorned the Stählin map. He had been in Bering Sea waters where many of the imagined islands were located and struck out a third of them as non-existent, and altered the location of others. "If Mr. Staehlin was not greatly imposed upon what could induce him to publish so erroneous a map?" Cook wrote. It was a map "without the least regard for truth ... a map that the most illiterate of his illiterate Sea-faring men would have been ashamed to put his name to." Cook no doubt wished he had met these people on his outward journey so that he had not paid attention to such a worthless document looking for nonexistent islands.[12]

Although strangers to anything on the American coast, the Russians had already fixed upon the name "Alaska" for the American continent to the east. "I have already observed that the American Continent is here called by the Russians as well as Indians *Alaska*," Cook observed, "which is the proper Indian name for it ... [they] call the whole by that name and know very well that it is a great land." While the Russians had not been to this great land, and offered no names for the places Cook had seen, they knew of its existence from the local people. Ismailov knew the largest of the Shumagin Islands was called "Kodiak" although it is now considered to be situated to the east of that group of islands. Since Cook had sailed by Kodiak without distinguishing it from the mainland, he could not place it on his map and of course did not know that Kodiak dominated the Shumagins in Alaskan geography.

Cook, Clerke and Ismailov were inseparable for three days, until the English were ready to leave for Hawaii. Cook learned the Russians limited their fur trading operations to the chain of islands between Kamchatka and Unalaska and that each hunter was required to complete a term of five years in the islands before they could return to Kamchatka. The hunters rarely saw more than one vessel in any year, using it to dispense supplies and pick up furs. Cook could only speculate about the way in which the Russians dominated the local people or how long they had been in control of Unalaska, but he knew these people were not hunting for the Russians solely for profit. "I never thought to ask how long it was sence they got a footing upon *Oonalaska* and the neighbouring isles, but to judge from the great subjection the Natives are under, it must have been some time."[13] Scholars now believe the Russians had been in control of Unalaska for no more than three years before Cook arrived.

Other English crewmen were more critical of the Russian treatment of the Aleuts. David Samwell, surgeon on the *Discovery*, wrote, "The Russians have been obliged to use harsh Methods to bring the Natives of Nawanalaska & the other Islands about into subjection & to make them honest. They told us that they never forgave a Theft but always punished it with instant death. ... the inhabitants of this Island are in a state of Subjection to the Russians," he continued, "and it should seem from what we observed amongst them that they are made to pay Tribute to their Masters, all their Arms of every kind are taken from them." Samwell said the Russians abducted many children from their parents to teach them to hunt for furs, to speak the Russian language and to practice the Orthodox religion.[14]

King likened the Aleuts to Russian slaves, reporting "that the Russians have cut many of their throats before they could subdue them." In fact the Russian technique was to exact tribute from the natives and to threaten and even enslave their families to assure their maximum effort in hunting sea otters.[15]

There were uprisings, to be sure, but the English could only speculate on the equilibrium they now observed since they could not speak either language. Thomas Edgar, master of the *Discovery* likened their plight to the American quest for independence:

> The first settlers on these Islands took from the natives their bows, Arrows, spears, & all other kind of warlike instruments and destroy'd them, by which means they keep them greatly under subjection making them pay tribute … It does not appear they have ever been able to get footing on the continent, but that the Americans by the russian's account have always been too powerful for them; they cry out most bitterly against them as savages & sad fellow, for defending themselves & driving off the invader of their country and preserving their native freedom; by this you will see that efforts for liberty are not confined totally to the east side of the continent.[16]

Clerke was told by the Russians that the Aleuts were unpredictable, that the Russians made "heavy Complaints of the treachery and perfidy, as they seem to deem it, of the Americans." By example the Russians recounted the story of the recent murder of a Russian captain "by stabbing him during a social Embrace," and the deliberate killing of a Russian seaman who was simply an observer to an Aleut demonstration of their bows and arrows. According to the Russians, "one of them, having presented his Bow and drawn it home to shoot up as the others had done, very suddenly brought it down again, to a level at the Russian, and shot him dead."

Clerke assumed the stories of Aleut mayhem were true, but felt the Aleut side had not yet been told, particularly since the Russians occupied these islands as conquerors. "There probably may be a great deal of truth in these Stories," Clerke wrote, "but these honest fellows of Russians think it, or at least call it, no provocation to take possession of these poor fellows Country, force them to become Tributaries to they don't know who, and if they attempt by stealth or any other Means to keep their own, destroy them without Mercy, which the Indians complain they do very readily." It seems there were two sides of the story and the English freely recognized the Russians had the upper hand with their superior firepower. The conquerors also made sure the Aleuts did not cause any further disturbance, "for they had deprived them of every article that bore the least resemblance to shooting materials."[17]

On their parting Cook gave Ismailov a letter to the Admiralty enclosing a chart of his discoveries to date, which Ismailov promised would be returned to Kamchatka, and then St. Petersburg the following year. Cook wanted to be sure the Admiralty had benefit of his geographic knowledge in case he did not return. Sketchy as it was, it showed "all the Northern coasts I visited" and for the first time put New Albion, Nootka, Prince William Sound, Cook Inlet, the Alaska Peninsula, and Bering Strait in their correct location. The map and letter arrived in London six months before the expedition's return in March 1780. Along with Cook's journal, it offers the best evidence of Cook's personal view of the outcome of his expedition to the West Coast of North America.[18]

By now Cook and many of his crew were superb ethnographers who wrote at length about the Aleut people they met at English Bay. In three voyages spanning a decade at sea, they had encountered dozens of cultures encompassing the far reaches of the Pacific. Yet these Aleuts held a special place in Cook's heart, and he gladly wrote of his pleasant experiences there. These were "the most peaceable inoffensive people I ever met with" he recalled, "they are remarkably cheerfull and friendly amongst each other and always behaved with great civility to our people." He had spent eight arduous months in the North Pacific since the landfall at Oregon, and his only other substantial contact was with the people at Nootka. The kind nature of the Aleuts and the bountiful harvest of fish in these islands bore little resemblance to Nootka Sound. In light of the disastrous experience that would soon befall him in Hawaii, one can only speculate what might be different if he had wintered instead at English Bay. But for the Russian presence in these islands, which presumably prevented Cook from considering such a prospect, the history of Pacific exploration might be quite different today.

The Aleut, or Unangan, "the original people" as they call themselves, have inhabited the Aleutian archipelago for thousands of years. They are descended from a population that was first established more then 7,000 years ago. Since the oldest known archeological site is located on the eastern Aleutian chain, near Alaska, anthropologists believe the Aleuts traveled outward from the Alaska Peninsula to settle the 1300-mile long island chain. They are distant relatives of the coastal Eskimo people of Alaska and western Canada. However, linguists believe the Aleut language separated from the earlier Eskimo languages about 4,000 years ago as the westward migration along the archipelago progressed.

When the Russians reached the Aleutian islands after Bering's voyage in 1741, the Aleuts inhabited all of the major Aleutian Islands, the Alaska Peninsula as far east as Port Moller, and the Shumagin Islands to the south of the Alaska Peninsula. The estimated population at first contact was 15-18,000. By 1799, when the Russian-American Company was formed, probably half of all Aleut males between 18 and 50 years of age were hunting for the Russians, enslaved to pay tribute in furs to protect their families from Russian conquest. The toll was appalling. Scholars believe at least 80 percent of the Aleut population was lost during the first and second generations of Russian contact. Further, even after the Russians moved their principal operations to Sitka, the continuing barbarities of the Russian traders and dramatic impact of foreign diseases reduced the population to less than one-tenth of the pre-contact number.[19] The 1910 U. S. Census accounted for just 1491 Aleuts, but the population has rebounded. Today there are about 8-10,000 Aleuts living in this same area.

Aleut settlements were usually located on bays where there was a good gravel beach for landing skin-covered watercraft. A good supply of fresh water would be nearby, presumably a bountiful salmon stream. Other important factors in locating a village was the availability of driftwood, access to stone materials suitable for making tools and weapons, sea mammal hauling grounds, and an elevated lookout post to watch for enemies and whales.

An Aleut house was called a "barabara," built in the ground as a rectangle, no more then fifty feet long and twenty-five feet wide. The structure of the roof was built with driftwood and whalebone, covered with sod and moss. Inside the house rooms were portioned off for the separate age groups occupying that house. Usually extended families (cousins, aunts, etc.) shared a house, usually along the matrilineal line, like many other Alaska native cultures.

The kayaks were a distinguishing feature of Aleut culture, as the unique split bow design increased the seaworthiness and speed of the craft. Aleut hunters wore distinctive bentwood visors with sea lion whiskers. These visors provided protection from glare as well as a visual symbol of the status of the hunter. Various portions of sea mammals were used for clothing and other utensils. The skins of seal, sea lion, sea otter, bear, birds, squirrels, and marmots were turned into clothing. Hats and baskets were woven from spruce roots and grass. Baskets were woven with geometric patterns, considered among the finest in the world with up to 2500 stitches per square inch.[20]

The ship journals described at length the people, their food, housing, furniture, tools, weaponry, boats, arts and culture. Cook noted the Russians had imported some Siberians to assist in the otter trade, then offered extensive praise for the local people.

> These people are rather low of Stature, but plump and well shaped, with rather short necks, swarthy chubby faces, black eyes, small beards, and straight long black hair, which the Men wear loose behind and cut before, but the women tie it up in a bunch behind. …the Womans frock is made of Seal skin and the Mens of birds skins and both reach below the knee. This is the whole dress of the Women but Over this frock the Men wear a nother made of Gut which resists water and has a hood to draw over the head; some of them wear boots and all of them a kind of oval snouted Cap made of wood, with a rim to admet the head… They make no use of paint but the Women punctulate their faces slitely and both men and Women bore the under lip to which they fix pieces of bone, but it is as uncommon at Onalaska to see a man with this ornament as a women without it.

The Aleuts did not seem to live as long as Europeans, as Cook observed only a few people in their fifties. "I no where saw a person, man or woman," he wrote, "which I could suppose to be sixty years of age and but very few that I thought above fifty, probably their hard way of living may be the means of shortening their days." [21] This seems ironic, as Cook was born in late October, 1728, and turned age 50 his first day at sea after leaving Unalaska.

Cook was fascinated by the bountiful harvest of plants and fish in these islands and spoke favorably of the earthen, communal, subterranean homes used by the natives, called *barabaras*. "Their food is fish, sea Animals, Birds, roots and berries and even sea-weed," he explained. They usually ate their food uncooked, but recently acquired brass kettles from the Russians so were able to boil and broil their food, which offered different methods of preparation pleasing to a European palate. The chiefs were apparently reserved the right to dine on halibut cheeks, a delicacy recognized even today by Alaskan gourmets who dine on fresh halibut.

The Aleuts were clean and kept their homes as neat and tidy as could be expected, unlike many other cultures Cook had observed. Their homes were huge dug out chambers measuring 50 by 20 feet, always located near the ocean to give quick access to the fish and other resources of the sea. Several families would live in each home, with separate apartments lining the edges. In the center the homes would have two holes to admit light, one for the ladder to gain entrance, and the other for smoke from their flat stone oil lamps. They did not have fires inside, which Cook assumed allowed for their clean and tidy appearance.

The household implements usually consisted of bowls, spoons, matted baskets and similar utensils made from local materials. The "mats and baskets of grass" were especially well made and intricately decorated. While some iron and pots had been acquired from the Russians, the Aleuts seemed to prefer more traditional implements. "They did not seem to wish fore more iron or want any other instruments," Cook explained, "except sewing needles, their own being made of bone, with which they not only sew their Canoes and make their cloaths, but make also very curious embroidery."

The English offered keen insights into the current state of the Aleut culture, a fascinating study of a culture in first contact with Europeans. Among other things, Cook noted they had no weapons of any kind, a state imposed upon them by the Russians for protection. "...we cannot suppose the Russians found them in such a defenceless state, but rather for their own security have disarmed them." He also correctly surmised that the Russians had taken all their large vessels, preventing their escape, leaving them only with kayaks to serve one or two people at a time near shore to capture sea otter.

Cook was nonetheless impressed with the capabilities of the kayak, remarking on its tight construction, maneuverability in the water, and the ability of the mariner to integrate his gut frock with the center hole to keep dry in the near constant rain. "The sleeves of his frock is tyed tight round his wrists, drawn close round his neck, the hood drawn over his head where it is confined close by his Cap, so that no water can penetrate either his body or into the Canoe." Cook also remarked on the ingenious engineering of the double bladed paddle and the fishing and hunting implements tied to the side of the kayak, including the "dart" used to spear fish and otter alike.

Cook was fascinated by the method by which the Aleuts buried and remembered their dead. He noted they were always buried at the highest points above the habitations, presumably so their spirits could continue to observe the sea. They covered the graves with hillocks of stones and frequently families would return to the hillocks with new stones, causing the graves to grow in size over the years. "I saw in the Country several stone hillocks," Cook remarked, "that seemed to have been raised by art. Many of them were of great antiquity; the stones being cemented together and become as it were one stone, but it was easy to see that the hillock was composed of a great number and variety of sorts, nor was it very difficult to separate them."

The captain also wrote of the Aleutian countryside and its marine environment. Cook observed whales, porpoises, sword fish, halibut, cod, salmon, trout, flat fish and others too numerous to list and "there may be many more that we had no opportunity of seeing." He was especially impressed by the quantities of halibut and salmon, and that some varieties of salmon were preferred. Today Unalaska still serves as the homeport to the greatest groundfish fisheries in the world. While Cook speculated that the North Atlantic of his day was even more plentiful in variety and quantity of fish resources than the North Pacific, the modern-day Bering Sea fishery has not been depleted by over harvest and is now probably unequalled in its annual fishery harvests.

Cook also noted the presence of several sea mammals, not only the plentiful otter, but also walrus and sea lions. He called the otter "Sea beaver," and the sea lions a "Sea Cow," probably relying on Steller's observations of the northern manatee. The sea cow was already extinct from Russian plundering of its populations, which were probably limited in range to the proximity of Bering Island and the western Aleutians. Cook's party did not notice many land mammals.[22]

On Monday, October 26, the explorers left for Hawaii. Gilbert wrote "This ended a very hazardous and disagreeable Season; wherein we surveyed an extent of Coast of 1200 Leagues which is far more than ever any navigator had done before." Cook and his crew longed for a long rest in warmer climates. "My intention was now to proceed to the *Sandwich Islands* to spend a few of the Winter Months," Cook wrote, "and then proceed to *Kamtschatka*, endeavoring to be there by the Middle of May next."[23] Although they returned to Kamchatka the following year and went on to chart the ice pack, it was a mission without full purpose, as they lost their commander in a dispute over a shore boat at Kealakekua Bay.

–Chapter 9–

Hawaii

After a summer of storms in Alaskan waters, the prospects of a warm retreat to the Hawaiian Islands lured the expedition south for a well-deserved holiday. But violent weather greeted them on their departure from Unalaska, an alarming storm that pitched the ships in every direction. Gale-force winds shredded the sails of both ships and, after being battered for two days, the main mast of the *Discovery* came out of its footings and crashed to the deck killing one crewman and injuring three others.

Such fall storms in the Aleutian Islands are known to be both fierce and frequent. In 1741 a similar storm drove Bering's vessel off course for nearly a month, preventing that expedition's safe return. This 1778 storm played similar havoc with Cook's expedition, and after a few days at sea, both ships were again in desperate need of repair. So with shortened sail and makeshift repairs, the ships staggered south.

By late November Cook's ships were in sight of Maui and the Big Island of Hawaii. The weather was hot again. In three weeks they had gone from freezing temperatures and gales in the Bering Sea to the mid 80's and sultry rains in the tropics. Clerke, aware of his failing health, welcomed the change, "we are now advancing toward a Climate, which we have all reason to suppose we shall find less turbulent & boisterous, than those we have just bid adieu to ..." Maui was rocky and steep, dominated by a huge extinct volcano, called Haleakala, some 10,000 feet high. The waves crashed against the shore in thunderous surf, offering no respite for the expedition. Cook wrote:

In the country was an elevated saddle hill whose summit appear'd above the Clouds, from the hill the land fell in a gentle sloap and terminated in a steep rocky coast against which the sea broke in a dreadfull surf ... It was not long before we saw people on several parts of the coast, some houses and plantations, and the Country seemed to be both well wooded and Watered, the latter was seen falling into the sea in several places.[1]

As they approached the western shore of Maui, natives came out in canoes and welcomed the seamen warmly, and there was regular trade in fish, fruit, hogs and roots. Midshipman George Gilbert summarized the sentiments of the men:

The joy that we experienced on our arrival here is only to be conceived by ourselves or people under like circumstances; for after suffering excess of hunger and a number of other hardships most severely felt by us for the space of near ten months, we had now come into a delightfull climate were we had almost every thing we could wish for, in great profusion...[2]

Like the Hawaiians of Kauai and Niihau the previous winter, the people who came on board were mainly interested in trading for iron. Each day visitors in scores of canoes would come alongside carrying, as Cook put it rather directly, "hogs and women." The women, he thought, were "more ready to bestow their favours" than any he had ever known. Upon sighting land he issued orders forbidding private trade, the use of firearms, and sexual relations. But the crew rebelled, and Cook finally relented. The crews were impatient to get ashore and for the first time Cook wrote of his "mutinous turbulent crew," stemming from their distaste for his impossible orders and their growing frustration over the failure to find an anchorage.[3]

The vessels continued south, ultimately spending the five weeks at sea in adverse winds circling the Big Island. When they ventured near shore, canoes came out from the fertile eastern side of the island. "The Natives came off to us in great numbers," Gilbert wrote, "and behaved in a very friendly manner; we traided with them as usual till we had purchased provisions enough for five or six days, which we did in three or four hours and might have gotten three times as much if we had chose, for the greater part of their Canoes were obliged to return to the shore with what they had brought off to us."[4]

On two occasions the ships came close to shore, only to be driven away by nearing breakers. As beguiling as these islands are, a safe place to anchor could not be found. So instead of lounging in exotic islands, they tacked until mid January in a zigzag fashion in maddening, unpredictable winds around the eastern, then southern shores of Hawaii. This island was dominated by two snow-capped peaks at its center, Mauna Kea and Mauna Loa, even loftier than Haleakala at nearly 14,000 feet. "There are hills in this island of a considerable height," Cook wrote, "whose summits were continually covered by snow, so that these people know all the climates from the Torrid to the Frigid Zones."

As the expedition rounded the southern cape of the huge island, the landscape changed from fruitful to desolate, almost a moonscape. Lava trails fell from the high peaks across barren valleys into the sea. Bligh was asked to reconnoiter several possible openings without success. There was no visible landing place, let alone sheltered harbor. They finally found a bay Bligh pronounced to be reasonably safe, and the broken ships and exhausted crew entered the luxuriant and inviting Kealakekua Bay on January 17, 1779. It was the last day Cook recorded an entry in his journal.[5] Kealakekua Bay or "Karakakooa" as Cook heard it, is not really a harbor, but it is the best anchorage on the Kona Coast, on the west side of the Big Island of Hawaii, a mile-wide bay protected at almost all times except from infrequent storms from the southwest.

The overwhelming and unprecedented reception at Kealakekua Bay was probably the most lavish welcome in the annals of Pacific exploration. Upwards of a thousand canoes, surfboard riders, and swarms of swimmers unable to find their own craft, greeted them "like shoals of fish," Cook wrote. Additional thousands lined the shores of the bay. King and Samwell each estimated as many as 10,000 natives were in attendance, virtually every resident of this region of the island. They crowded on board and nearly overwhelmed the ships. "... The decks both above and below were entirely covered with ... men, women and children," Gilbert wrote, "so that when we wanted to work the ship we could not come at the ropes without first driving the greatest part of them overboard; which they bore with the utmost cheerfulness and good nature...."[6]

Soon a high priest came to the ships and restored order. He then escorted Cook and some officers ashore to an elaborate ceremony given in Cook's honor. The assembled thousands prostrated themselves and priests greeted Cook with speeches of submission in which the word "Lono" was frequently repeated. From the beach the English visitors were taken to what seemed the island's most sacred place, where there were many carved wooden idols. The Hawaiians conducted a lengthy ceremony with processions and incantations. Cook was frequently the center of the service, wrapped in a bright cloth and offered hogs and vegetables but, in King's words, it was "a long & rather tiresome ceremony." The ritual baffled them for a time. Soon, however, it became clear that Cook was being revered as a superior being, and the ceremony was held to celebrate him as "Erono," the incarnation of their greatest god, "Lono," the god of light, peace, happiness and abundance. Lono's return to the islands in human form had been predicted for generations and his arrival was certainly foreshadowed by repeated sightings of the two ships as they sailed slowly around the island during the prior weeks.

"It is very clear ... from many ... Circumstances, that they regard us as a set of beings infinitely their superiors," wrote King. Like his experience in Kauai the previous winter, Cook noted an awe or respect that he could not understand. King spent the two weeks ashore at the expedition observatories that were set up near a compound of the priests.[7] The reverence offered to Cook was also bestowed on King and Clerke, who were deferentially regarded as Cook's sons. Clerke was not amused. He asked the chiefs to stop the prostrations in his honor. He wrote, "I disliked exceedingly putting so many people to such a confounded inconvenience."

While Cook was overwhelmed by the reception, he decided to keep up appearances, as in similar situations throughout the South Pacific. So instead of a simple interchange with the people, in their first days on shore the crew was on its best behavior, displaying their finest regimental uniforms. The obeisance to Cook continued whenever he stepped ashore. He was not a free agent. Whenever he approached, the crowds fell to the ground. As soon as he passed, they picked themselves up and followed. If he turned around, they fell to the ground again. It was hardly the treatment he sought, but he could do nothing to prevent it.

Trading continued on board the ships all day and into the night. Commerce was so frantic the first day that the crew ran out of room in the ships, so half of their new-found wealth had to be transported back to shore. "…in the evening we were again crowded with company," Ellis wrote, transfixed by the first evening in the bay, "especially the women, who were remarkably anxious to engage themselves to our people. As night came on, the men departed, but the ladies were so much attached to the ships, that they determined to spend the night there, a favour which was accordingly granted them." They were naturally attracted to the women, who usually only wore a small, open skirt or loincloth, and nothing covering their breasts. Samwell confided in his journal on that first night, "We had more young Women on board to night than we have had yet." Despite Cook's objections, the women stayed every night, offering their sexual favors below decks for nails and trifles or simply for the pleasure of English company. Sometimes the ship was so crowded with women in the late evenings "we were obliged to send them overboard." [8]

Soon the visit became like so many others, being occupied with the usual trading, ship repair and mainte-nance, salting of pork for later travels and astronomical observations. To minimize visitation, tents were set up on shore near the compound reserved for the priests and the ships were unrigged for a complete overhaul. The inter-change between the crew and islanders was exceptional. Trevenen summarized happy days of peace and trade with the islanders, "A constant exchange of good offices, & mu-tual little acts of friendship obtained among us." Samwell offered, "We live now in the greatest Luxury, and as to the Choice & number of fine women there is hardly any one among us that may not vie with the grand Turk himself." [9]

Most crew toured the islands unarmed and the fearless Ledyard trekked with a few of his mates deep into the island interior. There they observed expansive fields of sweet potatoes and plantations of breadfruit forests between walls of lava. They spent two nights away, hiking approximately 24 miles overland. They encountered deep tropical forests and lava fields, but fell about 10 miles short of Mauna Loa, their intended objective. "It was exquisitely entertaining," Ledyard wrote of the trip as he viewed the bay below, "Nature had bestowed her graces with her usual negligent sublimity. The town [below] and our ship in the bay created the contrast of art as well as the cultivated ground below, and as every object was partly a novelty it transported as well as convinced."[10]

Soon the monarch they called Terre'oboo (Kalani'opu'u), king of the island group, arrived in an elaborate procession in double-hulled sailing canoe with a host of priests and lesser chiefs. Another ceremony ensued. Cook was showered with gifts, including Terre'oboo's imposing cape and helmet of red and yellow feathers, the pride and glory of the islands. These garments were made of hundreds of thousands of brightly colored feathers from rare birds, ornamented by pearl oyster shells. Cook and his crew also received cloaks, hogs, fowl, coconuts, breadfruit, plantains, sugar cane, sweet potatoes, taro, and other gifts. The king insisted that his people feed the entire expedition during their time on shore. In time, the crew came to be treated as honored guests, to the point that they stopped carrying their weapons. They enjoyed dancing, wrestling, boxing matches, surfing demonstrations, and regular relations with the women; Cook responded with a fireworks display.

On February 4 the expedition prepared to depart for Kamchatka, having spent less time ashore than in Unalaska. They sensed they were wearing out their welcome as the Hawaiians tired of lavishing their gifts and foodstuffs on the captain and crew. When they announced their departure, there was another ceremony. At this time, the king gave them another 200 hogs, as well as large quantities of coconuts, breadfruit, tarrow and sweet potatoes, probably decimating the island of its remaining resources. An armada of crowded canoes followed them out of the bay as they left for Maui—probably with a mixed sense of relief and farewell.[11]

During the fourth night, February 7, 1779, disaster struck. As they sailed north, a gale arose that split *Resolution*'s rotten foremast, the spar that had been repaired at Nootka Sound. The mast was a comparatively new spar from the forests of Vancouver Island but it had been tested too many times in Arctic gales. While carefully splinted in the past weeks, the repairs did not hold in their first test, a modest storm in comparison to what would confront them in the North Pacific. Inspection aloft showed serious damage that could not be repaired at sea. The officers consulted on a weighty decision, knowing the Hawaiians would not understand their problem. "All hands much chagrined," King reported, "and damning the foremast."[12] Reluctantly, Cook retraced his steps to Kealakekua Bay, the only safe anchorage he had discovered in the islands. It was a fatal decision.

In stark contrast to their first arrival, this time a less enchanted island people coolly received the captain and his crew. There seemed to be a taboo about the ships, and no women or chiefs came aboard. While the carpenters busied themselves in making further repairs on shore, relations quickly deteriorated, and the crew found they had to carry arms while ashore. The reverence accorded the strangers had now turned to contempt and disdain. The native people were hostile and, when they came to the ships, it was usually with theft in mind. A native who had been caught stealing armorer's tongs was punished with forty lashes. Some of the people were insolent, even mean, and for the first time many natives carried weapons.

The problem with pilferage was especially great on the *Discovery*, in part because Cook was still considered as a god, but more likely because Clerke, weakened by tuberculosis, ran a much looser ship. On February 13 Cook, who was ashore with the carpenters, heard shots fired from the *Discovery*, and saw natives paddling franticly away from the ship with Edgar and Vancouver in hot pursuit. When the two seamen caught up to the fleeting thieves on shore, who had stolen the same armorer's tongs, an angry mob assembled. Efforts to seize the perpetrators and their canoe were rebuffed as the angry crowd pelted the seamen with stones, then the oars of the canoes. Although Vancouver and some of the seamen were badly injured, a priest advanced into the crowd and prevented further bloodshed.[13]

The unfortunate brawl put everyone on edge. Shocked and baffled by this sudden change in temperament, Cook that night lamented to King "I am afraid that these people will oblige me to use some violent measures; for they must not be left to imagine that they have gained an advantage over us." Clerke was likewise frustrated, "... our friendly connections having lull'd us into too great security." At dawn the next morning, Lt. Burney told Clerke that the cutter, the large shore boat critical to coastal explorations, had been taken from its mooring alongside the *Discovery*. "This was a loss which could not be overlooked on any account," Ellis later wrote to justify the response, "as the loss of so capital a boat might prove of great consequence to us in the remaining part of the voyage."[14]

When told of the treachery, Cook was enraged. It was a matter that Clerke should have handled, as the boat was stolen from his ship, but "Clerke was then in a deep decline in his health," Ledyard wrote, "and too feeble to undertake the affair."[15] So Cook took over, deciding to take Terre'oboo hostage until the craft was returned, a practice he used with other chiefs in similar situations throughout the Pacific. Unfortunately for him, the plan backfired. In an hour it would cost him his life.

Cook went ashore in full uniform with two officers, Phillips and Williamson, and nine armed red-coated marines in three small shore boats: a small cutter, launch and pinnace (a small sailboat). When awakened, Terre'oboo was terrified by the show of force, but seemed to oblige. But as he came to shore his wife and two chiefs intervened, suspicious of the early morning visit of armed marines, and prevented him from entering Cook's pinnace. The commotion caused a 2-3,000 strong horde of natives to assemble. They soon surrounded Cook and the chief, vastly outnumbering the captain and his small group of ill-equipped sailors. The mood was ugly and confrontational, and soon stones showered down, and a melee ensued. Cook, and even Terre'oboo, was unprepared for the hostilities of the mob.

At this point the marines thought Cook would retreat to the ships. Phillips later told Clerke that the Hawaiians at the water's edge had moved aside to allow Cook and the marines to pass. But a native approached from the multitude and threatened Cook with a dagger. In response, Cook fired his pistol. Loaded only with birdshot, it failed to wound the attacker, who was wearing matted armor. The gun's failure surprised the crowd, suggesting Cook was not invincible after all, so they were emboldened to attack.

Cook signaled for the marines to rescue him, but in the chaos they saw it as a signal to attack. The marines shot a single fruitless volley into the crowd and the natives reacted with force. At first they shoved and clubbed Cook. Then a chief stabbed him, ironically with a dagger from the ship. "The captain did not fall in consequence of his wound," Ellis wrote, "but still pressed towards the boats; the Indians however rushed upon him and, with clubs and stones, soon put a period to his existence!" The captain staggered into the surf and fell face down. The crowd then descended upon him and held him under, pounding his lifeless body again and again, killing the man they worshipped as a god.[16]

Samwell described the final attack:

> An Indian came running behind him, stopping once or twice as he advanced, as if he was afraid that he should turn round, then taking him unaware, he sprung to him, knocked him on the back of his head with a large Club taken out of a fence, & instantly fled with the greatest precipitation; the blow made Captain Cook stagger two or three paces, he then fell on his hand & one knee & dropped his musket. As he was rising another Indian came running at him, & before he could recover himself from the Fall, drew out an iron Dagger he concealed under his feathered Cloak & stuck it with all his force into the back of his Neck. This made Captain Cook tumble into the water where [it] is about knee deep.
> Here he was followed by a croud of people who endeavored to keep him under the water, but struggling very strongly with them he got his head up, & looking towards the Pinnace

which was not above a boat hook's Length from
him, waved his hands to them for Assistance,
which it seems was not in their power to give. ...
when a fellow gave him a blow to the head with
a large Club and he was seen alive no more.[17]

Cook's body lay lifeless in the water. In the space
of a few minutes, before eight o'clock in the morning on
February 14, 1779, Captain James Cook, 50, and four of his
marines were dead. The others, including the seriously
wounded Lt. Phillips and two others, hastily retreated
to the ships. Today there is a memorial to Cook on the
volcanic rocks where he fell. Although probably two
dozen Hawaiians were also killed in the melee, there is no
memorial to them.[18]

"Thus ended the life of the greatest navigator that
this or any other nation ever could boast," Rickman wrote,
"after having successfully led his crews of gallant British
seamen thrice round the World; had reduced to a certainty
the non-existence of a Southern Continent ..., had settled
the boundaries of the earth and sea.... Reader, if though
hast any feeling for thy country is the loss of so great, so
illustrious a navigator... thou will drop with me a tear at
this melancholy relation..."[19]

The shock overcame the people on both sides, who
were horrified by the tragedy. The crews lost their "father"
and commander, and the Hawaiians their legendary god
and many husbands and friends. Moans of grief came
from the island people, saddened by their loss and worried
about possible retribution from English cannons and
firearms. "I, as well as the others, had been so used to look
up to [Cook] as our good genius our safe conductor and as
a kind of superior being," King later wrote, "that I could
not suffer myself, I could not dare to think, he would fall

by the hands of the Indians, over whose minds and bodies he had been used to rule with absolute sway."

"When on the return of the boats informing us of the Captains Death," Gilbert wrote, "a general silence ensued throughout the ship for the space of a near half an hour; it appearing to us somewhat like a Dream that we could not reconcile ourselves to for some time. Grief was visible in every Countenance, some expressing it by tears, and others by a kind of gloomy dejection, more easy to be conceived than described, for as all our hopes centered in him, our loss became irreparable and the sense of it was so deeply impressed upon our minds as not to be forgot." As they returned from the skirmish, the retreating marines were heard to say, "We have lost our father! Our father is gone!"[20]

While the British contemplated an all out attack, cooler heads ultimately prevailed. The agitated Bligh wanted to lead a reprisal and was outraged when Gore and others urged caution. There were recriminations directed at the marines for failing to defend Cook and Phillips was quick to point to Williamson as the one to blame, as he had ordered the launch offshore and away from the mêlée at the critical moment that came before the commander's death. Clerke heard the evidence and ultimately found that Cook's own actions, unintended as they were, caused the incident and his death. "Upon the whole I firmly believe matters would not have been carried to the extremities they were had not Capt Cook attempted to chastise a man in the midst of this multitude," he concluded after a careful investigation.

In the custom of the British Navy, Clerke promptly took command and, as sick as he was, insisted on a peaceful, measured response. He redoubled the guard for the carpenters' work on shore and sent messages to Terre'oboo insisting on the return of Cook's remains. While there were some uneasy times, soon there was reconciliation. Several skirmishes occurred the first day. However, after a few days several priests came on board with hogs, vegetables and other gifts to express their sorrow and seek atonement. The women returned. Trade was plentiful and theft unknown. "From this night [the 16th] we may be said to have made peace with the Natives," King wrote, " for on the two following days all the remaining bones of Captn Cook were return'd, a Chief came with presents from Terreeoboo, & many others were brought from other Chiefs, which by being accept'd, & our original terms of peace being complied with, of course all Ideas of further Hostilities & satisfaction ceas'd."

The Hawaiians treated Cook's remains in the same manner reserved for their highest chiefs. On the sixth day following his death, a procession came out of the hills lead by a sorrowful priest. He presented all that could be found of Cook--his skull, hands, and some leg and arm bones. The remainder had been burned in religious ceremonies all over the island as the people came to grips with the loss of Cook, the human manifestation of their greatest god Lono. The ships' crews then committed these few remains to the sea in solemn ceremony. Clerke wrote, "I had the remains of Captain Cook committed to the deep with all the attention and honour we could possibly give it in this part of the World."[21]

Scholars have searched the voyage records and the many first and second-hand accounts of the skirmish that morning to learn why the great commander fell and whether the disaster could have been prevented. The principle cause is known. The broken spar required a return to Kealakekua Bay. Cook knew the reception would be far different on their return. When Clerke's shore boat was stolen,

Cook responded for the ailing Clerke with an excessive show of force that was poorly received by the gathered multitudes on shore. During the first visit he was revered as a reincarnated god and the Hawaiians overwhelmed him with gifts, but such worship came at a serious cost that depleted the island's meager resources. Now they mistrusted him. Even though Terre'oboo continued to support Cook on his return, the lesser nobles and priests grew weary of their own loss of power, authority, and respect among the people, and feared another prolonged visit from the English.

But there are other questions about the voyage and its impact on the commander that will probably never be fully answered. Cook was on his third voyage and, after a difficult year in the North Pacific, was tired and worn. Medical evidence suggests he might have been suffering from a parasitic infection of the intestine, causing irritability and loss of concentration. He had established a personal formula for interchange with the people of the Pacific islands that had served him well, particularly when confronted by thievery. His recent experiences in Nootka, Siberia and Unalaska contributed to his belief in his own invincibility, especially when he waded into the crowd of hostile Chukchi at St. Lawrence Bay. Given his godly status and the gentle nature of the Hawaiian people, he would not have expected such a ruthless response as occurred when confronted by the mob that morning. A number of eyewitnesses said he seemed to deliberately challenge the Hawaiian warriors to attack him and, with his soldiers too far away, the mob had the upper hand.

Readers of Cook's journals of Alaska and the North Pacific have another answer. The third voyage had been a disappointment from the start. Cook had been disillusioned too often and rarely enjoyed the excitement of discovery as in his earlier voyages. He left Plymouth alone, without

Clerke, and soon learned the *Resolution* was in a sorry state of repair. He had endured a summer of storms on the west coast of North America and, despite promising Russian maps, found that the Alaskan continental land mass prevented his discovery of the imagined northwest passage. He labored for fearful months in contrary winds and fog and he could have hardly anticipated a happy summer ahead in the Arctic ice pack. Quite simply, he was discouraged and fatigued and was in no mood to trifle with the mob.

The broken spar that forced him back to Kealakekua Bay was a sturdy Douglas Fur that had broken from the strain of Alaskan storms, a culmination of his terrible summer in the north. Alaska and the North Pacific, it seems, had defeated him. The loss was simply played out before the unsuspecting and unpredictable crowd in Hawaii.

Clerke moved to the *Resolution* with King as his first lieutenant. He appointed John Gore, Cook's irrepressible lieutenant, who thought Prince William Sound and Cook Inlet were entries to the great northern ocean, to command the *Discovery*. They now left Kealakekua Bay for a second time on February 23, 1779. Too sick to come on deck, Clerke had Bligh steer the vessel from the bay. Trevenen wrote of the emotions that fell to each sailor as they left, "An universal gloom and strong sentiments of grief and melancholy were very observable throughout all ranks on board the ship on our quitting this bay without our great and revered commander."[22]

The expedition did not leave Hawaii right away. For three weeks they continued their running survey of the Hawaiian Islands, sailing past Maui and the adjacent islands of Lanai and Molokai, but never coming to shore. They anchored briefly on the north shore of Oahu but could find no water. The only significant island coastline left unexplored was the south side of Oahu, so they missed Hawaii's finest anchorage at Pearl Harbor. They then returned to Waimea Bay on the southwest coast of Kauai, their first landing site a year earlier, and sent several parties ashore to collect wood, water and trade for other fresh provisions. Clerke said it was "the most extraordinary Hog Island we ever met with," so many hogs were purchased and salted for the journey north.[23]

Sadly, during their time on shore at Waimea Bay, another confrontation with an unhappy mob occurred and a Hawaiian was shot, but the incident passed without the recriminations of Kealakekua Bay. Samwell reported the event, reminiscent of the turmoil that ended in Cook's death:

> A great number of Indians were collected together at the Town of Owaimea and our people had hardly landed before the Natives stole a Bucket, and presently after attempted to snatch away the Cooper's Bag of Tools; they grew very troublesome & many of them were armed with Clubs and Spears, so that our people were obliged to be strictly on their guard to prevent a general attack from them; they made several attempts to seize their Arms from the Marines, one of them snatched the Serjeant's hat off his head & got clear off with it, for it would have been rash to fire at any of them while our people were ashore, as there could be no less than ten or twelve thousand Indians who could have easily destroyed the handful of Men we had there. As they were getting into the Boats they snatched the Lieut's Hanger from him, when our people had all embarked they fired three Muskets at them & killed one Man but not the Thief.[24]

If Samwell is to be believed, the landing party disarmed a crowd four times the size of the group that surrounded Cook, a formidable task that ended with just one dead. The following day there were further confrontations, but after careful diplomacy with the local chief, Clerke was able to restore order and normal trade. Leaving Waimea Bay in early March, the expedition spent its final week at Niihau in stormy weather, so windy few canoes came to trade, before beginning their melancholy return to the Arctic.

By now the shock of Cook's death had subsided and the journal writers could again attend to the customs and living conditions of the Hawaiians. King spent a considerable time in a series of Kauai communities, offering an incomparable record of first contact in the islands. Despite the conflicts, he wrote that the Hawaiians were like all Polynesians, agreeable and generally peaceable.

> From all our Transactions, we must I think allow the Natural dispositions of these people to be good, & on this point they are like their Brethern at the Society and Friendly Islands. I do not see that their conduct when we were at open hostilities ought to be brought as any Proof to the Contrary. If they are revengeful, cruel enemies, they are not implacable, nor Mistrustful. Although our situation made us under necessity of killing a man each time we were at Atou [Kauai] I, & of a much greater Slaughter at Owhyhee [the Big Island of Hawaii], yet in the former place it made no alteration in their friendly conduct toward us. They made us presents, sold us their Produce, & behav'd as if we had done them no injury.[25]

The winter in Hawaii had lasted three and one-half months, but it had been anything but a holiday. In mid-March the expedition turned back to their instructions and the plans of their dead captain as they bent their sails to steer back to Siberia.

~Chapter 10~

The Return North

With Cook dead and Clerke confined to his cabin, the prospects of an unproductive summer in the Arctic were high. The expedition had been at sea for three years and had spent a year investigating and tracing the Alaska coastline without finding the Northwest Passage. With the voyage objectives met, Clerke and Gore were well within their authority to abandon the voyage and return to England. But Clerke was implacable. The pact he and Cook made in Unalaska to return to the Arctic the next summer was binding. This second trip would determine whether the icepack could be penetrated at an earlier time of year. The time they spent the previous year surveying the Alaska coastline defeated them because they reached the icepack in late August. They hoped that an earlier trip would allow the ships to make further headway in the ice. So despite his failing health, Clerke resolved to go north again.

The expedition's officers were convinced this second voyage to the Arctic icepack would probably attain little. In their first venture the ice was as "compact as a wall," so many felt it was likely to be a permanent obstacle on this second foray. Many of them had also been with Cook on his second voyage where the ice served as a permanent barrier in the southern ocean. While he was still alive, Cook speculated about a second summer in the ice. He wrote the Admiralty from Unalaska, "I must confess I have little hopes of succeeding." As close as the two captains were, Clerke no doubt agreed.

Samwell was equally dubious about the venture as he ruminated about the expedition's purposes after leaving

Hawaii, "... our next Rendezvous being the Harbour of St. Peter and Paul in Kamchatka, from whence we are to proceed to the Northward to examine a narrow space between the two Continents which was left unexplored last Year," he wrote, almost to justify the unpopular decision, "tho' we have sufficient Reason from the shallowness of the Water, no Current & other Circumstances that there can be no Passage between them, which was the Opinion of Captn. Cook & the officers of both Ships; yet he himself had he lived intended to go to the Northward again this summer & settle this long disputed point of a North East & North West passage beyond the possibility of a doubt..."[1]

Clerke's decision was certainly made without consideration for his own health. Given the advanced state of tuberculosis plaguing him, he knew he could not survive another grueling season in the North Pacific. Consequently, as they set sail for Siberia from Niihau, Hawaii, he virtually sealed his own death warrant. Clerke was now so infirm that he rarely came on deck, turning all navigation over to Bligh. It is a tribute to the officers and crew, and English naval tradition, that the expedition followed the orders of one dead and a second dying captain to return to the Arctic once again.

Clerke's log offered little insight as they sailed north, recounting only a few sentences each day on the direction of travel. Though he never mentioned his own health, he was rapidly deteriorating and had less energy to devote to his journal. In five weeks the forlorn voyagers had ascended from the tropics back to Siberia, where Clerke could only lament the bitter wind and cold. His entry on April 23 advises "... during the night the Frost, Snow & Sleet were exceeding severe & cold; in the Morning our Ship appear'd a fair sheet of Ice, the Sleet & Snow as it fell having froze to the sails & Rigging." The temperature had plummeted 53 degrees, and it was now 28° in a blinding snow storm.[2]

Ledyard spoke for the crew, "I shall ... only simply observe that [this passage] was rendered extremely trying and severe not only from the sudden change of climate in leaving the tropical latitudes, and entering a winters coast, and a new coast, but from other circumstances; Our clothing ... was really miserable, our food was the same on Monday morning and Sunday evening—pork and yams begun, and pork and yams ended all our bills of fare, and we had besides but half an allowance of the latter ... Besides it was the month of March, and to crown the jest our ship was fairly worn out. We pumped and bailed her half the passage."[3]

In late April the Russian landscape appeared out of the fog. While there were frequent snow showers, the land, still locked in winter, could be made out through the mists. "...we stood in to take a view of the Land, and a more dreary prospect I never yet came in the way of," Clerke wrote pessimistically. "It makes strait having little or no Curve along the Sea side & rises in many distinct Hills of very mod[era]te elevation, behind which are ranges of Mountains whose Summits were lost in the Haze & Clouds, but to all appearance I should suppose them of great Altitude. Every atom of Earth was covered with Snow ..." King was similarly discouraged. "... All the Country was covered with Snow," he wrote, "& imagination could not paint a more dreary Prospect."[4]

The crew suffered the most. "The poor fellows after broiling as they have lately done several Months in the Torrid Zone are now miserably pinch'd with the Cold," Clerke wrote. "The Doctors list increases every day, several of them are frost bit."[5] To make matters worse, Captain Cook's favorite chronometer, which served the second voyage without incident, suddenly stopped working. The loss of such a vital navigational instrument was critical to the crew as they embarked on another summer in fog-enshrouded waters. The watchmaker on board cleaned, adjusted and repaired it several times on the way to Kamchatka, only for it to stop again and again. It was finally lost to the voyage until a broken spring was replaced in England. But the instrument's journey was not over, as it later accompanied Captain Phillip with the First Fleet to Australia.[6]

On April 27, 1779, the ships entered Avacha Bay, some 175 miles from the southern tip of the Kamchatka Peninsula, the only harbor on the east coast of the peninsula. Today this is the location of the thriving port of Petropavlovsk-Kamchatsky, a town of over 250,000 people, capital of modern-day Kamchatka. But in the early spring of 1779 it was a bleak and foreboding place, a bay choked in ice, with mountains covered in snow. Picking their way through the moving ice, the British finally saw the tiny village of St. Peter and St. Paul, named after Bering's ships.

Based on the grand reports of Ismailov in Unalaska, they had anticipated a significant and prosperous colony of Russians, but it was nothing like that. "We saw a few log houses, & Conic shaped huts upon Poles," King wrote, "but their miserable appearance, & Smallness in Number, would not allow us to take it for St. Peter and St. Pauls Village… with our glasses we could discern two men Walking about the huts; we look'd round the bay but saw no more huts, no boats, no living Soul. Some few flocks of duck was all that enlightened this very silent solemn, waste prospect." [7]

Ellis was similarly unimpressed. "We were anxious to find out the Russian ostrog, or town, which … we were lead to suppose was a capital one … and which was secured by a fortification that mounted forty guns. But how great was our surprise, when, upon examining every corner of the bay with our glasses, we could only discover a few huts at the bottom of a small bay, which proved to be the harbour of St. Peter and St. Paul. Upon our landing

... our laughter was sufficiently excited, upon finding this town dwindled to a poor forlorn hamlet, containing only twenty-one wooden buildings, including jourts, balagans, and houses, and the formidable battery shrunk up to two guns, one of which was a two-pounder, the other a swivel." [8] Ismailov had overstated the size and fortifications of the town, presumably fearing that Cook's two armed ships would overwhelm it. Cook had contemplated spending the previous winter in the village, a grim prospect now that it was seen in all its glory.

The solid shore ice stopped the ships almost a mile from land. Clerke sent King with John Webber, the ship's artist, and they trudged half a mile over the broken ice to the few huts at the center of the village. Although no one in the expedition could speak or read Russian, Webber was dispatched with the faint hope that someone would know German, which he spoke fluently. It took the party several hours before they reached shore, as they frequently broke through the crusted ice and soaked themselves to their knees.

They found a tiny garrison with a handful of Russians, fewer than at Unalaska, surrounded by a small native village. Samwell later counted 30 soldiers and another 20 people, Cossacks and others of uncertain origin, who made up the population of the village. Ledyard said the Russian guard amounted to "just 15 or 20 miserable looking men commanded by a serjeant and about 60 Indians." [9] Although friendly, the Russians were alarmed by the presence of two armed ships and resisted offers of assistance. The English wanted to purchase supplies for the journey north. Before they could agree, the sergeant explained, he would need approval from his commander at Bolsheretsk on the other side of the peninsula, nearly a hundred miles away on the Sea of Okhotsk. This would be a daunting task, given the deep and drifted snow along the route.

Clerke knew he could not spend another summer in the Arctic without fresh provisions and Ismailov had told him this port would offer sufficient beef and flour for the journey north. So he resolved to seek the approvals necessary, no matter the difficulty of the journey. He sent King, Gore and Webber with two Cossacks trudging overland on foot and by dogsled to Bolsheretsk. In the time they were gone, increased sunlight and spring temperatures improved the land and the men's dispositions. The carpenters again attended to the *Resolution*, while others harvested fish from the bay and found freshly sprouting edible plants that mended both their diets and temperament. The harvest was so bountiful they shared it with the meager garrison on shore, which had been suffering badly at the end of a long Siberian winter.

King's log offers a gritty report of a difficult four-day mountain journey over the spine of the Kamchatka Peninsula, navigating wild rivers and crossing wide banks of drifted snow. When they arrived, they found Bolsheretsk not much more impressive than the village of St. Peter and St. Paul, with just a few more buildings and a handful of cattle to distinguish it. But Major Magnus von Behm, the fort's commander, was "an agreeable, sensible well-bred man." He also spoke German, ending the difficulties in communication. He explained to Webber and the other Englishmen that he was eager to support the expedition, offering the emissaries hospitality and his own keen insights into current affairs. A party was given in their honor and the few women of the village attended in their finest gowns. Von Behm was taken by the importance of the expedition, and determined that he should support it to the maximum extent, and charge nothing for it. He had already learned of Captain Cook's visit to the Chukchi people at St. Lawrence Bay the prior summer. The Chukchi thought Cook was a Russian, and Cook impressed them so much that the natives had unexpectedly offered signs of friendship to the Russians, even the promise to pay tribute.

So von Behm returned the favor. He sent 20 head of cattle, 900 pounds of rye meal, 400 pounds tobacco, tea, fresh butter, rice, cordage and canvas, and other provisions overland through the broken snow to the ships. He even came along to make sure his decision to resupply the expedition was fully implemented. Since he spoke German, he and Webber were inseparable. Von Behm was surprised with the fitness of the English, particularly when he learned they had been away from home for three years. He compared their good health to the dismal record of the fur hunters sent to the Aleutians. "… nor was he less astonished to hear that we had lost but such a Small number of Men by sickness," Samwell reported, "telling us that the Russians sent their small Sloops with about 60 Men in them on a Summer's Cruise to the Coast of America and the adjacent Isles & that it often happens that not more than 20 or 30 of them return home alive, the rest dying from Scurvy & other Disorders."

Von Behm organized a substantial expedition from his meager colony that plodded back over the spine of the peninsula to resupply the vessels. Upon reaching the village of St. Peter and St. Paul, von Behm decided to stay a week and regularly dined with Clerke and the other expedition officers aboard the *Resolution.* When von Behm told them he was about to leave his post and return to St. Petersburg, Clerke entrusted him with Cook's journal and several expedition charts. King explained, "Capt Clerke, judging with what safety accounts of our discoveries could be trust'd to a man of the Majors private & publick Character, & that we had a very hazardous part of the Voyage yet to go thro, determin'd to send by him the Journal of our late Commander, with his own from his death to this time, & a Chart … by which should any misfortune attend us, the

Admiralty would have a detailed account of … the principal part of our discoveries."

Von Behm kept his word. Cook's journal and the other accounts entrusted to the major were delivered to the Admiralty in London seven months later, even before the Unalaska accounts sent the previous fall reached England. So it was von Behm, a Russian diplomat of German ancestry, who told the waiting world of Cook's untimely death and the expedition's failure to find the Northwest Passage.

King was astounded by von Behm's generosity. "If every country that the stranger may be driven to, had a von Behm to preside over their affairs," King wrote, "what honour would redound to their Soverigns, & to their Country, & what credit would it be to human Nature … the example of the Major must be of infinite use." Vancouver was so taken by the man, and his considerable largess in the face of a bleak Russian spring for his own starving colonies, he later honored him by naming a prominent Alaska water body after him. The name of Behm Canal, a broad inlet that stretches through the Tongass National Forest east of Ketchikan's Revillagigedo Island, survives today.[10]

By the middle of June the Russian landscape had changed from winter to summer and it was time to test the Arctic Sea. The two English ships had been in Avacha Bay for six weeks. Von Behm had fully resupplied the expedition, so it could be underway again. The day before they sailed a nearby volcano exploded. "The burning mountain to the Northward," Samwell wrote, "… which has emitted smoke more or less all the time we have been here, was observed… to throw out larger Columns than usual & last Night a rumbling noise was heard from it; soon after the Ship's Decks were covered with Ashes, which continue to pour down on us in a constant shower…"[11]

As they coasted out of the bay, the ash and cinders falling from the volcano intensified the gloom of the ever-present coastal fog. Clerke said there was thunder, lightning and a shower of cinders, and the cinders were "the size of a Pea." He described a foreboding sight: "Towards the Evening it thunder'd and Lightn'd prodigiously, which with the darkness of the Air cast the most dreadful Gloom & dismal Appearance I ever saw. The Effects of this Volcano must have been felt far off at Sea, for we were about 8 leagues from the Mountain, & as far as we could see to the Sea the Ashes must have fallen.[12]

"...we had again the small shock of an earthquake and heard a hollow rumbling noise in the air," Ledyard wrote, "it became almost as dark as night. ...the mountain exploded with a tremendous shock that convulsed everything around us ... the atmosphere was one continuous sheet of flame ... Soon after it began to thunder there fell showers of small fragments of lava about the size of a walnut." The travelers were about 20 miles from the volcano and soon the two ships and nearby shore were covered with mud and ash "which lay several inches thick on our decks."[13]

Leaving the eruption behind, for nearly three weeks the explorers followed the Kamchatka coast, usually enshrouded in a thick fog, passing Bering Strait on July 6. They then crossed over to Alaska to investigate the coast now known as Kotzebue Sound, which Cook missed the previous season. But the Alaska coastline was again embedded with ice, and they made little progress toward shore. Moving north, they soon came to the icepack, a continuous, impassable wall that prevented further progress. Cook had hoped entering the Arctic Sea in July would lead to further penetration in the ice, but the contrary was true. The ice held fast to shore with loose, drifting ice that impeded forward progress.

The penalty for arriving so early in the season was that the ice was farther south than the previous year. Undaunted, Clerke drove the ships against the ice to break through, but with little success. "We continued our endeavours to force our way through the Ice till we found the flakes very large," he wrote on July 10, "...they were so thick as not possibly to be avoided and when we did encounter them their weight was such as wholly to stop the Ship, the shocks we receiv'd by them ... damag'd the Sheathing about the Bows."[14] They also saw walrus and whales moving about the ice. Cook's regimen of fresh provisions for the crew continued. The captains insisted that walrus be shot and served to the crew, no matter the taste.

Moving away from Alaska the adventurers tested the ice pack again and again, finding the barrier obstinate and unconquerable. They faced a ridge of solid ice that frequently rose 20 feet out of the water, rough and unbroken, and it continued ahead as far as they could see. On July 19 they reached 70°33' in a deep bay formed by this solid ice, a few miles short of Cook's northernmost point from the prior summer.[15] Two polar bears appeared on the ice field, the first time such bears had been seen on the journey. "...a boat was sent after them which after 4 or 5 shots killed them both in the Water & brought them on board," Samwell wrote, "they were male & female, the latter which was the largest. ...the flesh of them was eaten both by the Officers & Men & tho' fishy was generally preferred to stale Meat..." [16]

Nothing could restore Clerke's health. On July 21, still anticipating another opening north, he considered his plans to move along the ice to the Siberian coast. He wrote:

> I therefore think it the best step I can take for the good of the service to trace the Ice over to the Asiatic Coast, try if I can find a Hole that will admit me any farther North, if not see whats to be done upon that Coast where I hope

but cannot much flatter myself with meeting better success, for this Sea is now so Choak'd with Ice that a passage I fear is totally out of the question.[17]

This was his final journal entry. Burney took up Clerke's pen to continue the log of the *Resolution*.

There was no hole admitting the ships to the north. They bore away to the west in a counter-clockwise arc from the Alaskan coast sailing in and out of floes against the impenetrable ice pack. At one point the ships were surrounded by ice, trapped by a driving wind forcing the ships against the pack. "..we found ourselves closely blocked up by the ice, and could see it all around us in a solid body to a great distance," Rickman wrote, "...in this horrid situation we ... moored out ship with both our ice anchors" unable to move. Waiting out the near disaster, the following day the wind finally shifted and "our Captain, looking over our starboard quarter, discerned the ice to the southward seemingly to leave the ship, and soon we heard a crash, as if a thousand rocks had been rent from their foundations." The ships were suddenly freed. The anchors were raised and the ships followed a narrow opening into the open sea. Although frequently stopped by huge bergs the expedition was underway again.[18]

The ice was "an obstinate and unconquerable barrier." They finally reached the Russian coast without making any progress through the ice. Clerke made one last desperate attempt to get through the drift ice that lay off the pack, but it was futile. In that final foray the *Discovery* crashed into an ice floe with such violence that it lost the protective sheathing. This suddenly ended the ships' efforts to breach the frozen wall. So on July 27 Clerke abandoned the search and ordered the ships to turn south. By July 30 they passed Bering Strait.

Clerke was now nearly dead and his mission nearly complete. On August 10 he wrote his final letter to King, anticipating his death and offering final commentary on the voyage, and the prospects for reaching England. He continued to command the ship until August 15, when he relinquished it to King and was confined to bed. On August 22 he died at age thirty-eight, in sight of the Kamchatka coast. King wrote of the sad affair, "Captain Clerke dyed on the 22 August when we were almost in sight of the bay of Awatshka; his disorder was a consumption of which he had lingered during the whole voyage, & his decay was so gradual, that he did the duty of his station till within a week of his death, when being no longer able to come on deck, he desired the officers to receive my orders & gave the command up to me."[19]

Samwell wrote confidently of Clerke's seamanship as the second in command to Cook, as well as his leadership after the death of Cook. "...his Perseverance in pursuing the Voyage after the death of Captn Cook, notwithstanding his own bad state of Health, will ever reflect Honour upon his Memory. The most remarkable part of his Character was his happy convivial Turn & humourous Conversation in which he excelled most Men; these, joined to an open generous Disposition, made his Company universally caressed and engaged him in excesses which laid the Foundation of the Complaint of which he died."[20]

Unlike Cook, whose few remains were committed to the sea in Kealakekua Bay, Clerke wanted to be buried ashore on the grounds of the nearby church in the village of Paratoonca. In two days the expedition reached the harbor of St. Peter and St. Paul and he was soon laid to rest in Kamchatka. Gore insisted the burial be given the most solemn ceremony, with all the pomp and dignity available in such a remote place. All the crew, even the local Russian soldiers, marched in procession with the local priest, offering "great respect and solemnity."

King wrote, "in the afternoon we paid our last offices to Captain Clerke, with all the decency and ceremony we could, the officers & men of both ships walking in procession to the Grave whilst the ships fyred minute guns, & the service being over, the marines fyred three vollies. Captain Gore was prevailed upon, by our good friend the priest, to bury Captain Clerke here, rather than at Paratoonca, as that church is so soon to be removed. This Reverend Gentleman walked in the procession with the gentleman who read the service, & all the Russians attended with a great deal of respect." After the burial the crews planted willows around the grave, and Gore inscribed a wooden plaque or escutcheon that was posted in the nearby Russian Orthodox Church.[21]

As King explained, the site of the grave was selected by Gore and the priest to be located on the grounds where a new church was to be built. The inscription on the headstone read:

> Beneath this Tree lies the Body of Captn Charles Clerke who succeeded to the Command of his Brittanic Majesty's Ships the Resolution and Discovery on the Death of Captn James Cook who was unfortunately killed at an Island in the South Sea on the 14th of Febry in the Year 1779 and died at Sea of a lingering Consumption on the 22d of August in the same Year aged 38.

The gravesite was also chosen because it was close to the grave of Louise Delisle de la Croyère, Chirikov's second in command, who died of scurvy in October 1741. Ironically, de la Croyère died as Chirikov's ship entered

Avacha Bay on its return from Alaska. As it turned out the church was constructed elsewhere, so by the middle of the nineteenth century, both graves fell into disrepair and have since been lost to the ages.[22]

After reaching the harbor of St. Peter and St. Paul, the British stayed for seven weeks, the longest stop on the voyage. The first day it was 70°, a marked improvement from two months in the ice. "The country now exhibited an aspect so different from what it was before, as not to appear like the same place" Ellis wrote, with some relief.[23] Gore was now in command of the expedition, returning to Cook's flagship, and King took command of the *Discovery.* Anxious to go home, the time ashore proved tedious to most of the crew. But after two months in the Arctic, with thunderous, desperate attempts to break through the ice, both ships required considerable overhaul: planks and iron sheathing were broken or lost, caulking missing, ironwork twisted, rudders broken, and sails and rigging in tatters.

Settling in for a long stay, Gore had tents erected for all the crew on shore, not just for the carpenters and sail makers. For a time, the captains considered scuttling the *Discovery* because of the damage it received in the Arctic. The most imminent repairs required were to the ruined sheathing and the broken hull where the ice had punctured the vessel below the water line. In addition, there were open uncaulked timbers throughout. When the officers found similar problems with the *Resolution,* the thoughts to abandon the consort ship were dismissed and the lengthy repair of both ships began. Crew not engaged in retrofitting the ships were free to explore the countryside, usually occupying their free time collecting berries, hunting bears and brewing spruce beer.[24]

The English did not have much interchange with the native people of the village, finding them peaceable and reserved, but usually keeping their distance. It is more likely they were so dominated by the Russian garrison that they were allowed little contact with the visitors. The seamen observed the homes of these natives to be much different than those on the mainland of Alaska and in the Aleutians. Ledyard wrote the local village "contains about 30 huts, some of which are built with logs, as we do in our new American settlements, and others are erected on posts about 14 feet from the ground, consisting of a slight frame of a conical form and thatch." These were the winter and summer homes of the people. The summer huts were called "balagans." Ledyard continued:

> The face of the country is high and mountainous, and thick covered with well grown woods, which chiefly consists of birch, pine and beach, and the internal parts of it abounds with a variety of wild animals ... As the inhabitants have no horses, they make use of a number of middling sized dogs: And as they travel mostly in winter, they use them mostly for that purpose in light sledges, with which they travel 40 or 50 miles a day very comfortably.[25]

The Russians, especially the soldiers, appeared to be a lazy, ineffectual people who relied on native servants to do most of their work. As a result, the Russians were roundly criticized in British journals. "The settlements at this Bay appear to be more in a state of decay than improvement," Gilbert wrote, "for the Russians don't seem to make any effort either to extend their Navigation, or increase the number of their vessels. And so great is their indolence that they rather choose to live in the most wretched state of any people we ever saw, than to be at the least labour to cultivate the Country."[26] Ellis noticed that, on their return to the bay in August, some of the Russians were confined to their beds with scurvy in the midst of a plentiful fall harvest of berries and vegetables. "...a stronger proof of their laziness cannot be produced," he concluded.[27]

It appeared that the Russian soldiers were present in these parts simply to collect tribute in furs from the local native people and to serve as a way station for the periodic supply ships calling in the Aleutians. Von Behm said the Russian Cossacks and soldiers controlling the region numbered about 400, with probably 3,000 native inhabitants on the entire peninsula. Apparently many of the Russians were "emigrants" from the east, banished from the Russian capital. "According to the Russian emigrants who occupy [Siberia]; and the dialect of the aborigines of the country Kamchatka," Ledyard wrote, "this is one of the southern circles of Russian Siberia, called thus from its being a place where malefactors of rank from the Court of Russia are exiled: the word 'Siberia' in Russ signifying a prison."[28]

So the Cossacks and misfits lived in tiny villages scattered throughout Siberia, serving simply as landlords for the Czar. The Russians seemed to keep an uneasy peace in the region but the English observed they were in constant fear of attack. King wrote, "These [garrisons] are to keep the rebellious Tchuskoi [Chukchi] as they call them not so much in obedience for they have not yet subdued them, but from attacking ... indian tribes who are subdued. ... although [the peninsula] had suffered greatly by a rebellion which had reduced it to a very low poor state to what it had been; the Russians for a long time after quelling that Rebellion could have no apprehensions of the Kamskadales, reduced as they were, making new efforts to shake off their slavery."

At one point King met the local chief on a return from an unsuccessful fishing trip. "I could not but observe how much inferior our Kamskadales were, at this method of fishing, to those at Oonalaska," he wrote. He later conferred with a local Russian who had been to Unalaska and was familiar with Aleut fishing practices. "I wanted to know the reason of this from the Corporal who had been many years amongst the Americans. He said that formerly the Kamskadales made use of the same darts & spears with bone barbs & points, & were once equally dextrous." The English attributed this malaise to a disintegration of the local culture. While probably true, King apparently gave little thought to the impacts of Russian enslavement.

King also learned of the dismal record of conquest in the Aleutians and Kodiak Island, particularly how the Russians had recently suffered a setback on Kodiak Island. "Here as also upon the continent opposite, they met with such a repulse as has frightened them ever since from going so far. They met with better success in the Islands to the West of Alashka having reduced them, tho without losing a number of men & killing still much a greater number of natives." The problem, as King understood it, was that the Russians simply could not explain to the native people of Alaska, and especially in Unalaska and Kodiak, the concept of paying tribute.

King speculated that the only way the Russians would come to dominate the Kamchatka region, and certainly the eastern Aleutian Islands and the Alaska mainland, would be through the passage of time. He learned of the ravages of small pox on the native people in the region near Okhotsk, where 20,000 died, but 7,000 remained. Whole villages were depopulated, and the people who survived intermarried with the Cossacks to form a new population. King lamented the outcome, and the implications for

Kamchatka and the Aleutians. "Such has been the effects of this terrible visitation which having so diminished them," he concluded, "& at the same time fresh supplies of soldiers Cossacks & banished men being sent here who intermix by marriage with the natives, that I should suppose in a short time there will be very few of the original natives remaining, which I think will be of little service to the country, for the Kamskadales are a laborious quiet set of people as I ever saw, whereas the Soldiers & Cossacks are the Idlest drones one can conceive, glad enough to connect themselves with the Kamskadales & to be kept by them."[29]

On October 5 the spruce beer ran out, about the same time the carpenters, coopers and sail makers completed refitting the ships. The Siberian terrain also began to turn to winter. "The Summer here is of a very short duration," Gilbert wrote, "being little more then four months; for by October the Country began to have quite a wintry appearance; the trees and Bushes having entirely lost their verdure, and the weather grown cold."[30] The time had come for the English to leave. The Russians again providently resupplied the vessels with fresh provisions, far beyond the means of their meager resources. By October 10 the two ships were underway, finally bound for England.

-Chapter 11-

The Voyage Home

Cook's instructions were understandably vague about the route the expedition should take back to England. It was assumed the intrepid mariner would find a direct passage home, sailing over the top of the world through an undiscovered passageway. No one contemplated Gore's predicament that autumn in Kamchatka. A northern passage had not been found, so the ships were required to return by the more circuitous but conventional means, taking nearly a year to go around the southern tip of either South America or Africa.

Gore consulted with the other officers on the best plan. They decided to sail down the coast of Russia, past the little-known Kurile Islands and Japan, then call at Canton for supplies. They quickly agreed to avoid Batavia, where Cook lost so many men at the end of the first voyage. The ships would instead sail directly for Cape of Good Hope and, eventually, England. In the first and second voyages, Cook successfully circumnavigated the globe. Gore's route of travel, returning by way of Africa the same way they came, kept them from achieving that distinction on the third voyage. Presumably sailing by way of China was the unstated objective that prevented the circumnavigation; after all, they had a considerable booty of sea otter furs on board and Chinese merchants would offer the best price.

Leaving Avacha Bay the sailors again found the interminable North Pacific fog and saw little more of Siberia or the Kurile Islands. While there were fleeting glimpses of the Japanese islands and a few vessels came out to see them, there was no recorded contact with any people. The first land the expedition clearly sighted came in late November when, after nearly two months at sea, a volcanic island southeast of Formosa stood out in stark relief in the China Sea. On December 4 they entered the Portuguese port of Macao at the mouth of the Canton River (Pearl River today), a few miles west of modern day Hong Kong. They stayed at Macao a month.[1]

After nearly four years away, in China they finally had some news from home. The greatest surprise was that the American colonies were in full rebellion against England and that the French had joined them. "Here we heard of the war with France," Gilbert wrote, "which was a very unexpected event to us; as in general we were of opinion that the Rebellion in American wou'd have been quell'd long before that time." Gore commanded the expedition and both he and Ledyard were Americans. So reports of a sustained rebellion between their fellow Americans and the English must have prompted a few anxious moments with their shipmates.[2]

"What a conflict of passions did this mighty flood of new matter occasion," King asked, "American declaring herself independent so soon after our departure, supporting for a length of time her declaration at last aided by France. England our dear long absent and distant country, so often wished for, to be so situated with Spain also preparing to annoy her was intelligence sufficient to rouse the dullest & most slavish mind amongst us."[3]

They soon learned from English traders on the Canton (Pearl) River that the French and Americans had already considered the plight of the British ships returning from this expedition. The Americans were apparently so captivated by Cook and the importance of his voyage they issued general orders that guaranteed the care and safety of Cook's ships, exempting them from possible capture.

Benjamin Franklin, then American ambassador to France, wrote the following letter of free passage distributed to all craft sailing for the American cause:

To all Captains and Commanders of armed Ships acting by Commission from the Congress of the United States of America now in War with Great Britain—

A Ship having been fitted out from England before the commencement of this War to make Discoveries of new Countries in unknown Seas, under the conduct of that most celebrated Navigator Capt. Cook; an undertaking truly laudable in itself, as the Increase of Geographical Knowledge facilitates the communication between distant nations, in the exchange of useful Products and Manufactures and the extension of Arts. Whereby the common enjoyments of human life are multiplied and augmented, and Science of other kinds increased to the benefit of mankind in general. This is therefore most earnestly to recommend to everyone of you that in Case the said Ship, which is now expected to be soon in the European seas on her return, should happen to fall into your Hands, you would not consider her as an enemy, not suffer any Plunder to be made of the effects contained in her, nor obstruct her immediate return to England by detaining her or sending her into any other part of Europe or to America, but that you would treat the said Captain Cook and his people with all civility and kindness, affording them as common friends to mankind all the Assistance in your power which they may happen to stand in need of. In so doing you will not only gratify the generosity of your own dispositions, but there is no doubt of your obtaining the approbation of the Congress and your other American Owners.

B. Franklin, Minister Plenipotentiary from the Congress of the United States to the Court of France
Given at Passy, Near Paris, this 10th day of March 1779.[4]

The crew was certain the sea otter pelts collected along the coast would be hotly contested by the merchants at Macao and upriver at Canton. Some had unluckily sold their furs in Kamchatka, but those who waited were handsomely rewarded, as the frenzy for the furs stimulated a brisk trade. "One of our Gentlemen purchase eleven prime Skins for double the number of large green beads," King wrote, "which here would have sold for 80 or 100 Dollars each…" Gilbert reported "We sold the remainder of our furs to much greater advantage than at Kamchatka, the Chinese being eager to purchase them and gave us 50 to 70 Dollars a skin … for what we bought with only a hatchet or a saw."

In the end, all the pelts were sold for an estimated £2,000, a handsome sum. By comparison, the Admiralty paid £2,800 for the *Endeavor*, Cook's first sailing ship, when it was commissioned from the coal trade. King complained, "the rage with which our Seamen were possessed to return to Cook's River and buy another cargo of skins to make their fortunes was at one time not far short of mutiny." He feared the sailors would insist on an immediate return north, despite the condition of the ships, but England was at war and the sailors were already "too much chagrined at having been so long out of the road of honourable achievements" that they continued home. Nonetheless, rumors of the fantastic profits made by the sailors in Canton soon fueled a new fur industry on the northwest coast.[5]

Leaving Macao in mid January, the ships made excellent progress to Africa, but a gale in the Indian Ocean forced them to put into port in South Africa to repair and refit the beleaguered *Resolution*. This was the *Resolution's* last renovation. And it was here that Williamson and Phillips allegedly fought a duel, though there is no record, as they bitterly and steadfastly blamed each other for the death of Cook.

In mid-July, four years after leaving England, the weary travelers entered the English Channel expecting a triumphant return. But yet another delay was in their path. An easterly storm arose and they were unluckily driven northwest into the Irish Sea. The storm did not abate for several days and finally they anchored in Stromness harbor in the Orkney Islands—in the farthest reaches of northern Scotland. King, Bayly and Webber were sent overland to deliver the journals, sketches and charts to the Admiralty, while Gore and the other crew waited for better weather. At last, after a month's time, favorable winds took them down the east coast of England. They nearly circumnavigated the island, appropriately passing the seacoast where Cook first learned the maritime trade 30 years earlier. Two months after first sighting England, on October 7, 1780, the ships anchored at the Royal Dockyards at Deptford, on the southern bank of the Thames River near Greenwich.[6]

Thanks to Major von Behm, the results of the voyage, and especially the death of Cook in Hawaii, was already known throughout England and the rest of Europe. Von Behm had passed Cook's journal to the Admiralty on

January 10, 1780 and Cook's earlier letter from Unalaska arrived in March. On January 11, 1780, the *London Gazette* gave the following report:

> Captain Clerke of His Majesty's Sloop *Resolution*, in a letter to Mr. Stephens, dated the 8th of June 1779, in the Harbour of St. Peter and St. Paul, Kampschatka, which was received yesterday, gives the melancholy account of the celebrated Captain Cook, late commander of that Sloop, with four of his private Marines having been killed on the 14th of February last at the island of O'Why'he, one of a group of new discovered Islands in the 22nd Degree of North Latitude, in an affray with a numerous and tumultuous Body of the Natives.

An obituary for Cook appeared the same day:

> This untimely and ever to be lamented Fate of so intrepid, so able, and so intelligent a Sea-Officer, may justly be considered as an irreparable Loss to the Public, as well as to his Family, for in him were united every successful and amiable quality that could adorn his Profession; not was his singular Modesty less conspicuous than his other Virtues. His successful Experiments to preserve the Healths of his Crews are well known, and his Discoveries will be an everlasting Honour to his Country.[7]

As a result, little excitement arose over the arrival of the vessels eleven months after the announcement of Cook's death, except for the pleasure of relatives and friends seeing the safe return of the weary sailors. Promotions and appointments were awarded, wages were paid, and the artifacts and collections of flora and fauna were sent to Banks and the Royal Society for safekeeping. But for Britons still at war with their rebellious colonies there was no reason to celebrate.[8] The Northwest Passage had not been found and Captains Cook and Clerke were dead.

"Thus ended a long, tedious and disagreeable voyage," Gilbert concluded, "of four years, and three months, during which we lost only seven persons by sickness, who all belonged to the Resolution, and three by accident belonging to Discovery, exclusive of those who were killed with our great and unfortunate Commander."[9] At that time the third voyage was the longest single exploring voyage in history. Remarkably, no one died from scurvy, a true testament to Cook's determination.

The news of Cook's death far overshadowed the results of the voyage and brought grief to many in England and throughout the world. Cook had come to represent the best of the Age of the Enlightenment in Europe, a humane explorer and great gentlemen. He singularly enjoyed the great variety of people, cultures and civilizations he met while, at the same time, introducing the western world to the near boundless limits of the globe. Just as important, he revolutionized shipboard hygiene. When news of his death reached London, the *London Evening Post* praised Cook for losing just one sailor to sickness on the entire second voyage.[10] A century earlier it would not be uncommon for such lengthy voyages to lose one-third of their crews to scurvy.

King George III, it was said, openly wept when told of Cook's death. He later granted a posthumous coat of arms for the family: a map of the Pacific showing the voyage with polar stars, palm wreaths, and two Latin mottos

"Around the globe" and "He left nothing untried." The Royal Society struck a medal in Cook's honor and Sir Hugh Pallister, Comptroller of the Navy, erected an obelisk on his personal estate, which reads in part:

> To the memory of Captain James Cook, The ablest and most renowned Navigator this or any country hath produced. He raised himself, solely by his merit from a very obscure birth, to the rank of Post Captain in the royal navy, and was, unfortunately, killed by the Savages of the island of Owhyhee, on the 14th of February, 1779; which island he had not long before discovered, when prosecuting his third voyage around the globe.

> He possessed, in an eminent degree, all the qualifications requisite for his profession and great undertakings. ... Traveller! Contemplate, admire, revere, and emulate this great master in his profession; whose skill and labours have enlarged natural philosophy; have extended nautical science; and have disclosed the long concealed and admirable arrangements of the Almighty in the formation of this globe...[11]

Samwell, Surgeon's mate on the *Resolution,* wrote:

> Nature had endowed him with a mind vigorous and comprehensive, which in his riper years he had cultivated with care and industry. His general knowledge was extensive and various: in that of his own profession he was unequalled. With a clear judgment, strong

masculine sense, and the most determined resolution: with a genius peculiarly turned for enterprise, he pursued his object with unshaken perseverance—vigilant and active in an eminent degree: cool and intrepid among dangers: patient and firm under difficulties and distress: fertile in expedients: great and original in all his designs: active and resolved in carrying them into execution. In every situation he stood unrivalled and alone: on him all eyes were turned: he was our leading star, which at its setting left us involved in darkness and despair.[12]

Even the gruff Johann Reinhold Forster, Cook's naturalist on the second voyage, who had a bitter disagreement with Cook over the publication of that voyage's journal, offered a touching eulogy:

If we consider his extreme abilities, both natural and acquired, the firmness and constancy of his mind, his truly paternal care for the crew entrusted to him, the amicable manner with which he knew how to gain the friendship of all the savage and uncultivated nations, and even his conduct towards his friends and acquaintances, we must acknowledge him to have been one of the greatest men of his age, and that Reason justifies the tear which Friendship pays to his memory.[13]

The British government appropriately granted Elizabeth Cook a handsome pension. They had been married 16 years but she had been with him less than five. She had already lost three of her six children and in the end she outlived them all. In 1780, even before the *Resolution* and the *Discovery* returned to London, young Nathaniel Cook drowned at age 16 on the vessel *Thunderer* in a hurricane off the coast of Jamaica. In 1793 his brother, Hugh, died of scarlet fever in his first few months at Cambridge College. The Captain's namesake, the oldest son James, was already a commander in the Navy when he was drowned in 1794 at the Isle of Wight, near Portsmouth, on the way to join his ship. Elizabeth lived to be 93 years of age, 56 years alone after the death of her husband in Hawaii.

"She kept her faculties to the end," a friend wrote on her death, "I remember her as a handsome and venerable lady, her white hair rolled back in ancient fashion, always dressed in black satin, with an oval face, an aquiline nose, and a good mouth. She wore a ring with her husband's hair in it; and she entertained the highest respect for his memory, measuring everything by his standards of honour and morality." Overwhelmed by her love and admiration for her dead husband's memory, she never remarried. Apparently every man she met suffered in the comparison.[14]

At the end of the voyage, the crew quickly dispersed. Some of them were promptly assembled and sent off in warships for America. Gore was given Cook's now vacant position as captain of Greenwich Hospital, where he served another ten years until his death in 1790. King was also promoted to captain and sailed the following year to the West Indies. For Gore, the third voyage had taken its toll. He died from tuberculosis in 1784. Midshipmen Trevenen, Vancouver and Riou were appointed to the rank of lieutenant. There were 17 such promotions in all but for some unknown reason the uncompromising Bligh was overlooked for another year. Lieutenant Phillips, who nearly died alongside Cook in Hawaii, was later promoted to the rank of captain. When he died in 1832 he was the last surviving officer of the voyage.[15]

The two ships had similar fates. The *Resolution* was converted into an armed transport, sent to the East Indies, and disappeared. Some reports suggest she may have served as a coal transport in Rio de Janeiro. The *Discovery* was disassembled and soon became a prison ship, permanently moored in the mud of the Deptford dockyards near London. For years she housed convicts awaiting transportation to Botany Bay and Port Jackson, Australia.[16]

The published accounts of the first and second voyages had already gone into several editions so the anticipated demand for the published account of the third voyage was high. The Admiralty hired John Douglas, who had helped Cook with the second voyage account and he merged Cook's manuscript with the entries from King's journal after Hawaii. King received credit as coauthor. John Webber oversaw the engravings, selecting several dozen from his stunning portfolio of voyage drawings, but it took several London engravers four years to complete the task. Webber later published other sketches into engravings and aquatints that sustained him in his later life until his death in 1793.

Despite a discouraging delay, the official account of the third voyage finally appeared in June 1784. It was the most lavish of the three voyage accounts, three quarto volumes and a separate folio atlas of maps and the engraved drawings. The published version sold in record numbers. At a cost of £5 it was too expensive for most Britons but the first edition still sold out in three days, with disappointed buyers offering twice the retail price to get their hands on a set. Second and third editions, and even French and German editions, appeared within two years, and all sold as promptly as the first edition. Later some smaller and cheaper versions appeared, and popular magazines reprinted the maps and charts, making the voyage chronicles available to the average Englishman.[17]

Gore and King were supposed to collect all the personal journals of the officers and crew as they approached Macao. British tradition demanded that such accounts of exploration would be combined into a single voyage journal issued in the name of the captain. But several of Cook's crewmen kept and ultimately published personal memories of the voyage. The men certainly understood from the beginning the importance of their task in charting the Pacific. Their stories became only more compelling after Cook's death on the voyage, as an insatiable public sought the details of his murder in Hawaii. Ledyard, Ellis and Rickman published unauthorized versions and they were roundly chastised for doing so. Gilbert, who died a year after the voyage ended, left unpublished memoirs that his family later printed in his memory. The more lucid recollections of Clerke, King, Samwell and Anderson were not made available until many years later.

The consequences of the third expedition were evident and quickly played out in the confluence of nations that occupied the Northwest coast of America, including Alaska, as they searched for furs and scientific knowledge. Like the second voyage, the principal accomplishment was to prove a negative, that is, there were no northern passages navigable by sailing ships from the North Pacific to the Atlantic. But the voyage also offered important positive results. It proved that, despite erroneous Russian maps, Bering had accurately reported the location of the strait that separated Asia from America. Despite a summer of storms in and out of constant fog and rain, the expedition also yielded a comprehensive running survey of the landforms of Alaska and the North Pacific and, though much was yet to be learned, it offered the first chart that made sense of this farthest shoreline from the capitals of Europe. The voyagers also found the Hawaiian Islands, which quickly proved to be of considerable economic, scientific, and strategic significance to the world.

The greatest measure of any man, and particularly James Cook, may be to consider those who served in the third voyage and followed him to greatness. Gore, King and Burney later rose to the rank of Post Captain in the Royal Navy, Cook's rank, and served distinguished careers. Bligh gained his own distinction with the mixed reviews that came from his breadfruit expedition. For all his qualities as a navigator, his difficult personality led him into more than one famous mutiny and several courts martial.

John Ledyard sought greatness as well. After the Revolutionary War he moved to Paris and befriended Thomas Jefferson, then American ambassador to France. The far reach of the American continent fascinated Jefferson and the two Americans often discussed commercial ventures in the Pacific Northwest. Unknown to Jefferson, however, Ledyard decided to undertake an incredible plan to walk 4,500 miles from Paris to Kamchatka across the spine of Russia, there to enter the sea otter trade from Kamchatka. He nearly reached the Sea of Okhotsk before he was arrested and sent back the way he came. Undaunted, Ledyard decided to explore the interior of Africa. He stopped briefly in Paris to tell Jefferson of his plans, where they agreed he would return from Africa to explore the trans-Mississippi west. But before any of these impractical schemes materialized he died of a mysterious illness, suddenly and alone, in Cairo, Egypt.[18]

Several of the crew, the most notable being Dixon and Portlock, captained their own ships and returned to survey the Northwest coast and capitalize on the fur trade. Trevenen and Billings became captains in the Russian Navy, thanks mainly to their reputations as sailors with Cook, and Billings sailed with distinction in the North Pacific. The most famous of all, George Vancouver, emulated the great captain on his own voyage of distinction by conclusively charting the Northwest coast from San Diego to Cook Inlet.

-Chapter 12-

In the Wake of Cook

Cook's final voyage was of critical importance to the European exploration of the west coast of North America. He was the first captain to sail the full reach of the coast and record its principal features, setting the standard for those who followed. In the subsequent decade the coast became a virtual crossroads of empires, as most of the major European seafaring nations, as well as the fledgling American nation, sent ships to assert claims of sovereignty, pursue passions for science and ethnography, or simply to harvest furs for commercial gain.

It was the French who first followed Cook to Alaska in the single, desperate voyage of Jean François Galaup, Comte de La Pérouse. La Pérouse was an accomplished French seaman, who had risen through the ranks by defeating British warships. In 1785 he was asked by Louis XVI to mirror Cook and sail around the world, promoting science and French trade. His expedition was conducted on the finest scientific principles of the Enlightenment and fueled by the fervent desire to explore nature and the inhabitants of newfound lands. While the expedition's principal geographic discoveries were near Japan, La Pérouse was the second European to command an expedition to Hawaii and was the first to visit the fledgling Spanish colonies of Alta California.

La Pérouse came to the Gulf of Alaska from Hawaii in July 1786, eleven months after leaving France. The expedition sailed in two ships, the *Boussole* (Compass) and the *Astrolabe*. Their landfall was within sight of Mount St. Elias. Even though surrounded by whales, seals, sea otter, ducks and other marine creatures, La Pérouse was disappointed with his first view of Alaska, "The sight of land, after a long voyage, usually excites feelings of delight;" he wrote, "but on us it had not this effect. The eye wandered with pain over masses of snow, covering a barren soil, unembellished by a single tree. The mountains appeared to be a very little distance from the sea, which broke against the cliffs of a table-land ... totally destitute of greenery."[1]

The two ships coasted to the east, then entered Lituya Bay west of Mt. Fairweather. The bay is guarded by a narrow entrance and, given its considerable tides, the tidal rips nearly capsized the vessels as they passed into the estuary. La Pérouse called the tiny bay Port des Français, or Frenchman's Harbor. The ships were soon surrounded by the local inhabitants who were excited by the visit. They first took the French for the servants of *Yehlh*, their bird creator, but soon decided these were just men in gigantic canoes. The French and the local people then commenced trade, so intense that the crew was forced to post a continuous guard to avoid theft. The natives' principal interest was adzes, hatchets and iron bars, and they freely offered salmon, otter pelts and other valuable skins in return.

The expedition stayed at Lituya Bay for four weeks. While wood and water were replenished, the commander set up observatories on the central island in the bay and charted glaciers at the edge of the surrounding waters, hoping to penetrate into the interior of North America. Although La Pérouse was discouraged that they could not find an outlet, he collected a comprehensive catalog of the flora and fauna of the area. Despite being at similar latitudes, he found the Alaska climate milder than Hudson's Bay. Plant growth seemed to be very rapid during the four month summer season, he concluded, and the crew gorged themselves on berries, celery, wild peas and other local vegetables. In the forests French hunters saw bears, martens and squirrels, and the natives traded pelts of lynx, ermine and fox.[2]

The expedition left France at the height of the Enlightenment, when most educated Europeans believed in the concept of the "noble savage" unsullied by the travails of western culture. Bougainville's voyage to Tahiti, supported by the reports of Cook's first voyage there, only cemented this perception. But on the Northwest coast of America, the French could not find much to praise in the local people. They seemed gloomy, dirty, ungrateful, thieving and temperamental, and their language was shrill. They lived in large wooden sheds with fires in the center over which fish was smoked, explaining their grimy appearance. The women adorned themselves with stone labrets in their lower lips, and both men and women wore tattoos, rings, bones and other body ornaments. All of this disillusioned the French visitors.

La Pérouse wrote, "I am willing to admit that it is impossible for a society to exist without some virtues, but am forced to state that I did not have the wisdom to notice any." Yet the French acknowledged the locals were excellent traders with a keen eye for metal and had extensive skill in wood carving, building canoes and even working with iron and copper. These were the coastal Tlingit, the northernmost nation of the people of the Northwest coast, who shared many of the same customs as the Nootka observed by Cook. They lived on the beaches and islands throughout the southeastern Alaska Panhandle, tucked between the tidewater and the rugged coastal mountains, and created complicated and elaborate societies founded upon the abundant resources of the forest and the sea.

When the size of the harbor at Lituya Bay became clear to La Pérouse, he hoped his expedition had discovered the entrance to the imagined northwest passage. "Imagine a vast basin, whose depth in the centre is impossible to estimate, edged by great, steep, snow-covered mountains," he wrote, "this is the channel by which we plan to enter into the heart of America." But in following each of the two arms of the bay he soon learned, like Cook before him, that the passageway could not be found. Instead the surveyors found that huge glaciers blocked further progress from the bay.

Disaster struck the expedition as the ships prepared to leave, July 13, 1786, while their two long boats were making final soundings at the outlet. Despite written warnings given to the officers in charge about the tidal rip, the small vessels were engulfed and 21 men drowned. Even the local people observed the disaster in anguish, but there were no survivors. In profound despair, the crew erected a monument with the inscription: "Twenty one brave sailors perished at the entrance to this harbor; whosoever you may be, mingle your tears with ours."[3]

Overcome by the tragedy, La Pérouse made no further explorations in Alaska. He sailed along the northwest coast, mostly in dreary weather of fog and rain, observing Cross Sound, the Queen Charlotte Islands, then Nootka Sound. Six weeks later he entered Monterey Bay, where the Spanish had built a fort in 1778. This was the first foreign ship to visit the California colonies and they were greeted by the Spanish friars as if fellow countrymen. The French were surprised how few Spaniards lived in the colony, controlling thousands of Indians within the mission enclaves. They were also disturbed by the drudgery imposed on the Indians, wishing that the friars cared as much for their material welfare as for their salvation.[4]

In a month they sailed west, to Macao, then Japan, and finally Petropavlovsk, Kamchatka in September, 1787. The fledgling Russian colony was still the humble village Clerke visited nearly a decade earlier, composed of only a few Russian and native cabins. The French took the time to replace the plaque at Clerke's tomb, visit a nearby volcano, and attend a modest ball held in their honor. Like the British, the French decided to dispatch a member of their crew to St. Petersburg to return the journals of the voyage to France. It was a good thing. After a brief stop in January, 1788 at Botany Bay, where they came in contact with Commodore Phillip's First Fleet on its arrival in Australia, La Pérouse and his expedition were never seen again.

For more than forty years, the whereabouts of his ships remained a mystery to a curious French public. Finally the wreckage was found at Vanikoro in the Fiji Islands. Local legend was that the frigates were destroyed in a storm. As the crew fell into the water, they were attacked by sharks and then by the natives as they reached shore. Those who survived constructed a small vessel from the wreckage but never returned home. Although a few of the crewmen may have stayed behind, they died before any European again encountered that lonely shore. The reports carried home from Kamchatka by the voyage's sole survivor did not encourage French colonial enterprise on the Northwest coast.[5]

Although the Russian occupation of the North Pacific was not significant at the time of Cook's voyage, the advance of the promyshlenniks led to the establishment of the tiny community of "Three Saints Bay," the first permanent settlement in Alaska. Although local tradition disputes the story, the principal Russian factor, Grigorii Ivanovich Shelikhov claimed he wanted peace with the local people. But the Koniag people, known today as Alutiiq, massed in formidable numbers to destroy his settlement. One night they attacked; arrows reigned down upon the encampment. The Russians responded with their own firepower and the islanders retreated to a nearby rocky promontory, where Shelikhov routed them with cannon-shot and heavy arms.

Hundreds were shot or died as they fell into the ocean, and 1,000 prisoners were taken.

The colony at Three Saints Bay was thus born. It was a small village, with seven or eight dwellings. A school was constructed first and then an orthodox church. The teaching of the local children and later the adults was begun. Shelikhov decided the education and conversion of the natives would lead to peaceful and permanent colonization in his colony. But Shelikhov's primary interest was furs and he mounted expeditions into the far corners of Kodiak Island. These hunting parties soon expanded to Cook Inlet and Prince William Sound. During the second winter the colony suffered from lack of food with scurvy threatening every resident. Instead of taking advantage of their weakened condition, the Koniags rescued the colony with fresh provisions. The following summer Shelikhov returned to Kamchatka, discharging his bountiful cargo of sea otter pelts. He then began to press his case for a trading monopoly that, in time, led to the Russian American Company.[6]

Even though the Spanish missionaries were consumed by their drive to impose religion on the California Indians, the Age of Enlightenment was not lost in New Spain. Aware of Cook's departure from Europe in 1776, Viceroy Bucareli decided to intercept him as he reached America. In 1779 the viceroy sent two frigates north, commanded by Lt. Ignacio de Arteaga, with Juan Francisco Bodega y Quadra his second in command. In May, when Clerke was in Kamchatka, the Spaniards put into Bucareli Bay in southeast Alaska. After initial contacts with the natives proved friendly, a major epidemic broke out. Some of the local people died, even after a barracks for the sick was constructed on shore and used to isolate the infirm. Trade also progressed poorly, so the natives grew restless. Hostages were taken, then hostilities broke out. Finally the ship cannons were fired to stop advancing war canoes, killing many natives, and the Spanish quickly departed.

In July the frigates advanced to Prince William Sound, taking formal possession at Port Etches, the northernmost point ever claimed by the Spanish. A storm drove them along the Kenai Peninsula until they reached Afognak Island. Heavy rains, seven deaths and many grave cases of scurvy convinced the Spanish to give up the search for Cook. Despite his presence in these waters, neither fleet was aware of the other, and the Spanish returned confident that Cook had not reached the coast and that the Russians were confined to the Aleutians.[7]

Official accounts of the Cook and La Pérouse expeditions challenged scientists in Europe while giving critical acclaim to their governments. To prove it was a world power, the Spanish created their own academic institutions and, despite hundreds of years of secrecy, sought to publicize their findings on the coast. A Royal Expedition was sent to New Spain in 1785, and a second, more expansive expedition was initiated by Alejandro Malaspina. His two corvettes, the *Descubierta* (Discovery) and the *Atrevida* (Daring or Audacious), were well outfitted for coastal examinations, and botanists, cartographers, astronomers and artists were gathered to record events.

They arrived at Port Mulgrave, or Yakutat Bay, in late June, 1791. Malaspina had hoped to find the elusive Northwest Passage in the bay but his ships were stopped by glaciers, one of which was later named for him. He named the inlet "Bahia del Desengano" (Disenchantment Bay). Hundreds of Tlingit Indians arrived in wooden canoes for trade, offering fishing implements, domestic articles, and apparel for old clothing, nails, buttons, and other prizes. But as time passed, the natives concentrated on iron goods and those not proffered by the Spanish were soon pilfered. Still the Spanish persevered in the name of science, gathering native weapons, articles of dress, manufactured items and other artifacts for display in Madrid. They even attempted to learn the local language. Like the French before them, the Spanish were overwhelmed by the filthy appearance of the Tlingit and their clever trading strategies.

Leaving Yakutat Bay, Malaspina's expedition first turned west, searching in vain for the imagined passage of Lorenzo Ferrer Maldonado, whose sixteenth century report claimed the discovery of a water route between Hudson Bay and the Pacific. They searched near the region of Prince William Sound. Like Cook before him Malaspina was doubtful, and soon resolved that Maldonado's accounts were fictitious and there was no passageway. He later reflected in his journal that modern readers would be surprised by the seriousness early European explorers gave to these imagined straits and waterways "in an age which we call scientific and enlightened."[8]

The expedition turned south, passing Bucareli Bay, then entering Nootka Sound, the site of a short-lived Spanish colony. Here the Spanish learned the language and customs of the Nootka people, comparing their culture favorably to the Tlingit in Alaska. After a few weeks, the Spanish sailed in constant fog to California, noting but not entering the Strait of Juan de Fuca and the Columbia River. Reaching Monterey, Malaspina visited several missions, writing a generous, if not simplistic report of California Indian life with the Franciscans. From California, the corvettes returned to Mexico, and eventually to the Philippines and Spain.

Upon his return, Malaspina was embroiled in political intrigue. He joined those who sought to bring about Spain's resurgence as a world power, criticizing the inattention to its New World colonies. But his liaison with the Queen, discovered by the ruthless Manuel Godoy, abruptly ended his rise to power. Tried and convicted of treason for the indiscretion, Malaspina was imprisoned, then banished, and the manuscripts of the expedition languished. The scientific momentum in Spain during the Enlightenment thus came to an abrupt end.[9]

The Russian government also mounted expeditions to their newfound colonies, although it is unclear whether they were for the lofty objectives of the Enlightenment, or to assure the proper collection of tribute. The most notable effort was by an Englishman, Joseph Billings, whose voyage was stimulated by La Pérouse's departure from France. Although authorized in 1785, it required an overland march from the Baltic and construction of new ships on the Siberian coast. So the expedition did not sail until May 1790, but in four weeks it reached Unalaska and in two more weeks it was at Three Saints Bay. The Billings expedition made a careful record of the native people and their customs, as well as Russian commerce. Billings later wrote that over 600 kayaks were in the waters surrounding Kodiak Island at the time, hunting sea otters, sea lions and fur seals.

In mid-July Billings was anchored at Montague Island. The natives were peaceful, and engaged in a lively trade for furs, although some were embittered about earlier Russian visits. Gavriil Sarychev went out with a boat's crew and in two days found Kayak Island. While reconnoitering there, he spoke with an old native man, who remembered Steller's visit when he was a boy. The expedition returned to Kamchatka but, like Bering fifty years before, adverse winds blunted the advance and, before regaining Kamchatka in October, scurvy was rampant.[10]

In 1784, when the official publication of Cook's last voyage was finally released, merchants and traders from a host of nations were inspired to launch expeditions to the West Coast in search of sea otter furs. The greatest stir came within the offices of Richard Cadmon Etches, who thrived in the center of the London's historic financial and trading center. In May 1785 he gathered several London traders to form the King George's Sound Company (King George's Sound being Cook's name for Nootka Sound) to collect furs on the northwest coast of America. Joseph Banks, who was elected president of the Royal Society in 1778, continued to advocate Cook's discoveries in further exploration of the coast and joined Etches to hasten both commercial and scientific investigations.

They hired Nathaniel Portlock and George Dixon, both of whom had sailed in Cook's last voyage. The two captains left in companion trading vessels the same month that La Pérouse left France. Portlock, who was master's mate aboard the *Discovery*, was given command of the 320-ton *King George*, larger than Cook's consort on the third voyage. Dixon, a mere armorer on the *Discovery*, commanded the smaller *Queen Charlotte*. Later captains James Hanna and James Strange were dispatched from China in separate trading expeditions for the East India Company. Sailing for the same company, John Meares was sent to the North Pacific from Bombay.

In all, seven English trading expeditions arrived on the coast in 1786 in the race for furs. But there was significant competition from the Russians, who had the advantage of using the indigenous populace in vast, sweeping hunting expeditions that often wiped out whole populations of otters. Hanna was the first and most successful. Dixon and Portlock found little fur in two summers in Alaska and had the good sense to spend the winter in Hawaii.[11] But Meares, unaware of the severity of Alaskan winters, unwisely decided to remain in a cove in Port Fidalgo in Prince William Sound. He built a cabin on shore, anticipating an idyllic winter in the woods, but by early spring the dark, deep snow, and cold prevented the captain and his crew from hunting game or even leaving the ship.

By spring the lack of fresh provisions took its toll in scurvy and decimated his men. In all twenty-four died, nearly half the crew. His desperate condition the next spring made it clear that the traders needed a more temperate port on the coast, distant from the Russian settlements in Alaska.

Like other merchants in the sea otter trade, Meares, Portlock and Dixon were primarily concerned with commerce so exploration and charting were secondary. However, each captain published his own voyage journal and at least Portlock and Dixon were credible, as they included many landmarks of southeast Alaska on their charts that Cook bypassed in the stormy weather encountered in the spring of 1778. Meares journal is not only tainted by his misguided decision to spend a winter in Alaska, but also offers an improbable map of the North Pacific that boldly depicts a waterway from Hudson Bay to the west coast of North America. In his map a great river flows westward from the Great Slave Lake with three imagined outlets into Prince William Sound and both the Knik and Turnagain Arms of Cook Inlet. Not finished with such fanciful inland connections, halfway between the lake and the outlets Meares inserted in the legend: "Falls said to be the Largest in the Known World."[12]

The traders and captains soon learned that the Russians had already depleted much of the Alaska fur population and, after Meares' experience, found Alaska's climate too cold and harsh for most Europeans. So the merchant fleet centered its activities at Nootka Sound. The local chieftain, Maquinna, became the gatekeeper of the trade as his small tribe acquired the treasures of Europe in exchange for sea otter furs. Captain Hanna was the first to enter the harbor in 1785; soon others came. Although most of the trading vessels were British, before long American, Spanish, Portuguese, and even Swedish vessels stopped at Nootka. Unlike the others, the irrepressible Meares decided to establish a colony in the tiny bay, without the slightest support of his government. Indeed, Meares was uncertain of his allegiances, as he often disguised his vessels by flying the Portuguese flag.[13]

The first Americans in the fur trade were John Kendrick and Robert Gray in the ships *Columbia* and *Lady Washington*; they reached Nootka Sound in 1788. During the summer of 1788 Gray went as far north as Bucareli Bay, Alaska, while Kendrick stayed in Nootka Sound. Their two ships wintered in Nootka Sound until late 1789, when they returned to Boston via China with a considerable number of sea otter furs. Gray was the first to circumnavigate the world flying the Stars and Stripes. [14]

The Spanish launched an expedition in 1788 to determine the extent of the English fur trade, and to learn the reach of the Russians on the coast. Estéban José Martínez, who was pilot to Perez in 1775, had for the past decade steered supply ships between Mexico and Alta California. In command of two ships, in eight weeks he reached Prince William Sound. But relations with his officers broke down, as the intoxicated Martínez ordered the logging of false courses. The consort, under López de Haro, then abandoned Martínez and continued to the west, sighting the Russian outpost at Three Saints Bay on southwestern Kodiak Island and landing at Unalaska. He mapped seven Russian outposts reporting 460 inhabitants en route.[15]

Meanwhile Martínez sailed separately to the west, reaching Unalaska, where the Russian manager there told him of a growing British merchant fleet in the China-Nootka trade. These reports alarmed the new viceroy, Conde Revillagigedo, who sought to protect Spain's claims to the coast against British, and even Russian designs. So in early 1789 Martínez was instructed by Revillagigedo to sail for Nootka to establish permanent fortifications.

When Martínez arrived, he found that Meares had already erected at least one building to help in the construction of a small ship, but Meares was gone and the building seemed abandoned.

So the Spaniard and his crew constructed Fort San Miguel and other permanent habitations to take formal possession of the harbor. Like the Russians to the north the Spanish reasoned that their best claim to sovereignty over the region was to establish occasional fortifications along the coast and establish peaceful relations with the local people. This was the strategy already employed with the missions and presidios of Alta California and now Martínez was asked to implement it at Nootka Sound. The Spanish assumed this would confirm their claims to the Northwest coast to Bucareli Bay.[16]

James Colnett, captain of the *Argonaut* and a partner of Meares, entered the bay in June, a month after Martínez. He brought Chinese workmen to help him build a settlement to serve as a base for shipbuilding. Colnett was outraged that the Spanish were building a fort and confronted Martínez. He insisted that the port belonged to Britain by virtue of the discoveries of Captain Cook. However, Martínez had been at Nootka with Perez four years earlier than Cook, so he was certain of Spain's prior claim. Maquinna was the ultimate arbiter, confirming Perez' earlier voyage. Still, Colnett refused to present his papers to recognize Spanish authority to the port, which incensed the Spaniard. Tensions flared between the impetuous and unstable Europeans, probably the result of a night of heavy drinking in Martínez' cabin.

Ultimately the Spaniard arrested Colnett and his ship. A week later, another British trading vessel that entered the port was detained. The local residents, especially Maquinna, were stunned that Europeans could act in such an erratic way. In the midst of the debate, Martínez shot a local chief who publicly heckled the Spaniard for his rogue conduct, thereby infuriating the local tribes. The only innocents were the Americans, John Kendrick and Robert Gray, who watched the growing fracas from their two ships with growing concern. To their credit, they never took sides and, after collecting a paltry number of furs, abandoned Nootka to continue the fur trade elsewhere. Martínez later wrote that he should have seized the American vessels as well but his orders were limited to confronting British traders. Martínez also had a personal interest. He had consigned 137 sea otter skins to Kendrick for resale in China.

Claims and counter claims continued to erupt from both sides through the summer, fodder for newspapers and soap operas. A Spanish supply ship arrived in the fall and, rather than resupplying the Spanish fortifications, it came with an order from the viceroy to abandon the fort. The viceroy had reversed himself, uncertain of the crown's ability to support colonies so far from Mexico. Martínez was confused and enraged. He had arrested the English and built the fort to assert Spanish claims to the Northwest coast and now Revillagigedo abandoned the plan before it could be put in place. Frustrated, he finally relented, dismantled the fort, and returned to Mexico. Uncertain about Colnett's status, he hauled the two captains and their ships back to Mexico.[17]

The crisis in Nootka now broke on the international scene. The British were enraged by the insult. Etches, who stood to gain a great deal if Nootka was available to his trading ships, goaded the English Prime Minister, William Pitt, into a propaganda campaign over the Spanish seizure. John Meares was so agitated by the arrest he came to London to plead his case. At Pitt's request, Meares submitted an account of the Nootka "incident" to the British cabinet, which then disseminated it to the public. Since Meares was not actually present at Nootka, and had no first hand evidence, his claims were vastly overstated. But the publication was intended by Pitt to embolden the British public. It was very effective.

Sensing a weakening Spanish position in world affairs, Pitt threatened war. Although the Spanish may have had a prior right to Nootka, those claims were empty, as they kept their many expeditions secret. So they agreed to a truce. In the Nootka Convention of 1790, each country abandoned its claim to Nootka, with reparations paid to Colnett. Further, the two countries agreed to restore the structure and land that Meares possessed at the port and Etches was assured free access to the port and the furs along the vast unoccupied stretch of coast north of California.[18]

Unaware of the diplomatic agreements being made in Europe, in 1790 Revillagigedo and Bodega determined to refortify Nootka, so they sent all their ships and senior captains to the north. They had tired of Martínez, who had falsified records and arrested the English ships with little justification, so Martínez returned to Nootka only as a supernumerary. On the way, one of the captains surveyed the Strait of Juan de Fuca. Another, Salvador Fidalgo, was ordered north into Alaskan waters to give further credence to Spanish claims to the region. Fidalgo not only carried out useful surveys of Prince William Sound and Cook Inlet but also took possession of several Alaska landmarks for the Spanish crown. When he took possession in Prince William Sound, he named his bay "Cordova" and the narrow inlet to the north "Valdez" to honor members of the Spanish cabinet. Fidalgo's names are still in use for the two largest communities in Prince William Sound— Cordova and Valdez. [19]

While the Admiralty was already planning an expedition to follow Cook, the Nootka Convention gave added impetus, since supervision was required to restore Meares' possessions. George Vancouver was chosen to command the expedition because of his experience on Cook's last voyage to the northwest coast. In fact Vancouver had been with Cook on the second voyage as well, where Vancouver claimed he had been nearer the South Pole than any other man. When Cook decided that they could go no farther than 71°10' south latitude, Vancouver bragged he climbed out on the bowsprit to reach the southernmost point of any of the crew aboard.[20]

Now on his own voyage, Vancouver sailed in a vessel named after Cook's consort, the *Discovery*. The ship was accompanied by the armed tender *Chatham*, commanded after the first year by Lieutenant Peter Puget. The two ships carried 145 men, 40 fewer than on Cook's final voyage. Under his instructions, Vancouver was to assist at Nootka, then undertake a detailed survey from California to Cook's River in Alaska. The theoretical geographers were still at work, particularly as a result of Meares' claims about Cook's River. The Admiralty wanted to put all the theories to rest. So Vancouver was given the most capable surveyors, astronomers, and mapmakers of the day, with instructions to survey every inlet on the coast. This formidable task was intended to take two summers on the Northwest coast, but ultimately required a third season.[21]

The ships sailed April 1, 1791, around the Cape of Good Hope to Australia, New Zealand, Tahiti and finally Hawaii, which they reached in eleven months. During the first survey season, landfall in North America came in April, 1792, north of San Francisco Bay. Following the coastline to the north, the English saw the mouth of the flooded Columbia River. The volume of water in spring runoff kept them from approaching the river, so they continued north into the Strait of Juan de Fuca. There they met the Boston trader *Columbia*, commanded by Robert Gray, now on the coast in his second voyage. Gray had spent several days in the strait, but now had turned south. He waited for the floodwaters of the Columbia River to subside and made the first entry into the Columbia River on May 11, 1792. The vast river was named by Gray after his ship.[22]

When Vancouver reached the end of the strait the coastline led to Port Townsend and the inner reaches of the series of islands and channels that make up today's Puget Sound. His crew went to work in the shore boats conducting the first of forty-six coastal surveys, some of them lasting weeks at a time. The surveys were usually commanded by the masters of the two vessels, Joseph Whidbey of the *Discovery* and James Johnstone of the *Chatham*. They were not "running" surveys, like those performed by Cook as the master mariner coasted in and out of storms away from the shore. Instead, Vancouver's men rowed their shore boats along every waterway, landing frequently to establish their positions by triangulation, until each coastal feature was surveyed and added on to the expedition's master maps. In this way the expedition's meticulous survey settled all doubts about the principal bays and inlets on the ragged Northwest Coast. [23]

As Puget was in command, his name was bestowed upon the first inlet surveyed, Puget Sound, now the shoreline of modern-day Seattle. In less than a month Vancouver found and named Whidbey and Vashon islands, Mt. Rainier, Mt. Olympus, Mt. Baker, Hood Canal, Port Orchard, Port Discovery, Possession Sound, Restoration Point, Deception Pass, Bellingham Bay, and Admiralty Inlet, names for some of the most prominent landmarks along the coast of modern-day Washington state. These were just the first of over three hundred names, most of which continue in use today, that Vancouver gave to the mountains, headlands, waterways, and islands along the coast. As a part of this remarkable journey, Vancouver took formal possession of the region on June 4 at Tulalip Bay, near the modern-day city of Everett, in Washington state. The expansive area he claimed for England encompassed the stretch of coastline and the internal bays and inlets from Oregon to southern Canada, a land he called "New Georgia" after the British monarch, George III. By mid-June Vancouver's expedition had passed the San Juan Islands and explored what is now downtown Vancouver, Canada. He named the Gulf of Georgia, which divides the modern-day British Columbia mainland from Vancouver Island. In a week the English made another contact with a foreign fleet, finding two Spanish schooners, the *Sutil* and the *Mexicana*, commanded by Dionisio Alcalá Galiano and Cayetano Valdés. Looking for a site to replace their Nootka fortifications, the Spaniards missed Puget Sound. Cordial relations were established and the four ships moved through the narrows that separate Vancouver Island from the mainland, surveying the coastline. Ultimately the Spaniards turned back, leaving Vancouver with the distinction of being the first to circumnavigate the island that bears his name. He then sailed to Nootka Sound to supervise the restoration of Meares' meager possessions and to rendezvous with his store ship *Daedalus*.[24]

In 1792 Nootka had expanded to a small colony of 200 Spaniards with as many as fifty homes, some with gardens, with an even larger compliment of local native people nearby, led by Chief Maquinna. It also served as an international gathering place, where in the few summer months five Spanish, eleven English, two Portuguese, one French, and eight American vessels anchored.[25] In this scene Vancouver met with Captain Bodega y Quadra, who as the senior naval officer in Mexico represented Revillagigedo, as well as Maquinna. Negotiations were so amicable that out of mutual respect the two captains named the island "Quadra and Vancouver Island." But neither captain was given adequate instructions to negotiate restitution of British property in the cove, nor discretion to find a common ground, so the negotiations finally ended without agreement, and Vancouver left Nootka for California.

While Vancouver sailed ahead, his consort entered the mouth of the Columbia River, struggling past dangerous breakers and a sand bar. Gray had accomplished the task in May, reaching 20 miles upriver. Now the *Chatham* anchored, and its shore boats went 100 miles upriver to the location of modern-day Vancouver, Washington. Meanwhile, in November Captain Vancouver was warmly received upon entering San Francisco Bay, the first foreign ship to visit the mission and presidio there. After ten days, he sailed south to Monterey, where he was shocked by the deplorable conditions of the missions and the treatment afforded the Indians. Even more, he was amazed by the undermanned presidio garrisons and speculated they might be easily conquered.[26]

In January he sailed to Hawaii, where the crew spent two months refitting the vessels, while the captain advised King Kamehameha of the benefits of combining the warring tribes into a single nation, then ceding the islands to Great Britain for their protection. In early March 1793, the expedition spent a week at Kealakekua Bay, receiving a tumultuous welcome that rivaled the first visit by Cook. Nonetheless, the English were wary of the surly attitude of some in the crowd, so posted a continuous guard. The fickle and uncertain attitude of the local people was reminiscent of the fatal Cook encounter that had occurred here fourteen years earlier.

Vancouver returned with some trepidation to the place where Cook was murdered in 1779 and even met with the Hawaiian who was said to have thrust the fatal dagger into the captain. Although the Hawaiian was sorry about Cook's death, the native expressed no remorse. Vancouver wrote that he visited, "...first of all the fatal spot, where Captain

Cook so unexpectedly, and so unfortunately for the world, was deprived of his valuable life. This melancholy, and ever to be deplored event, the natives are at much pains exactly to represent, to produce reasons for its taking place, and the shew that it fulfilled the prophecies of the priests, who had foretold this sad catastrophe."[27]

In April the expedition returned for a second season on the Northwest coast with surveys commencing along Vancouver Island and proceeding into Southeast Alaska. Vancouver was in charge of a survey party on Revillagigedo Island in southern Alaska when Tlingit Indians surrounded them. He attempted to fend them off with trinkets and then shouts, but finally he gave orders to fire. As many as ten Indians were killed and the others broke off the attack. This was the only bloodshed in the expedition's three years charting the Northwest coast. Vancouver soon left the area, returning to San Francisco and Monterey. He then sailed south to Santa Barbara, Ventura and San Diego, the first foreign expedition to modern-day Southern California.

In late December he reached Hawaii again. In two months he achieved the Hawaiian cession, confirmed by the islands' king and his ruling council. It is unknown why Great Britain failed to follow up on this important feat, never recognizing the annexation of Hawaii. The British certainly took advantage of Vancouver's similar claims to the ownership of Western Canada.[28]

From Hawaii, in February 1794 Vancouver sailed to the far north to begin his third and final survey season, reaching Cook Inlet in winter. After completing the survey that disproved the Northwest Passage, Vancouver met with Russian traders at the mouth of the Kenai River. He wanted to meet their manager, Alexander Baranov. Having no interpreter, after several days Vancouver gave up hope of any meeting and the expedition abandoned Cook Inlet.

Passing Port Dick at its outlet on the Kenai Peninsula, the English observed a fleet of over 400 sea otter hunters. After sailing past Resurrection Bay, the expedition entered Prince William Sound. Local fur hunters reported there were just 466 Russians in all of Alaska at the time, dispersed in three forts at Kenai, Port Etches (Prince William Sound) and in Bristol Bay. The hunters also seemed well acquainted with the geography of the region, explaining the proximity of the Sound to Turnagain River, and that the Kenai Peninsula was almost an island, but for a short portage. "The two extensive inlets appeared," according to Vancouver, "to be separated from each other by a narrow isthmus of mountainous land." Later the English learned that the local people regularly portaged their canoes over the isthmus. Vancouver surveyed the area in considerable detail, giving names for the principal landmarks, all of which survive to this day. The area features the popular receding glacier, Portage Glacier, and the adjacent Portage Pass, east of Anchorage. It is just a few miles from Passage Canal, so-named by Vancouver, and the small community of Whittier, in the western extremity of Prince William Sound.

The expedition sailed for Mt. St. Elias, where in late June they entered Yakutat Bay. Here they found a massive Russian hunting party of over 900 Kodiak Islanders hunting sea otters in kayaks. Vancouver was surprised at the overwhelming size of this expedition, certain that it would anger the local Tlingits and wreak havoc with the sea otter populations. Later the expedition entered Icy Strait, where Whidbey began a survey eastward from the entrance to Cross Sound. At first the survey was hampered by ice calving from the glacier that extended to the entrance of Glacier Bay. Today this strait is ice-free. In two centuries the glacier has retreated an astounding sixty miles into smaller tideland glaciers occupying the separate fjords and inlets of the bay.

After examining Lynn Canal, leading north from modern-day Juneau to Skagway, Whidbey proceeded down Chatham Strait between Baranof and Admiralty Islands. Finally, by late August Vancouver and his crewmen completed the three-year coastal survey at Port Conclusion, on the inner coast of Baranof Island. In his penultimate journal entry at Port Conclusion, Vancouver spoke of the finality of his work. Despite Meares' fanciful map, no passage through the continent was found:

> I trust the precision with which the survey of the coast of North West America has been carried into effect, will remove every doubt, and set aside every opinion of a north-west passage, or any water communication navigable for shipping, existing between the North Pacific, and the interior of the American continent, within the limits of our researches. The discovery that no such communication does exist has been zealously pursued, and with a degree of minuteness far exceeding the letter of my commission or instructions.[29]

Unlike Cook, Vancouver and his crew found the local people to be an ever-present distraction, but they did little to investigate or report native languages, habits or cultures. The sailors encountered the full range of people who lived on the coast, Salish, Kwakiutl, Haida, Tlingit, Alutiiq and Dena'ina, but little is known of the encounters except, on rare occasions, when the meetings turned hostile. Instead these contacts were regarded as just one element of risk in the daily grind of coastal surveying and, now that the examination was complete, the people of the coast were left in peace.[30]

The expedition proceeded south, anchoring in Nootka Sound, then Monterey, California, before returning to England the following September. At four years, six months, the expedition was the longest in the annals of British exploration, covering an estimated 65,000 miles. By comparison, Cook's second expedition covered 55,000 miles and the third voyage lasted four years and three months. Despite minor outbreaks of scurvy and a few skirmishes with natives, Vancouver and the sailors who accompanied him suffered just six fatalities, one-third the normal mortality rate in all of England at the time.[31]

Vancouver devoted the last two years of his life to the preparation of his journal, but died before its publication, a month before his 41st birthday. The consequences of his voyage were unmatched. He helped implement the Nootka Convention, or at least asserted claims of British sovereignty to the area, and concluded a meticulous survey of the Northwest coast, dashing Spanish claims to sovereignty over the region. More important, the accuracy and completeness of Vancouver's survey were critical to future commerce and coastal navigation in the region. William Dall, an Alaskan explorer, stated in 1870 that Vancouver's explorations "have not been excelled by any other navigator," and he found in the 1880s that Vancouver's charts were still the most trusted authority on Alaskan waters. Indeed, these charts were still the official maps of the coast well over a century after their initial publication.[32]

When Vancouver left North America in 1794 he concluded an intense period of exploration on the Northwest coast that had lasted twenty years. While fur-trading expeditions continued for several more decades, and many vessels followed Vancouver's, they usually had only commercial objectives. It was mostly the Russian Navy that continued the spirit of scientific observation in expeditions that circumnavigated the globe and gave further certainty to the outlines of the Alaska coastline in the Bering Sea.

In the spirit of the European Enlightenment, Captain James Cook initiated the campaign of discovery in his peripatetic survey of coastal Alaska in 1778. His map was sketchy and incomplete, often showing only general trends of the coast. Ships from a host of nations then followed and each in their own way considered the geography, ethnography and commercial opportunities of this farthest temperate shore from Europe, the so-called "backside" of America. But none of them attempted a complete survey, so only a part of the coastline was revealed. It was only after Cook's midshipman, the determined and tireless George Vancouver, completed three seasons of painstaking travail that the coastal outlines were conclusively resolved.

~Appendix 1~

Third Voyage Chronology

1768-1771	First Voyage to Tahiti, New Zealand and Australia
1772-1775	Second Voyage to South Pacific, circling the Antarctic Continent
February 10, 1776	Captain Cook receives Third Voyage commission from the British Admiralty
July 12, 1776	The *Resolution* sails from England; the *Discovery* sails August 1
January 26, 1777	Arrival at Adventure Bay, Tasmania
February 12, 1777	Arrival at Queen Charlotte Sound, New Zealand
March 29, 1777	Arrival at the Cook Islands
April 28, 1777	Arrival at Nomuka, Tonga (the "Friendly Islands")
August 23, 1777	Arrival at Matavai Bay, Tahiti (the "Society Islands")
November 2, 1777	Depart Huahine after returning Omai to his homeland
January 18, 1778	Arrival at Hawaiian Islands
March 7, 1778	Landfall at Cape Foulweather, Oregon Coast
March 29, 1778	Arrival at Nootka Sound, Vancouver Island, British Columbia
May 1, 1778	Observe Mt. Edgecumbe, Alaska
May 12, 1778	Enter Prince William Sound
May 25, 1778	Enter Cook Inlet
June 1, 1778	King performs ceremony of possession at Pt. Possession, Cook Inlet

July 1, 1778	First visit to English Bay, Unalaska
July 16, 1778	Leave Bristol Bay waters at Cape Newenham
August 10, 1778	Arrive at St. Lawrence Bay, Kamchatka
August 18, 1778	Furthest north in pack ice, 70°44'
September 2, 1778	Expedition passes Cape Dezhnev (East Cape), Siberia, sailing south
September 8, 1778	Arrival at Norton Sound, Alaska
October 2, 1778	Second visit to English Bay, Unalaska
November 26, 1778	Observe Island of Maui, Hawaii
January 17, 1779	Arrival at Kealakekua Bay, Hawaii
February 11, 1779	Return to Kealakekua Bay
February 14, 1779	Death of Captain Cook at Kealakekua Bay
March 16, 1779	Depart Island of Kauai
April 24, 1779	Arrival at Harbor of St. Peter and St. Paul, Avacha Bay, Kamchatka
June 16, 1779	Depart Avacha Bay to sail north to the Arctic
July 19, 1779	Furthest north in pack ice, 70°33'
August 22, 1779	Death of Captain Clerke in sight of Avacha Bay
August 24, 1779	Second visit to Harbor of St. Peter and St. Paul, Avacha Bay, Kamchatka
October 10, 1779	Depart Avacha Bay
October 26, 1779	Observe Honshu Island, along Japanese coastline
December 4, 1779	Arrive at Macao and Canton River, China
April 11, 1780	Arrive at Cape of Good Hope, South Africa
August 21, 1780	Diverted by weather to Stromness,

| | Orkney Islands, Scotland |
| October 7, 1780 | Return to Royal Dockyards at Deptford, England |

—Appendices 2—

Names

Place Names on the Northwest Coast
Resulting from Cook's Third Voyage

Oregon and Washington:

Cape Foulweather (Expedition landfall in Oregon)
Cape Perpetua
Cape Gregory (now Gregory Point)
Cape Flattery (northwestern coastal point of
Washington state)

British Columbia:

Woody Point (now Cape Cook)
Resolution Cove (within Nootka Sound)
Bligh Island (within Nootka Sound)

Alaska:

Near Sitka:	**Mt. Edgecumbe** (after George Edgecumbe, commander of the Plymouth dockyard and later British admiral)
	Cape Edgecumbe
Gulf of Alaska:	**Mt. Fairweather**
	Cape Fairweather
	Cross Sound (observed on the day of the Holy Cross)
	Kaye's (Kayak) Island (Richard Kaye was Cook's personal friend from Yorkshire, an English reverend who was chaplain

to King George III)

Cape Suckling (after Captain Maurice Suckling, uncle of Lord Nelson and Comptroller of the British Navy)

Controller Bay

Prince William Sound:

Prince William Sound (Cook named it "Sandwich Sound;" it was renamed by the Admiralty after the king's third son)

Cape Hinchinbrook

Snug Corner Cove

Bligh Island (a second island with the same name on the Northwest coast after the self-important *Resolution* master who was later destined for fame and mutiny on the *Bounty*)

Montague Island (Montagu was Lord Sandwich's family name)

Green Island

Cook Inlet:

Cook Inlet (named "Cook's River" by the Admiralty, then "Cook Inlet" by Vancouver in 1794)

Turnagain Arm (named "Turnagain River" by Cook)

Point Possession (where Lt. King took formal possession of the upper Cook Inlet area, burying some bottles with a scroll)

Anchor Point

Cape Bede (north of Cape Elizabeth on Kenai Peninsula—observed on St. Bede's day, May 27)

Mt. St. Augustine (observed on St. Augustine's Day, May 26, 1778)

Barren Islands
Cape Elizabeth (Kenai Peninsula, on eastern side of entrance to Cook Inlet—observed on the day of Princess Elizabeth's birthday on May 21, 1778)
Cape Douglas (Alaska Peninsula, on western side of entrance to Cook Inlet—named after Canon Douglas of Windsor, editor of Cook's second voyage journal)
Point Banks (Northeastern Shuyak Island—named after the esteemed Joseph Banks, President of the Royal Society, who accompanied Cook on the first voyage)

Kodiak Island: **Cape Barnabas** (Cook called it "Cape St. Barnabas")
Twoheaded Island (Cook named it "Twoheaded Point")
Trinity Islands

Southwestern
Alaska: **Foggy Cape**
English Bay, Unalaska (named by the Russians after Cook's expedition)
Bristol Bay (named after Cook's friend, Augustus John Hervey, third Earl of Bristol)
Round Island
Cape Newenham (named after Sir Edward Newenham, an Irish friend of Cook)

St. Matthew Island:	**Cape Upright**
	Pinnacle Island
Seward Peninsula:	**Cape Rodney**
	Sledge Island
	King Island (named after Lt. King, who sailed on the *Resolution*)
	Cape Prince of Wales (named after the King's son)
	Cape Darby (named after Vice-Admiral George Darby)
Chukchi Sea:	**Mulgrave Hills** (named after a mutual friend of Cook and Banks, Constantine John Phipps, second Lord Mulgrave)
	Icy Cape
	Cape Lisburne
Norton Sound:	**Norton Sound** (named after Sir Fletcher Norton, Speaker of the House of Commons)
	Norton Bay
	Besboro Island (named after William Ponsonby, Second Earl of Bessborough, a member of the Irish and English Parliaments)
	Cape Denbigh (named after Basil Fielding, the sixth Earl of Denbigh, another friend of Banks)
	Stuart Island (named after James A. Stuart, a fellow member of the Royal Society)
	Cape Stephens (named after Sir Philip Stephens, Secretary of the Admiralty)

~Footnotes~

Given the nature of this book as a travel journal of Captain Cook and his crew while they sailed in the waters of Alaska and the North Pacific, footnotes have been minimized. However, references are provided when necessary to support significant pieces of information. Hopefully the subject matter of this publication will be compelling enough to some readers that they will wish to pursue it further.

While there are countless books written about Captain Cook and the other explorers of the North Pacific, the suggested biography and these footnotes should provide adequate resources for further study.

Chapter 1
New Albion

1 J. C. Beaglehole, The Voyage of the Resolution and Discovery, Cambridge University Press, 1967 (hereafter Beaglehole, Voyage Journal), Part I, p. 384. This is the edited version of the voyage journal, written by Captain Cook until just before his death in early 1779. J. C. Beaglehole, The Life of Captain James Cook, Stanford University Press, 1974 (hereafter Beaglehole, Life of Cook), p. 610. Beaglehole, Life of Cook, is the accepted bibliographical reference work on Cook.

2 Beaglehole, *Voyage Journal*, Part I, pp. 388-89.

3 Christine Holmes, ed., *Captain Cook's Final Voyage, the Journal of Midshipman George Gilbert*, University Press of Hawaii, 1982 (hereafter Holmes, *Gilbert Journal*), p. 83.

4 John Ledyard, *A Journal of Captain Cook's Last Voyage ... in the Years 1776, 1777, 1778, and 1779*, Hartford, 1783

(hereafter Ledyard, *Journal*), pp. 83-84.

5 William Ellis, *An Authentic Narrative of a Voyage ... in Search of the Northwest Passage*, 1782 (hereafter Ellis, *Journal*), Vol. I, pp. 278-79.

6 Beaglehole, *Voyage Journal*, Part I, p. 389, n. 1.

7 Beaglehole, *Life of Cook*, the prize offered by Parliament is discussed at pp. 477-78; the Admiralty instructions are found at pp. 490-91.

8 Beaglehole, *Voyage Journal*, Part I, pp. ccxx-ccxxiv.

9 Beaglehole, *Voyage Journal*, Part II, pp. 1087-88.

10 Beaglehole, *Voyage Journal*, Part I, pp. 289, 292.

11 Beaglehole, *Voyage Journal*, Part I, p. 292, n. 4.

12 Beaglehole, *Voyage Journal*, Part I, p. 292, n. 3.

13 Ellis, *Journal*, Vol. I, p. 183.

14 Ledyard, *Journal*, p. 69.

15 Francis Fletcher, *The World Encompassed by Sir Francis Drake*, Nicholas Bourne, 1628, p. 42.

16 Bernal Díaz, *The Conquest of New Spain*, 1568, J. M. Cohen, ed. Díaz was with Cortés during the siege and capture of Mexico City. See also Henry R. Wagner, *Spanish Voyages to the Northwest*, California Historical Society, 1929 (hereafter Wagner, *Spanish Voyages*), pp. 1-11, 94-96.

17 Juan Páez, *Cabrillo's Log, 1542-43*, The Western Explorer, 1968. See also Warren L. Cook, *Flood Tide of Empire, Spain and the Pacific Northwest 1543-1819*, Yale University Press, 1973 (hereafter Cook, *Flood Tide of Empire*), pp. 4, 25.

18 An excellent, recent report on the voyage is found in Laurence Bergreen, *Over the Edge of the World, Magellan's Terrifying Circumnavigation of the Globe*, William Morrow, 2003.

19 Cook, *Flood Tide of Empire*, pp. 5-37. Wagner, *Spanish Voyages*, pp. 129-31.

[20] John Sugden, *Sir Francis Drake*, Henry Holt and Company, 1990, pp. 132-38. Samuel Bawlf, *The Secret Voyage of Francis Drake*, Penguin Books, 2003, pp. 267-326. Bawlf places the northern reach of Drake's voyage in southern Alaska, and the anchorage of New Albion in British Columbia. *See also* Norman J. W. Thrower, *Sir Francis Drake and the Famous Voyage, 1577-80*, University of California Press, 1984. The linkage between Drake's voyage and the instructions given to Cook are discussed at pp. 164-65.

[21] A good discussion of Drake's California anchorage is found in Derek Wilson, *The World Encompassed, Drake's Great Voyage, 1577-1580*, Harper and Row, 1977, pp. 151-65. See also Alexander McKee, *The Queen's Corsair, Drake's Journey of Circumnavigation, 1577-80*, Stein and Day, 1978, pp. 265-74. The debate over the exact location of the anchorage is discussed in the seminal Drake work, Henry R. Wagner, *Sir Francis Drake's Voyage Around the World, Its Aims and Achievements*, John Howell Books, 1926, pp. 154-69, and in the lively and entertaining investigatory work, Warren L. Hanna, *Lost Harbor, The Controversy over Drake's California Anchorage*, University of California Press, 1979. After weighing all the evidence, the author decides in a close call the anchorage was within Drake's Estero, at Drake's Bay, Point Reyes National Seashore, California. Bawlf's conclusions surfaced over twenty years later.

[22] Wagner, *Spanish Voyages*, pp. 168-272. Cook, *Flood Tide of Empire*, pp. 10-27.

[23] Beaglehole, *Voyage Journal*, Part I, p. 289, n. 2.

[24] Beaglehole, *Voyage Journal*, Part I, p. 293. Beaglehole, *Life of Cook*, p. 582.

[25] Beaglehole, *Voyage Journal*, Part I, pp. 293-4.

Chapter 2
Master Mariner

[1] Beaglehole, *Life of Cook,* pp. 1-98. There have been many biographies of Cook. Please refer to the Bibliography. The first was published less than a decade after his death, written by Andrew Kippis, *The Life of Captain James Cook,* London, 1788. The Kippis biography is as collectable as the published accounts of the voyage. See also Richard Hough, *Captain James Cook, A Biography,* Hodder & Stoughton, 1994 (hereafter Hough, *Cook Biography*), pp. 1-44. Lynne Withey, *Voyages of Discovery, Captain Cook and the Exploration of the Pacific,* University of California Press, 1987 (hereafter Withey, *Voyages of Discovery*), pp. 75-90.

[2] Beaglehole, *Life of Cook,* pp. 100-44.

[3] Beaglehole, *Life of Cook,* pp. 163-68. See also Hough, *Cook Biography,* pp. 45-95. Withey, *Voyages of Discovery,* pp. 93-125.

[4] Beaglehole, *Life of Cook,* pp. 145, 155, 178 and 231. The artists both died during the voyage, Buchan at Tahiti and Parkinson in Batavia. See also Hough, *Cook Biography,* pp. 96-112.

[5] J. C. Beaglehole, *The Voyage of the Endeavour,* Cambridge University Press, 1955 (hereafter Beaglehole, *Endeavour Journal*), pp. cxliv-cxlv.

[6] Beaglehole, *Life of Cook,* pp. 196-236. Beaglehole, *Endeavour Journal,* pp. cxlix, clv. See also Hough, *Cook Biography,* pp. 113-41. Withey, *Voyages of Discovery,* pp. 126-68.

[7] Beaglehole, *Life of Cook,* pp. 236-52. Beaglehole, *Endeavour Journal,* p. clvii. See also Hough, *Cook Biography,* pp. 142-56.

[8] Beaglehole, *Life of Cook,* pp. 257-72. See also Hough, *Cook Biography,* pp. 157-84.

[9] Beaglehole, *Life of Cook,* pp. 273-305. See especially p. 276.

[10] Hough, *Cook Biography,* pp. 185-90.

[11] Beaglehole, *Life of Cook,* pp. 306-356. The discussion of Furneaux's brush with death in New Zealand and purported Maori cannibalism is p. 446. See also Hough, *Cook Biography,* pp. 222-33. Withey, *Voyages of Discovery,* pp. 199-235

[12] Beaglehole, *Life of Cook,* pp. 447-49. Withey, *Voyages of Discovery,* pp. 301-19.

[13] Beaglehole, *Life of Cook,* pp. 380-441. See also Hough, *Cook Biography,* pp. 234-56. Withey, *Voyages of Discovery,* pp. 236-73.

[14] Beaglehole, *Life of Cook,* pp. 442-71.

[15] Beaglehole, *Voyage Journal,* Part I, pp. xxix-lxviii. Glyndwr Williams, *Voyages of Delusion, The Search for the Northwest Passage in the Age of Reason,* Harper Collins, 2002 (hereafter Williams, *Voyages of Delusion*), pp. 239-86.

[16] The "dinner for four" that convinced Cook to lead the third voyage is discussed in Richard Hough, *The Last Voyage of Captain James Cook,* William Morrow and Company, 1979 (hereafter Hough, *Last Voyage*), pp. 9-17.

[17] Beaglehole, *Life of Cook,* pp. 472-512. Preparation of the *Resolution* in Deptford Yard was substandard, even disgraceful, nothing like what was necessary for a multi-year voyage in remote parts of the globe. Beaglehole, *Voyage Journal,* Part I, pp. lxviii-lxxi. The complement of officers is discussed at Beaglehole, *Voyage Journal,* Part I, pp. lxxi-xc. The ships' companies are listed in Beaglehole, *Voyage Journal,* Part II, pp. 1457-80.

[18] Beaglehole, *Life of Cook,* pp. 523-70. The departure of Omai in Tahiti is discussed at pp. 549-62. Hough, *Cook Biography,* pp. 302-15. Withey, *Voyages of Discovery,* pp. 342-58. See also Daniel Conner and Lorraine Miller,

Master Mariner: James Cook and the Peoples of the Pacific, Douglas & McIntyre, 1978 (hereafter Conner and Miller, *Master Mariner*), pp. 35-48; 66-79.

[19] Beaglehole, *Voyage Journal,* Part I, pp. cii-cvii. Hough, *Last Voyage,* pp. 90-95. Withey, *Voyages of Discovery,* pp. 323-41. Williams, *Voyages of Delusion,* p. 307.

[20] This occurred on May 20, 1777. Beaglehole, *Voyage Journal,* Part I, pp. ciii-iv. Plotting against Cook continued in Raiatea. Beaglehole, *Voyage Journal,* Part I, pp. cxiii. Conner and Miller, *Master Mariner,* pp. 49-65.

[21] Beaglehole, *Voyage Journal,* Part I, pp. cxvii-cxx.

[22] Beaglehole, *Life of Cook,* pp. 571-80. See also Beaglehole, *Voyage Journal,* Part I, pp. cxix and 279-82. Conner and Miller, *Master Mariner,* pp. 81-89. Withey, *Voyages of Discovery,* pp. 359-64.

[23] Beaglehole, *Voyage Journal,* Part I, pp. 289-90.

Chapter 3
Nootka Sound

[1] Beaglehole, *Voyage Journal,* Part I, pp. 295-96.

[2] Beaglehole, *Voyage Journal,* Part II, p. 1394.

[3] Beaglehole, *Voyage Journal,* Part I, pp. 297-98.

[4] Beaglehole, *Life of Cook,* p. 590.

[5] Beaglehole, *Voyage Journal,* Part I, p. 295. Beaglehole, *Life of Cook,* pp. 583-84.

[6] George Dixon, *A Voyage Round the World: But More Particularly to the North-West Coast of America,* George Goulding, 1789. Dixon was in the area of the Queen Charlotte Islands in July and August 1787, see pp. 210-34. Nathaniel Portlock, *A Voyage Round the World; But More Particularly to the North-West Coast of America: Performed in 1785, 1786, 1787, and 1788,* John Stockdale, 1789. Chapters X to XII cover the voyage on the Northwest Coast, see pp. 201-96.

7   George Vancouver, *A Voyage of Discovery to the North Pacific Ocean and round the World, 1791-95*, W. Kaye Lamb, Ed., four volumes, Hakluyt Society, 1984 (hereafter Lamb, *Vancouver's Voyage*). *See especially* Volume II, the chapter on Nootka Sound, pp. 658-87.

8   Beaglehole, *Voyage Journal*, Part I, pp. 298-99.

9   John Rickman, *Journal of Captain Cook's Last Voyage to the Pacific Ocean*, E. Newberry 1781 (hereafter Rickman, *Journal*), p. 239.

10 See generally the appendix, *Sense of the Sailing Ship*, in Alan Villiers, *Captain James Cook*, Charles Scribner's Sons, 1967, pp. 287-98.

11 A. P. McGowan, *Captain Cook's Ships*, in David Cordingly, ed., *Capt. James Cook, Navigator*, National Maritime Museum, 1988, p. 55. Roger Morris, *Pacific Sail, Four Centuries of Western Ships in the Pacific*, International Marine Publishing Company, 1987. Cook's ships are discussed at pp. 104-09. See also John Kendrick, *the Evolution of Shipbuilding in the Eighteenth Century*, in Stephen Haycox, James Barnett and Caedmon Liburd, eds., *Enlightenment and Exploration in the North Pacific 1741-1805*, University of Washington Press, 1997, pp. 88-102.

12 See generally, Andrew S. Cook, *James Cook and the Royal Society*, in Glyndwr Williams, ed., *Captain Cook, Explorations and Reassessments*, Boydell Press, 2004, pp. 37-55.

13 Alan Stimson, *Captain Cook and the New Navigation*, in David Cordingly, ed., *Capt. James Cook, Navigator*, National Maritime Museum, 1988, pp. 73-79. David Waters, *Navigational Problems in Captain Cook's Day*, in Antoinette Shalkop, ed., *Exploration in Alaska, Captain Cook Commemorative Lectures*, Cook Inlet Historical Society, 1980, pp. 41-56. See also Alun C. Davies, *Testing a New Technology: Captain George*

Vancouver's Survey and Navigation in Alaskan Waters, 1794, in Stephen Haycox, James Barnett and Caedmon Liburd, eds., *Enlightenment and Exploration in the North Pacific 1741-1805,* University of Washington Press, 1997, pp. 103-115.

14 Holmes, *Gilbert Journal,* p. 67. Much has been written about Cook's ministrations of fresh provisions to his crew to prevent scurvy, including the "blunderbuss approach," that is, he tried everything in hopes that something would work. Sir James Watt, *Medical Aspects and Consequences of Cook's Voyages,* in Robin Fisher & Hugh Johnson, eds., *Captain James Cook and his Times,* University of Washington Press, 1979, pp. 129-57. Wayne W. Myers, *Cook the Physician,* in Antoinette Shalkop, ed., *Exploration in Alaska, Captain Cook Commemorative Lectures,* Cook Inlet Historical Society, 1980, pp. 59-66. See also Beaglehole, *Voyage Journal,* Part II, pp. 1455-56 and 1489, entry for February 29, 1776. Vancouver's later voyage was even more remarkable in this respect. John M. Naish, *The Health of Mariners: Vancouver's Achievement,* in Stephen Haycox, James Barnett and Caedmon Liburd, eds., *Enlightenment and Exploration in the North Pacific 1741-1805,* University of Washington Press, 1997, pp. 79-87.

15 Beaglehole, *Voyage Journal,* Part II, pp. 1095, 1100. Beaglehole, *Life of Cook,* pp. 584-85.

16 Ledyard, *Journal,* p. 70.

17 Beaglehole, *Voyage Journal,* Part I, pp. ccxxii-ccxxiii.

18 Beaglehole, *Voyage Journal,* Part II, pp. 1329-33.

19 Rüdiger Joppien and Bernard Smith, *The Art of Captain Cook's Voyages, Volume Three, the Voyage of the Resolution and Discovery, 1776-1780,* Oxford University Press, 1987 (hereafter Joppien and Smith, *The Art of Captain Cook's Voyages*), pp. 171-203. See also John Frazier Henry,

Early Maritime Artists of the Pacific Northwest Coast, 1741-1841, Univ. of Washington Press, 1984, pp. 74-79.

20 Joppien and Smith, *The Art of Captain Cook's Voyages*, pp. 204-213. Ellis work was heavily influenced by Webber, who was the more accomplished artist. Ellis may have copied some of Webber's work, especially at Nootka Sound. See Joppien and Smith, *The Art of Captain Cook's Voyages*, pp. 214-15. See also John Frazier Henry, *Early Maritime Artists of the Pacific Northwest Coast, 1741-1841*, Univ. of Washington Press, 1984, pp. 67-70.

Chapter 4
People of the Coast

1 Robin Fisher, *Cook and the Nootka*, in Robin Fisher & Hugh Johnson, eds., *Captain James Cook and his Times*, University of Washington Press, 1979 (hereafter Fisher, *Cook and the Nootka*), pp. 81-98. Williams, *Voyages of Delusion*, pp. 309-11.

2 Beaglehole, *Voyage Journal*, Part I, pp. 311-30. Beaglehole, *Life of Cook*, pp. 583-90.

3 Beaglehole, *Voyage Journal*, Part II, pp. 1394-95.

4 Beaglehole, *Voyage Journal*, Part II, pp. 1323-24.

5 Ledyard, *Journal*, pp. 71-7.

6 Fisher, *Cook and the Nootka*, pp. 86-87. J. C. H. King, *The Nootka of Vancouver Island*, in Hugh Cobbe, ed., *Cook's Voyages and the Peoples of the Pacific*, British Museum, 1979 (hereafter, King, *Nootka of Vancouver Island*), pp. 89-108.

7 Beaglehole, *Voyage Journal*, Part I, p. 319.

8 Beaglehole, *Voyage Journal*, Part I, pp. 302-03. See also Fisher, *Cook and the Nootka*, pp. 92-93. Beaglehole, *Life of Cook*, pp. 583-84.

9 Beaglehole, *Voyage Journal*, Part I, p. 299. See also Fisher, *Cook and the Nootka*, pp. 90-91.

10 Samwell's report is at Beaglehole, *Voyage Journal*, Part II, pp. 1092-94. Ellis can be found at Ellis, *Journal*, Vol. I, pp. 197-99. The Gilbert quotations are Holmes, *Gilbert Journal*, pp. 69-71.

11 C. E. Chapman, *The Founding of Spanish California*, Macmillan, 1916, pp. 96-101. See also H. E. Bolton, *Fray Juan Crespi, Missionary Explorer of the Pacific Coast, 1769-1774*, University of California Press, 1927. Crespi was with Portolá, then with Pérez at Nootka in 1774.

12 Herbert K. Beals, trans., *Juan Pérez on the Northwest Coast*, Oregon Historical Society, pp. 33, 75-117. The Spanish crew observed an old bayonet and pieces of other iron implements in the hands of the Natives at Nootka. Because Pérez was the first European in these waters since Chirikov, the Spanish assumed these implements were from Chirikov's lost boats (pp. 111, 247, n. 17). See also Christon I. Archer, *The Spanish Reaction to Cook's Third Voyage*, in Robin Fisher & Hugh Johnson, eds., *Captain James Cook and his Times,* University of Washington Press, 1979, pp. 99-119. Williams, *Voyages of Delusion*, pp. 295-97.

13 Cook, *Flood Tide of Empire*, pp. 69-84. Though the Spanish denied it, Captain Nathaniel Portlock was convinced this voyage caused the smallpox epidemic. See p. 80, n. 69, describing Portlock's claim ten years later.

14 Henry R. Wagner, *The Cartography of the Northwest Coast of America to the Year 1800*, University of California Press, 1937 (hereafter Wagner, *The Cartography of the Northwest Coast*), Volume I, p. 184.

15 Cook, *Flood Tide of Empire*, pp. 93-98. Wagner, *The Cartography of the Northwest Coast*, Volume I, p. 191-96.

16 Beaglehole, *Voyage Journal*, Part I, pp. 303-05, 311. See Samwell's comments, Beaglehole, *Voyage Journal*, Part

II, pp. 1099-1100. See also Fisher, *Cook and the Nootka*, pp. 94-96.

17 Beaglehole, *Voyage Journal*, Part I, p. 303, n. 2. Beaglehole, *Life of Cook*, p. 588.

18 Beaglehole, *Voyage Journal*, Part II, pp. 1396, 1404-14.

19 Rickman, *Journal*, pp241-42, 246.

20 Beaglehole, *Voyage Journal*, Part I, p. 307. Beaglehole, *Life of Cook*, pp. 589-90.

21 J. C. H. King, *First Peoples, First Contacts, Native Peoples of North America*, Harvard University Press, 1999, pp. 122-75, where the author discusses the Mowachaht and their interplay with Captain Cook, including the quoted passage at pp. 123-24, as well as contacts between Natives and Europeans along the coast. The record of artifacts and drawings is remarkable and well displayed. See also Daniel Clayton, *Captain Cook's command of knowledge and space: chronicles from Nootka Sound*, in Glyndwr Williams, ed., *Captain Cook, Explorations and Reassessments*, Boydell Press, 2004, pp. 110-33. This article offers an enlightened view from the perspective of the Native observers of Cook, including new perspectives on European and Native views of "first contact" exploration encounters. See also King, *Nootka of Vancouver Island*, pp. 89-108.

22 Cook, *Flood Tide of Empire*, pp. 432-33. King, *Nootka of Vancouver Island*, p. 108.

Chapter 5
Southern Alaska

1 Beaglehole, *Voyage Journal*, Part I, p. 333.

2 Beaglehole, *Voyage Journal*, Part I, p. 333, n. 1.

3 Ledyard, *Journal*, pp. 77-78.

4 Beaglehole, *Voyage Journal*, Part I, p. 334.

5 Holmes, *Gilbert Journal*, p. 75.

6   Beaglehole, *Voyage Journal,* Part I, p. 335.

7   Beaglehole, *Voyage Journal,* Part I, p. 336.

8   Beaglehole, *Voyage Journal,* Part I, p. 336, n. 5.

9   Williams, *Voyages of Delusion,* p. 313.

10 Beaglehole, *Voyage Journal,* Part I, p. 338.

11 Evgenii G. Kushnarev, *Bering's Search for the Strait: The First Kamchatka Expedition, 1725-1730,* ed. E. A. P. Crownhart-Vaughn, Oregon Historical Society, 1990. Bering's apprehensions that ended that brief, fifty-one day expedition at sea are described on pp. 101-12.

12 F. A. Golder, *Bering's Voyages* (two volumes), American Geographical Society, 1922. The journal of the *St. Paul* is in Chapter 7 of Volume I. On July 27 Chirikov decided to retreat without the men left on shore, as he only had forty-five casks of water remaining. Consult the Note on the loss of Chirikov's men, p. 311, where tidal rips are offered as the likely explanation for the loss of the two vessels and their crew. See also Glynn Barratt, *The Afterlife of Chirikov's Lost Men,* in ed. O. W. Frost, *Bering and Chirikov, The American Voyages and Their Impact,* Alaska Historical Society, 1992 (hereafter Frost, *Bering and Chirikov*), pp. 265-66.

13 Georg W. Steller, *Journal of a Voyage with Bering, 1741-42,* ed. O. W. Frost, Margritt A. Engel and O. W. Frost, translators, Stanford University Press, 1988 (hereafter Steller, *Journal*), p. 61.   See also Golder, *Bering's Voyages,* Volume II, p. 34.

14 Steller, *Journal,* pp. 65-72.   See also Sven Waxell, *The American Expedition,* Hodge and Company, 1952 (hereafter Waxell, *American Expedition*), p. 106.

15 Waxell, *American Expedition,* p. 108. Golder, *Bering's Voyages,* Volume I, p. 140. Steller, *Journal,* p. 94. See also Robert Fortuine, *The St. Peter's Deadly Voyage Home: Steller, Scurvy and Survival,* in Frost, *Bering and Chirikov,* pp. 204-28. This excellent article provides the

medical setting for Steller's attributes as a physician and his ministrations in the spread of scurvy with the crew.

16 Waxell, *American Expedition*, p. 135. Golder, *Bering's Voyages*, Volume I, p. 230. Steller, *Journal*, pp. 134-41.

17 Waxell, *American Expedition*, p. 136-58. Golder, *Bering's Voyages*, Volume I, p. 231-61. Steller, *Journal*, pp. 142-69.

18 Glynn Barratt, *Russia in Pacific Waters, 1715-1825*, University of British Columbia Press, 1981, pp. 42-66.

19 Cook and King introduce the Müller and Stählin maps in the voyage journal at Beaglehole, *Voyage Journal*, Part I, p. 338, n. 5, and p. 342, n. 9. They soon came to lament the maps for their inaccuracy, especially the Stählin version, beginning on p. 414. See also Beaglehole, *Voyage Journal*, Part I, pp. cxxiv-cxxvi and Beaglehole, *Life of Cook*, p. 593. An analysis of the maps and how they came to be so inaccurate, can be found in Glyndwr Williams, *Alaska Revealed, Cook's Explorations in 1778*, in Antoinette Shalkop, ed., *Exploration in Alaska, Captain Cook Commemorative Lectures*, Cook Inlet Historical Society, 1980, pp. 69-87. Glyndwr Williams, *Myth and Reality: James Cook and the Theoretical Geography of Northwest America*, in Robin Fisher & Hugh Johnson, eds., *Captain James Cook and his Times*, University of Washington Press, 1979, pp. 58-80, and Carol Urness, *Russian Mapping of the North Pacific to 1792*, in Stephen Haycox, James Barnett and Caedmon Liburd, eds., *Enlightenment and Exploration in the North Pacific 1741-1805*, University of Washington Press, 1997, pp. 132-46.

20 Beaglehole, *Voyage Journal*, Part I, p. 358.

21 Beaglehole, *Voyage Journal*, Part I, p. 342, n. 9.

22 Beaglehole, *Voyage Journal*, Part I, p. 338, n. 3.

23 Beaglehole, *Voyage Journal*, Part I, pp. 341-42.

[24] Beaglehole, *Voyage Journal,* Part I, pp. 342-43. Beaglehole, *Life of Cook,* pp. 594-95.

[25] Holmes, *Gilbert Journal,* p. 76.

[26] Holmes, *Gilbert Journal,* p. 77.

[27] Beaglehole, *Voyage Journal,* Part I, pp. 346-47. Beaglehole, *Life of Cook,* pp. 596-97. Samwell's report on the encounter with the people of Prince William Sound is Beaglehole, *Voyage Journal,* Part II, pp. 1106-14. Ledyard, *Journal,* p. 80.

[28] Beaglehole, *Voyage Journal,* Part II, pp. 1414-21. Williams, *Voyages of Delusion,* pp. 313-15.

[29] Ellis, *Journal,* Vol. I, p. 237.

[30] Ellis, *Journal,* Vol. I, pp. 240-41.

[31] Beaglehole, *Voyage Journal,* Part I, p. 349.

[32] Rickman, *Journal,* p. 248-49.

[33] William W. Fitzhugh, *Eskimos: Hunters of the Frozen Coasts,* Lydia Black, *The Story of Russian America,* and Aron Crowell, *Prehistory of Alaska's Pacific Coast,* in William W. Fitzhugh and Aron Crowell, eds., *Crossroads of Continents, Cultures of Siberia and Alaska,* Smithsonian Institution, 1988, pp. 42-51, 70-82, 130-41.

[34] Shelikhov's personal account of the conquest of Alaska at Kodiak, and the Russian occupation of Prince William Sound, which he called Chugatsk Bay, is found in Basil Dmytryshyn, E. A. P. Crownhart-Vaughan, and Thomas Vaughan, *Russian Penetration of the North Pacific Ocean, 1700-1797: A Documentary Record,* Oregon Historical Society, 1988 (hereafter Dmytryshyn and Vaughan, *Russian Penetration*), pp. 296-320. See also P. A. Tikhmenev, *A History of the Russian-American Company,* R. A. Pierce and A. S. Donnelley, eds., University of Washington Press, 1978 (hereafter Tikhmenev, *Russian-American Company*), pp. 416-34.

35 Beaglehole, *Voyage Journal*, Part I, pp. 352-4, n. 1 and n. 4.
36 Williams, *Voyages of Delusion*, pp. 316-17.
37 Ellis, *Journal*, Vol. I, p. 246.
38 Beaglehole, *Voyage Journal*, Part I, p. 356 n. 2. Beaglehole, *Life of Cook*, pp. 597-98.

Chapter 6
Turnagain River

1 Beaglehole, *Voyage Journal*, Part I, pp. 356-60. Beaglehole, *Life of Cook*, pp. 598-99.
2 Beaglehole, *Voyage Journal*, Part I, p. 359, n.1. Beaglehole, *Life of Cook*, p. 599.
3 Beaglehole, *Voyage Journal*, Part I, p. 359, n.1. Beaglehole, *Life of Cook*, p. 599.
4 Ellis, *Journal*, Vol. I, p. 253.
5 Beaglehole, *Voyage Journal*, Part I, pp. 360-61.
6 Beaglehole, *Voyage Journal*, Part I, p. 363, n.1. Williams, *Voyages of Delusion*, pp. 317-18.
7 Beaglehole, *Voyage Journal*, Part I, pp. 364-65.
8 Beaglehole, *Voyage Journal*, Part I, p. 366.
9 Beaglehole, *Voyage Journal*, Part I, p. 367.
10 Williams, *Voyages of Delusion*, pp. 318-19.
11 Holmes, *Gilbert Journal*, p. 81.
12 Beaglehole, *Voyage Journal*, Part II, p. 1421.
13 Cook Inlet Historic Sites Project 1975:59, interview with Feodoria Pennington Kallander of Point Possession, Alaska.
14 Russian penetration of Cook Inlet is discussed in Shelikhov's personal account of the conquest of the inlet, which he called Kamysh Inlet, in Dmytryshyn and Vaughan, *Russian Penetration*, pp. 296-320. See also Tikhmenev, *Russian-American Company*, pp. 415-16.
15 Beaglehole, *Voyage Journal*, Part I, p. 371.
16 Beaglehole, *Voyage Journal*, Part II, pp. 1111-12.

[17] Ledyard, *Journal*, pp. 81-82.

[18] William Workman, *Human Colonization of the Cook Inlet Basin Before 3000 Years Ago,* in Nancy Yaw Davis and William E. Davis, eds., *Adventures Through Time: Readings in the Anthropology of Cook Inlet, Alaska,* Cook Inlet Historical Society, 1996. Lydia Black, *The Story of Russian America,* and Aron Crowell, *Prehistory of Alaska's Pacific Coast,* in William W. Fitzhugh and Aron Crowell, eds., *Crossroads of Continents, Cultures of Siberia and Alaska,* Smithsonian Institution, 1988, pp. 70-82, 130-41.

[19] Dmytryshyn and Vaughan, *Russian Penetration,* pp. 296-320, 385. Tikhmenev, *Russian-American Company,* pp. 45-46.

[20] Beaglehole, *Voyage Journal,* Part I, p. 368.

[21] Beaglehole, *Voyage Journal,* Part I, p. 368, n. 2. Beaglehole, *Life of Cook,* pp. 604-05.

[22] Beaglehole, *Life of Cook,* p. 604. Ellis, *Journal,* Vol. I, p. 249.

[23] Lamb, *Vancouver's Voyage,* Volume IV, p. 1243. Weather conditions in Cook Inlet were reported by Archibald Menzies, the botanist on the voyage, in Wallace M. Olson, ed., *The Alaska Travel Journal of Archibald Menzies, 1793-94,* University of Alaska Press, 1993, p. 91.

[24] Beaglehole, *Voyage Journal,* Part II, p. 1424.

Chapter 7
The Arctic Sea

[1] Beaglehole, *Voyage Journal,* Part I, pp. 374-77.

[2] Beaglehole, *Voyage Journal,* Part I, p. 379, n. 1.

[3] Lamb, *Vancouver's Voyage,* Volume III, p. 1209.

[4] Beaglehole, *Voyage Journal,* Part I, p. 383, n. 4.

[5] Beaglehole, *Voyage Journal,* Part I, p. 384, n. 1.

6   Beaglehole, *Voyage Journal*, Part I, p. 384, n. 1.

7   Tikhmenev, *Russian-American Company*, pp. 9-15.

8   Beaglehole, *Voyage Journal*, Part I, p. 386.

9   Beaglehole, *Voyage Journal*, Part I, p. 389. Beaglehole, *Life of Cook*, pp. 608-11.

10 Beaglehole, *Voyage Journal*, Part I, p. 390, n. 3 and n. 5.

11 King's description of the first visit is especially descriptive. Beaglehole, *Voyage Journal*, Part II, pp. 1424-28.

12 Beaglehole, *Voyage Journal*, Part I, pp. 397, 400.

13 Beaglehole, *Voyage Journal*, Part I, pp. 402-03.

14 Beaglehole, *Voyage Journal*, Part I, p. 403, n. 1.

15 Beaglehole, *Life of Cook*, p. 614.

16 Beaglehole, *Voyage Journal*, Part I, p. 409.

17 Raymond H. Fisher, *The Voyage of Semen Dezhnev in 1648: Bering's Precursor*, Hakluyt Society, 1981, pp. 197-239.

18 Beaglehole, *Voyage Journal*, Part I, pp. 410-11.

19 Beaglehole, *Voyage Journal*, Part II, pp. 1132-33.

20 Beaglehole, *Voyage Journal*, Part I, p. 412. Beaglehole, *Life of Cook*, pp. 618-24.

21 S. A. Arutiunov, *Even: Reindeer Herders of Eastern Siberia*, and *Chukchi: Warriors and Traders of Chukotka*, in William W. Fitzhugh and Aron Crowell, eds., *Crossroads of Continents, Cultures of Siberia and Alaska*, Smithsonian Institution, 1988, pp. 35-42.

22 Beaglehole, *Voyage Journal*, Part I, p. 416. Williams, *Voyages of Delusion*, pp. 322-24.

23 Rickman, *Journal*, pp. 275-76..

24 Beaglehole, *Voyage Journal*, Part I, p. 418.

25 Williams, *Voyages of Delusion*, pp. 408-09.

26 Beaglehole, *Voyage Journal*, Part I, pp. cxxxiii-cxxxv. Beaglehole, *Life of Cook*, pp. 616-17.

27 Beaglehole, *Voyage Journal*, Part I, pp. 419-20.

28 Holmes, *Gilbert Journal*, pp. 90-92.

29 Beaglehole, *Voyage Journal,* Part I, pp. 419-20, n. 3.
30 Beaglehole, *Voyage Journal,* Part I, p. 420.
31 Ledyard, *Journal,* pp. 87-88.
32 Beaglehole, *Voyage Journal,* Part I, p. 427.

Chapter 8
English Bay Unalaska

1 Beaglehole, *Voyage Journal,* Part I, p. 430.
2 Beaglehole, *Voyage Journal,* Part I, p. 439.
3 Beaglehole, *Voyage Journal,* Part I, p. 439. See also King's extensive notes on the visit to Norton Sound, Beaglehole, *Voyage Journal,* Part II, pp. 1431-41.
4 Beaglehole, *Voyage Journal,* Part I, pp. 441-42. Beaglehole, *Life of Cook,* pp. 626-27.
5 Beaglehole, *Voyage Journal,* Part II, p. 1565.
6 Beaglehole, *Voyage Journal,* Part I, p. 444, n. 2. For further discussion of Bligh's outrage over the map-making, see Beaglehole, *Voyage Journal,* Part I, pp. cxxxvi-cxxxvii. See also Beaglehole, *Life of Cook,* pp. 628-29.
7 Beaglehole, *Voyage Journal,* Part I, p. 446, n. 3.
8 Beaglehole, *Voyage Journal,* Part I, p. 448.
9 V. N. Berkh, *A Chronological History of the Discovery of the Aleutian Islands,* R. A. Pierce, ed., Limestone Press, 1974, pp. 2, 98-105.
10 Ledyard, *Journal,* pp. 91-100.
11 Beaglehole, *Voyage Journal,* Part II, p. 1449. King's complete notes on the second visit to Unalaska are found at pp. 1441-55.
12 Williams, *Voyages of Delusion,* pp. 325-32.
13 Beaglehole, *Voyage Journal,* Part I, p. 458. Beaglehole, *Life of Cook,* p. 630.
14 Beaglehole, *Voyage Journal,* Part II, p. 1142.
15 Beaglehole, *Voyage Journal,* Part II, p. 1442.
16 Beaglehole, *Voyage Journal,* Part II, p. 1355.

17 Beaglehole, *Voyage Journal*, Part II, pp. 1335-36.
18 Beaglehole, *Voyage Journal*, Part I, pp. cxxxix-cxl. Beaglehole, *Life of Cook*, p. 635.
19 See James R. Gibson, *Otter Skins, Boston Ships and China Goods*, University of Washington Press, 1992, pp. 12-18
20 Lydia T. Black and R. G. Liapunova, *Aleut: Islanders of the North Pacific*, Lydia Black, *The Story of Russian America*, and Aron Crowell, *Prehistory of Alaska's Pacific Coast*, in William W. Fitzhugh and Aron Crowell, eds., *Crossroads of Continents, Cultures of Siberia and Alaska*, Smithsonian Institution, 1988, pp. 52-57, 70-82, 130-41.
21 Beaglehole, *Voyage Journal*, Part I, p. 468.
22 Cook's thorough description of the Aleuts of Unalaska is found at Beaglehole, *Voyage Journal*, Part I, pp. 459-468.
23 Holmes, *Gilbert Journal*, p. 97. Beaglehole, *Voyage Journal*, Part I, p. 470.

Chapter 9
Hawaii

1 Beaglehole, *Voyage Journal*, Part I, pp. 473-74.
2 Holmes, *Gilbert Journal*, p. 99.
3 Beaglehole, *Voyage Journal*, Part I, pp. 475-79 and cxli.
4 Holmes, *Gilbert Journal*, p. 100.
5 Beaglehole, *Voyage Journal*, Part I, pp. 490-91.
6 Beaglehole wrote, *Voyage Journal*, Part I, pp. cxli, "no place in the eighteenth century Pacific has been more fully described for us than this bay, the northern half of which stands for so much in the history of exploration." Beaglehole, *Life of Cook*, pp. 648-51. Cook's description of the reception on the Big Island is located at Beaglehole, *Voyage Journal*, Part I, pp. 490-91. Samwell's entry for this is found at Beaglehole, *Voyage Journal*, Part II, pp. 1158-59. King's journal continues with

exceptional descriptions of the landscape and people, but as of November 26, 1778, it is the official supplement to Cook's journal as the approved, published voyage record. King's description of the lavish greeting is found at Beaglehole, *Voyage Journal,* Part I, pp. 502-04. The Gilbert quote is found at Holmes, *Gilbert Journal,* p. 101. See also Hough, *Cook Biography,* pp. 330-64. Conner and Miller, *Master Mariner,* pp. 125-141. Withey, *Voyages of Discovery,* pp. 376-98.

7 Beaglehole, *Voyage Journal,* Part I, pp. 504-09 and cxliii.

8 Ellis, *Journal,* Vol. II, p. 85. Beaglehole, *Voyage Journal,* Part II, pp. 1158-59.

9 Beaglehole, *Voyage Journal,* Part II, p. 1159.

10 Ledyard, *Journal,* the journey into the hills is at pp. 117-23, the quotation can be found at p. 120.

11 Beaglehole, *Voyage Journal,* Part I, p. 520.

12 Beaglehole, *Voyage Journal,* Part I, p. 527.

13 King was in the Observatories, on the south side of the bay, so his view of the incident was from shore. Beaglehole, *Voyage Journal,* Part I, pp. 528-31. Samwell was aboard the *Discovery,* so observed the incident close at hand. It turns out that Edgar and Vancouver gave chase to the thief to avoid bloodshed, as the culprit could have easily been killed as he jumped into his small craft alongside. Samwell's description of the events of February 13, 1779, is found at Beaglehole, *Voyage Journal,* Part II, pp. 1191-94.

14 Ellis, *Journal,* Vol. II, p. 105.

15 Ledyard, *Journal,* p. 143.

16 The death of Cook has been described by many onlookers, and repeated by biographers, all carefully examining the facts and implications, looking for a rationale for the loss. Beaglehole's accounts are at Beaglehole, *Voyage Journal,* Part I, pp. cxlvii-clvii and Beaglehole,

Life of Cook, pp. 662-72. Clerke's account carefully reconstructed events from the English perspective, almost as a court of inquiry, and can be found at Beaglehole, *Voyage Journal,* Part I, pp. 531-39. King was with Cook on the *Resolution* when events unraveled that morning. His version is at Beaglehole, *Voyage Journal,* Part I, pp. 549-61.

[17] Beaglehole, *Voyage Journal,* Part II, p. 1198. Samwell's account of the death of Cook is found at Beaglehole, *Voyage Journal,* Part II, pp. 1194-1207.

[18] The myths and reality of the death of Cook and whether the Hawaiians really looked upon him as a reincarnated god, as well as British and Hawaiian versions of the death, have been discussed in a lively debate found in Marshall Sahlin, *How "Natives" Think, About Captain Cook, For Example,* University of Chicago Press, 1995 and Gananath Obeyesekere, *The Apotheosis of Captain Cook, European Mythmaking in the Pacific,* Princeton University Press, 1992 (new preface in 1997). See also Pauline Nawahineokala'i King, *Some Thoughts on Native Hawaiian attitudes towards Captain Cook,* in Glyndwr Williams, ed., *Captain Cook, Explorations and Reassessments,* Boydell Press, 2004, pp. 94-109. See especially p. 103, discussing the Sahlin- Obeyesekere controversy on whether the Hawaiians accepted Cook as a god. A full examination of the people of Hawaii Island, their ancient history, contact with Cook and crew, and the later conquest of the island chain by Kamehameha in the decades after Cook's death, can be found in Ross Cordy, *Exalted Sits the Chief, the Ancient History of the Hawai'i Island,* Mutual Publishing, 2000.

[19] Rickman, *Journal,* p 320.

[20] Holmes, *Gilbert Journal,* p. 107-08.

[21] It was February 22, 1779. Beaglehole, *Voyage Journal,* Part I, p. 548.

22 Beaglehole, *Voyage Journal*, Part I, p. 568, n. 1.
23 Beaglehole, *Voyage Journal*, Part I, p. 575.
24 Beaglehole, *Voyage Journal*, Part II, pp. 1222-23. Beaglehole, *Life of Cook*, pp. 676-79.
25 Beaglehole, *Voyage Journal*, Part I, pp. 612-13.

Chapter 10
The Return North

1   Beaglehole, *Voyage Journal*, Part II, p. 1235.
2   Beaglehole, *Voyage Journal*, Part I, p. 642.
3   Ledyard, *Journal*, p. 164.
4   Beaglehole, *Voyage Journal*, Part I, p. 643.
5   Beaglehole, *Voyage Journal*, Part I, p. 644.
6   Beaglehole, *Life of Cook*, p. 679.
7   Beaglehole, *Voyage Journal*, Part I, p. 650. Beaglehole, *Life of Cook*, p. 679.
8   Ellis, *Journal*, Vol. II, pp. 204-05.
9   Beaglehole, *Voyage Journal*, Part II, p. 1240. Ledyard, *Journal*, p. 165.
10 King's two-week journey is described in his narrative, Beaglehole, *Voyage Journal*, Part I, pp. 659-70. Behm's reactions to Cook's earlier contact with Siberian people is found at Beaglehole, *Voyage Journal*, Part I, p. clxiii and Beaglehole, *Life of Cook*, p. 680. On his return, King noted that Clerke's sickness had deteriorated substantially, p. 671. Vancouver named Behm Canal in August, 1793, Lamb, *Vancouver's Voyage*, Volume III, p. 1033.
11 Beaglehole, *Voyage Journal*, Part II, p. 1257.
12 Beaglehole, *Voyage Journal*, Part I, p. 677.
13 Ledyard, *Journal*, p. 169.
14 Beaglehole, *Voyage Journal*, Part I, p. 691.
15 Beaglehole, *Voyage Journal*, Part I, p. 695 and clxiv-clxv. See also Beaglehole, *Life of Cook*, pp. 681-82.
16 Beaglehole, *Voyage Journal*, Part II, p. 1266.

[17] Beaglehole, *Voyage Journal,* Part I, pp. 696-97.

[18] Rickman, *Journal,* p 353.

[19] King's voyage journal was lost to Beaglehole in preparing the four-volume set, which troubled him a great deal. See Beaglehole, *Voyage Journal,* Part I, p. clxxxii. In 1973 Andrew David later found it in the British Hydrographic Office and published it in Andrew David, *The Charts and Coastal Views of Captain Cook's Voyages,* Hakluyt Society, 1997, Vol. III (hereafter David, *Charts and Coastal Views*), pp. 267-310. King's commentary on Clerke's death is found at David, *Charts and Coastal Views,* p. 273.

[20] Beaglehole, *Voyage Journal,* Part II, pp. 1271-72.

[21] David, *Charts and Coastal Views,* pp. 274-76.

[22] Ledyard, *Journal,* p. 181. David, *Charts and Coastal Views,* p. 273.

[23] Ellis, *Journal,* Vol. II, p. 295. Samwell's inscription reads a bit differently, Beaglehole, *Voyage Journal,* Part II, p. 1280.

[24] David, *Charts and Coastal Views,* pp. 276, 280.

[25] Ledyard, *Journal,* pp. 163, 185-86.

[26] Holmes, *Gilbert Journal,* p. 140, 147.

[27] Ellis, *Journal,* Vol. II, p. 304.

[28] Ledyard, *Journal,* pp. 167-69.

[29] See King's general remarks on the return visit to the Bay of Avacha, David, *Charts and Coastal Views,* pp. 282-87.

[30] Holmes, *Gilbert Journal,* p. 149.

Chapter 11
The Voyage Home

[1] David, *Charts and Coastal Views,* pp. 287-97. Beaglehole, *Life of Cook,* p. 684.

[2] Holmes, *Gilbert Journal,* p. 154.

3 David, *Charts and Coastal Views*, p. 297.

4 Beaglehole, *Voyage Journal*, Part II, p. 1535. Beaglehole, *Life of Cook*, p. 685. Conner and Miller, *Master Mariner*, pp. 35-36.

5 David, *Charts and Coastal Views*, p. 301.

6 David, *Charts and Coastal Views*, pp. 304-10. Holmes, *Gilbert Journal*, pp. 154-58. On the duel, and arrival in England, see Beaglehole, *Life of Cook*, pp. 685-86.

7 Hough, *Cook Biography*, pp. 45-112.

8 Beaglehole, *Life of Cook*, p. 364.

9 Holmes, *Gilbert Journal*, p. 158.

10 Withey, *Voyages of Discovery*, pp. 401-02. See generally Bernard Smith, *Cook's Posthumous Reputation*, in Robin Fisher & Hugh Johnson, eds., *Captain James Cook and his Times*, University of Washington Press, 1979, pp. 159-85. A fascinating look at Cook's contribution to the Pacific, particularly in light of recent changes in historiography, can be found in Glyndwr Williams, *"As befits out age, there are no more heroes, reassessing Captain Cook*, in Glyndwr Williams, ed., *Captain Cook, Explorations and Reassessments*, Boydell Press, 2004, pp. 230-45.

11 Beaglehole, *Life of Cook*, pp. 696-97.

12 Conner and Miller, *Master Mariner*, pp. 160.

13 William R. Gray, *Voyages to Paradise, Exploring in the Wake of Captain Cook*, National Geographic Society, 1981, p. 210.

14 Beaglehole, *Life of Cook*, pp. 689-96. See also Hough, *Cook Biography*, pp. 368-70.

15 Conner and Miller, *Master Mariner*, pp. 159. Withey, *Voyages of Discovery*, pp. 402-05.

16 Richard Hough, *The Last Voyage of Captain James Cook*, William Morrow and Company, 1979, p. 256.

17 Withey, *Voyages of Discovery*, pp. 403-06. Williams, *Voyages of Delusion*, pp. 336-38. See also Anthony Payne, *The Publication and Readership of Voyage Journals in the*

Age of Vancouver, 1730-1830, in Stephen Haycox, James Barnett and Caedmon Liburd, eds., *Enlightenment and Exploration in the North Pacific 1741-1805,* University of Washington Press, 1997, pp. 176-86. Rüdiger Joppien, *The Artistic Bequest of Captain Cook's Voyages— Popular Imagery in European Costume Books of the Late Eighteenth and Early Nineteenth Centuries,* in Robin Fisher & Hugh Johnson, eds., *Captain James Cook and his Times,* University of Washington Press, 1979, pp. 187-210.

[18] Hough, *Cook Biography,* pp. 365-66.

Chapter 12
In the Wake of Cook

[1] Jean François Galaup, Comte de La Pérouse, *A Voyage Round the World Performed in the Years 1785, 1786, 1787 and 1788 by the Boussole and Astrolabe,* A. Hamilton, 1799 (hereafter La Pérouse, *Voyage Round the World*), pp. 358-59.

[2] Julius S. Gassner, *Voyages and Adventures of La Pérouse,* translation of 1839 edition of F. Valentin, University of Hawaii Press, 1969 (hereafter Gassner, *Voyages and Adventures*), pp. 27-43. John Dunmore, *Pacific Explorer, the Life of Jean François de La Pérouse, 1741-1788,* Dunmore Press, 1985 (hereafter Dunmore, *Pacific Explorer*), pp. 229-31. See also Robin Inglis, *Lapérouse 1786: A French Naval Visit to Alaska,* in Stephen Haycox, James Barnett and Caedmon Liburd, eds., *Enlightenment and Exploration in the North Pacific 1741-1805,* University of Washington Press, 1997, pp. 49-64. Williams, *Voyages of Delusion,* pp. 340-48.

[3] La Pérouse, *Voyage Round the World,* p. 387. Gassner, *Voyages and Adventures,* pp. 33-34.

4   Gassner, *Voyages and Adventures,* pp. 43-51. Dunmore, *Pacific Explorer,* pp. 232-43.

5   Gassner, *Voyages and Adventures,* pp. 135-56. Dunmore, *Pacific Explorer,* pp. 276-95.

6   The war with the local people and establishment of the fledgling colony on Kodiak Island is described in Shelikhov's personal accounts in Dmytryshyn and Vaughan, *Russian Penetration,* pp. 296-320, 326-33, 352-53. See also Tikhmenev, *Russian-American Company,* pp. 410-14.

7   Cook, *Flood Tide of Empire,* pp. 93-98. Wagner, *The Cartography of the Northwest Coast,* Volume I, p. 191-96. Williams, *Voyages of Delusion,* p. 316.

8   Cook, *Flood Tide of Empire,* pp. 306-309. Wagner, *The Cartography of the Northwest Coast,* Volume I, p. 225-28. Williams, *Voyages of Delusion,* pp. 371-84. See also Iris H. W. Engstrand, *Spanish Scientists in the New World, The Eighteenth Century Expeditions,* University of Washington Press, 1981, and Andrew David, Felipe Fernandez-Armesto, Carlos Novi, and Glyndwr Williams, eds., *The Malaspina Expedition,* Vol. II, Hakluyt Society, 2003, pp. 100-60. Malaspina's doubts about Maldonado's claims are stated at pp. 139 and 159. See also pp. 468-80.

9   Cook, *Flood Tide of Empire,* pp. 309-20. Wagner, *The Cartography of the Northwest Coast,* Volume I, p. 228-29. Williams, *Voyages of Delusion,* pp. 384-85.

10 Martin Sauer, *An Account of a Geographical and Astronomical Expedition to the Northern Parts of Russia,* T. Cadell, 1802, pp. 148-209. See also G. Sarychev, *Voyage of Discovery to the Northeast of Siberia, the Frozen Ocean, and the North-East Sea,* Richard Phillips, 1806, Vol. 2, pp. 19-28.

11 Cook, *Flood Tide of Empire,* pp. 100-06. Derek Pethick, *The Nootka Connection: Europe and the Northwest*

Coast, 1790-95, Douglas & McIntyre (hereafter Pethick, *The Nootka Connection*), pp 12-23. Lamb, *Vancouver's Voyage*, Volume I, pp. 15-27. Williams, *Voyages of Delusion*, pp. 348-58.

[12] John Meares, *Voyages Made in the Years 1788 and 1789 from China to the North West Coast of America*, J. Walter, 1790. His notes from the earlier voyage (including the winter in Prince William Sound), and speculation about the northwest passage, are at the introductory pp. i-lxvi. Barry Gough, *The Northwest Coast, British Navigation, Trade and Discoveries to 1812*, University of British Columbia Press, 1992 (hereafter Gough, *The Northwest Coast*), pp. 87-95.

[13] Cook, *Flood Tide of Empire*, pp. 136-45. Gough, *The Northwest Coast*, pp. 96-115.

[14] Frederic W. Howay, ed., *Voyages of the "Columbia" to the Northwest Coast*, Massachusetts Historical Society, 1941 (hereafter Howay, *Voyages of the "Columbia"*). The first voyage log of Robert Haswell, first mate of the *Columbia*, is at pp. 3-107. J. Richard Nokes, *Columbia's River, The Voyages of Robert Gray, 1787-1793*, Washington State Historical Society, 1991 (hereafter Nokes, *Columbia's River*), pp. 59-79. Williams, *Voyages of Delusion*, p. 350.

[15] Cook, *Flood Tide of Empire*, pp. 119-29. Wagner, *The Cartography of the Northwest Coast*, Volume I, p. 202-05.

[16] Cook, *Flood Tide of Empire*, pp. 129-60. Wagner, *The Cartography of the Northwest Coast*, Volume I, p. 214-18.

[17] Cook, *Flood Tide of Empire*, pp. 160-99. Gough, *The Northwest Coast*, pp. 127-45.

[18] Cook, *Flood Tide of Empire*, pp. 200-49. Gough, *The Northwest Coast*, pp. 127-45.

[19] Cook, *Flood Tide of Empire*, pp. 271-84. Wagner, *The Cartography of the Northwest Coast*, Volume I, p. 219-22.

Pethick, *The Nootka Connection*, pp 32-33.

[20] Lamb, *Vancouver's Voyage*, Volume I, p. 5. The purposes and consequences of the Vancouver voyage are described in Glyndwr Williams, *George Vancouver, the Admiralty, and Exploration in the Late Eighteenth Century,* in Stephen Haycox, James Barnett and Caedmon Liburd, eds., *Enlightenment and Exploration in the North Pacific 1741-1805,* University of Washington Press, 1997, pp. 38-48.

[21] Lamb, *Vancouver's Voyage*, Volume I, pp. 27-54.

[22] Lamb, *Vancouver's Voyage*, Volume II, pp. 502-03. Howay, *Voyages of the "Columbia."* John Boit's log of the entry into Columbia River is found at pp. 393-97. Haswell's second voyage log is found at pp. 293-359. Nokes, *Columbia's River*, pp. 179-91. Williams, *Voyages of Delusion*, pp. 386-88.

[23] Andrew David, *Vancouver's Survey Methods and Surveys,* in Robin Fisher and Hugh Johnston, eds., *From Maps to Metaphors, The Pacific World of George Vancouver,* University of British Columbia Press, 1993, pp. 51-69.

[24] Lamb, *Vancouver's Voyage*, Volume II, pp. 500-687, which covers the expedition's exploration of Puget Sound and the circumnavigation of Vancouver Island. There is a separate voyage journal for the two Spanish ships, John Kendrick, ed., *The Voyage of the Sutil and Mexicana in 1792,* Arthur H. Clark, 1991. Their first meeting with Vancouver, June 21, 1792, is found at pp. 130-31. Vancouver's report of the meeting is found at Lamb, *Vancouver's Voyage*, Volume II, pp. 591-93. See also Gough, *The Northwest Coast*, pp. 156-63. Williams, *Voyages of Delusion,* pp. 386-95. Wagner, *The Cartography of the Northwest Coast*, Volume I, p. 239-43.

[25] José Mariano Moziño, *Noticias de Nutka, An Account of Nootka Sound in 1792,* Iris H. W. Engstrand, ed., University of Washington Press, 1991, pp. xli, 87.

[26] Cook, *Flood Tide of Empire,* pp. 362-82. Ultimately the Spanish withdrew from Nootka of their own accord, pp. 397-433. Pethick, *The Nootka Connection,* pp 135-43. Gough, *The Northwest Coast,* pp. 163-65. See Lamb, *Vancouver's Voyage,* Volume II, pp. 688-746, which chronicles Vancouver's impressions of the Spanish fortifications and missions of California, and pp. 747-70, which gives Lt. Broughton's account of the Columbia River voyage.

[27] See Lamb, *Vancouver's Voyage,* Volume III, pp. 797-898, which sets forth Vancouver's journal for that winter in Hawaii, and particularly pp. 831-32, where Vancouver revisits the death of Cook. See also note, p. 1164, where Lamb notes that several Hawaiians claimed to strike the fatal blow.

[28] See Lamb, *Vancouver's Voyage,* Volume III, pp. 899-1135, which chronicles Vancouver's second survey season, including his travels in Southern California, and pp. 1136-1205, which narrates the final visit to Hawaii. Wagner, *The Cartography of the Northwest Coast,* Volume I, p. 243-46.

[29] See Lamb, *Vancouver's Voyage,* Volumes III-IV, pp. 1206-1391, which governs Vancouver's third and final survey season on the coast, including pp. 1206-63 in Cook Inlet. Contacts with Purtov in Yakutat Bay are described on pp. 1313, 1329-31. Baranov apparently sent three messages to Vancouver via Purtov suggesting they meet, but Baranov never kept the appointments (pp. 1259-60). The final survey at Port Conclusion is found at pp. 1371; the quoted passage follows final survey deliberations and is found at pp. 1390. Pethick, *The Nootka Connection,* pp 188-93. Williams, *Voyages of Delusion,* pp. 401-05. Wagner, *The Cartography of the Northwest Coast,* Volume I, p. 246-50.

[30] Robin Fisher, *George Vancouver and the Native Peoples of the Northwest Coast,* in Stephen Haycox, James Barnett and Caedmon Liburd, eds., *Enlightenment and Exploration in the North Pacific 1741-1805,* University of Washington Press, 1997, pp. 198-209..

[31] Bern Anderson, *Surveyor of the Sea: The Life and Voyages of George Vancouver,* University of Toronto Press, 1960 (hereafter Anderson, *Surveyor of the Sea*), p. 213.

[32] Anderson, *Surveyor of the Sea,* p. 232. William H. Dahl, *Alaska and its Resources,* Lee and Shepard, 1870, p. 316.

-Bibliography -

The main source document for Cook's third voyage is the original three volume account published four years after the expedition returned to England, John Douglas, ed., *A Voyage to the Pacific Ocean in the years 1776, 1777, 1778, 1779 and 1780...Vol. I and II written by James Cook, Vol. III by Captain James King*, 3 vols., London, 1784. It is difficult to find, particularly in the prized first edition, and any edition is very expensive.

The more reasonably priced version is the comprehensive and annotated two-volume work edited by J. C. Beaglehole, *The Voyage of the Resolution and Discovery*, Cambridge University Press, 1967, which is part of a larger series published for the three voyages. Beaglehole (1901-71) was professor of British Commonwealth History at the Victoria University of Wellington, New Zealand. His unparalleled work contains Cook's journal, extracts from several other journals kept by members of the expedition, the list of seamen on the voyage, the voyage instructions, and letters and other documents from members of the expedition. It is supplemented by the author's biography of the explorer, J. C. Beaglehole, *The Life of Captain James Cook*, Stanford University Press, 1974.

In addition to the journals reprinted by Beaglehole, the following first-hand voyage journals are available:

- William Ellis, *An Authentic Narrative of a Voyage ... in Search of the Northwest Passage*, 1782.
- Christine Holmes, ed., *Captain Cook's Final Voyage, the Journal of Midshipman George Gilbert*, University

Press of Hawaii, 1982.

• John Ledyard, *A Journal of Captain Cook's Last Voyage ... in the Years 1776, 1777, 1778, and 1779,* Hartford, 1783.

• John Rickman, *Journal of Captain Cook's Last Voyage to the Pacific Ocean*, E. Newberry 1781.

A comprehensive catalog of the original drawings and engravings from the third voyage is Rüdiger Joppien and Bernard Smith, *The Art of Captain Cook's Voyages,* Oxford University Press, 1987. Two of the four volumes are dedicated to the third voyage drawings, principally those of John Webber and William Ellis. See also John Frazier Henry, *Early Maritime Artists of the Pacific Northwest Coast, 1741-1841,* University of Washington Press, 1984.

The charts and coastal views made by Cook and his officers can be found in the three-volume work edited by Andrew David, *The Charts and Coastal Views of Captain Cook's Voyages,* Hakluyt Society, 1997. Volume III is dedicated to the third voyage and includes original maps, coastal views drawn on the voyage, and the "lost" journal of Captain King beginning at the time of Captain Clerke's death in August, 1779, until the end of the voyage.

An excellent presentation on the early native cultures in contact with Europeans, including a display of artifacts collected by the explorers on the Northwest coast, can be found in J. C. H. King, *First People First Contacts, Native Peoples of North America,* Harvard University Press, 1999, and Steven C. Brown, ed., *Spirits of the Water, Native Art Collected on Expeditions to Alaska and British Columbia, 1774-1910,* University of Washington Press, 2000.

Numerous biographies exist on Cook, probably more than any other explorer in history. Only a few focus on the third voyage let alone Cook's expedition of Alaska and the west coast of North America. The reader should consider the range of the following ten selected titles:

- Daniel Conner and Lorraine Miller, *Master Mariner*, University of Washington Press, 1978.
- Paul W. Dale, *Seventy North to Fifty South, Captain Cook's Last Voyage*, Prentice-Hall Inc., 1969.
- Martin Dugard, *Farther Than Any Man, The Rise and Fall of Captain James Cook*, Pocket Books, 2001.
- Tony Horowitz, *Blue Latitudes, Boldly Going Where Captain Cook Has Gone Before*, Henry Holt and Company, 2002.
- Richard Hough, *Captain James Cook, A Biography*, Hodder & Stoughton, 1994.
- Richard Hough, *The Last Voyage of Captain James Cook*, William Morrow and Company, 1979.
- Nigel Rigby and Pieter van der Merwe, *Captain Cook in the Pacific*, National Maritime Museum, 2002.
- Nicholas Thomas, *The Extraordinary Voyages of Captain Cook*, Walker & Co., 2003.
- Thomas Vaughan and A. A. St. C. M. Murray-Oliver, *Captain Cook, R. N., The Resolute Mariner*, Oregon Historical Society, 1974.
- Lynne Withey, *Voyages of Discovery, Captain Cook and the Exploration of the Pacific*, University of California Press, 1987.

Hundreds of books consider topics presented in this book. The reader should consider the range of the following thirty selected titles:

- Glynn Barratt, *Russia in Pacific Waters, 1715-1825*, University of British Columbia Press, 1981.
- Richard Batman, *The Outer Coast*, Harvest/HBJ

Book, 1985.

- Warren L. Cook, *Flood Tide of Empire, Spain and the Pacific Northwest 1543-1819*, Yale University Press, 1973.
- Andrew David, Felipe Fernandez-Armesto, Carlos Novi, and Glyndwr Williams, eds., *The Malaspina Expedition*, Vol. II, Hakluyt Society, 2003.
- Basil Dmytryshyn, E. A. P. Crownhart-Vaughan, and Thomas Vaughan, *Russian Penetration of the North Pacific Ocean, 1700-1797: A Documentary Record*, Oregon Historical Society, 1988.
- John Dunmore, *Pacific Explorer, the Life of Jean François de La Pérouse, 1741-1788*, Dunmore Press, 1985.
- Raymond H. Fisher, *Bering's Voyages--Whither and Why*, University of Washington Press, 1977.
- Robin Fisher and Hugh Johnson, eds. *Captain James Cook and His Times*, University of Washington Press, 1979.
- Robin Fisher and Hugh Johnston, eds., *From Maps to Metaphors, The Pacific World of George Vancouver*, University of British Columbia Press, 1993.
- William W. Fitzhugh and Aron Crowell, *Crossroads of Continents, Cultures of Siberia and Alaska*, Smithsonian Institution Press, 1988.
- Corey Ford, *Where the Sea Breaks Its Back*, Little, Brown and Company, 1966.
- Julius S. Gassner, *Voyages and Adventures of La Pérouse*, translation of 1839 edition of F. Valentin, University of Hawaii Press, 1969.
- James R. Gibson, *Otter Skins, Boston Ships, and China Goods, The Maritime Fur Trade of the Northwest Coast, 1785-1841*, University of Washington Press, 1992.

- F. A. Golder, *Bering's Voyages* (two volumes), American Geographical Society, 1922.
- Barry Gough, *The Northwest Coast, British Navigation, Trade and Discoveries to 1812*, University of British Columbia Press, 1992.
- Warren L. Hanna, *Lost Harbor, The Controversy over Drake's California Anchorage*, University of California Press, 1979
- Stephen Haycox, James Barnett and Caedmon Liburd, eds., *Enlightenment and Exploration in the North Pacific 1741-1805*, University of Washington Press, 1997.
- Wallace M. Olson, ed., *The Alaska Travel Journal of Archibald Menzies, 1793-94*, University of Alaska Press, 1993.
- Derek Pethick, *The Nootka Connection, Europe and the Northwest Coast, 1790-1795*, Douglas & McIntyre, 1980.
- Nigel Rigby, Pieter van der Merwe, and Glyn Williams, *Pioneers of the Pacific, Voyages of Exploration, 1787-1810*, University of Alaska Press, 2005.
- Antoinette Shalkop, ed., *Exploration in Alaska, Captain Cook Commemorative Lectures*, Cook Inlet Historical Society, 1980.
- Georg W. Steller, *Journal of a Voyage with Bering, 1741-42*, O. W. Frost, Ed., Margritt A. Engel and O. W. Frost, translators, Stanford University Press, 1988.
- John Sugden, *Sir Francis Drake*, Henry Holt and Company, 1990.
- George Vancouver, *A Voyage of Discovery to the North Pacific Ocean and Round the World, 1791-95*, W. Kaye Lamb, Ed., four volumes, Hakluyt Society, 1984.
- Thomas Vaughan and Bill Holm, *Soft Gold, the Fur*

Trade and Cultural Exchange on the Northwest Coast of America, Oregon Historical Society, 1990.

- Henry R. Wagner, *Cartography of the Northwest Coast of America to the Year 1800,* University of California Press, 1937.
- Henry R. Wagner, *Spanish Voyages to the Northwest,* California Historical Society, 1929.
- Sven Waxell, *The American Expedition*, William Hodge and Company, 1952.
- Glyndwr Williams, ed., *Captain Cook, Explorations and Reassessments,* The Boydell Press, 2004.
- Glyndwr Williams, *Voyages of Delusion, The Search for the Northwest Passage in the Age of Reason,* Harper Collins, 2002.

~ *Index* ~

~ *A – C* ~

- *I - K* -

- L -R -

– S -Z –